W9-CDS-435

WRITING
THROUGH
SEQUENCE

A Process Approach

WRITING THROUGH SEQUENCE

A Process Approach

Charles R. Duke

MURRAY STATE UNIVERSITY

LITTLE, BROWN AND COMPANY   Boston · Toronto

Library of Congress Cataloging in Publication Data

Duke, Charles R.
   Writing through sequence.

   1. English language--Rhetoric.   I. Title.
PE1408.D75   1983   808'.042   82-24876
ISBN 0-316-19484-0

Library of Congress Catalog Card Number: 82-24876

ISBN 0-316-19484-0

9   8   7   6   5   4   3   2   1

ALP

Published simultaneously in Canada by Little, Brown & Company (Canada) Limited

Printed in the United States of America

ACKNOWLEDGMENTS

Chapter 2

"Writing Apprehension Survey" from "The Empirical Development of an Instrument to Measure Writing Apprehension" by John A. Daly, *Research in the Teaching of English* (Winter 1975). Reprinted by permission of the author.

Excerpt from "The Writing Autobiography of Bobbie Wimberley." Reprinted by permission of the author.

Excerpt from "Norman Mailer" in *Writers at Work: The Paris Review Interviews*, 3rd Series, edited by George Plimpton. Copyright © 1967 by The Paris Review, Inc. Reprinted by permission of Viking Penguin Inc.

Excerpt from "Writing Autobiography" by Mary Yokel. Reprinted by permission of the author.

(Continued on page 265)

Preface

When a person begins to learn to drive an automobile, a driving instructor does not place the person on a busy street corner, point to a passing,
expert driver and say, "See, like that, do it like that, d'ja see the way that
driver signalled the right turn? Now, you go do it exactly that way and
let me know next week if you had any problems." Fortunately, not many
driving instructors turn their students loose on the highway with that
minimal advice. Sometimes, though, it seems as if many students have
been turned loose on paper with little more preparation than the poor
driving student. If, as writers, students view only the perfection of the
final written product and then set out to try their hands at writing,
never understanding the process that led to the product, they may
become discouraged and fail.

Students often believe that writing is a precise product, an endeavor
to be admired and envied, perhaps, but more likely to be dreaded, and
finally, a feat to be imitated awkwardly in a theme a week. Small wonder
that many students' minds and pens quit in disgust when a first draft
does not approximate the quality and control of language found in an
original by Hemingway, Baldwin, Updike, Dillard, or Ellison.

Not surprisingly, many students also believe in the notion that a
person must possess some superior genetic traits to become an effective writer. For such students, the mystery of how a piece of writing got
to be so clean, so well formed, so precise, remains the secret of the
author—and of the writing instructor. But to write well, one has to
understand and practice the process of writing, not simply read and
critically appreciate someone else's efforts.

Writing Through Sequence: A Process Approach has as its basis
three broadly conceived categories or stages that closely parallel those

found in any creative process. The first stage is an opening outward, or a freeing of the individual to think about past, present, and future experiences. In traditional writing classes much time is devoted to reading and discussing writing, but writing students should actually spend more of that time in the writing process itself. Only in this way can they begin to explore what their experiences have to tell about themselves and others. The exploratory stage of this process, often called prewriting or rehearsing, becomes the first crucial step toward making discoveries that become important guides and sources for the writing that must yet be done.

The drafting stage—the placing of experience on paper—often comes about as a result of time spent in the first stage. The writer places on a blank page words that reveal preliminary decisions about the projected piece of writing. In the creative process, considerable restlessness and frustration characterize this stage of expression. Viewed in this light, then, first drafts rarely can be regarded as a writer's best effort. However, much present-day writing instruction ends with a graded evaluation of the first draft. Nothing could be more damaging to the student writer.

In the process of a person's creating anything of lasting value, preliminary evaluation and alteration usually figure prominently. For almost all writers, reformulating a first draft is necessary. In this stage the writer painstakingly checks, tests, criticizes, elaborates, and polishes until satisfied with the quality of writing. Only after these steps should the writer begin to think that his or her written efforts might become a finished product.

Writing Through Sequence: A Process Approach takes the student through a series of writing experiences, each one designed to expand a bit further the writer's skills in each stage of the writing process. These writing experiences begin with the writers themselves, drawing upon what they know best to form the basis of initial written communication. After this introduction, they are gradually guided to adopt perspectives on their experiences as a basis for analysis and commentary. Each writing experience follows a carefully defined sequence that reinforces the idea of process and emphasizes the responsibilities the writer must accept to insure that his or her experience clearly and effectively communicates with the audience.

In Chapter 1, "Making Sense of the Writing Process," students begin with a discussion of what characterizes an effective writer and tie those characteristics into the text as a whole; then they move to a discussion of the stages in the writing process and an explanation of each stage. The chapter concludes with a discussion of seven key questions used to determine what makes an acceptable paper.

Chapter 2, "Writing—How Do You Feel About It," presents the first writing situation; the student recalls past experiences with writing and relates these to his or her writing process. Students use listing and clustering as two prewriting strategies and have their first experience in sharing their writing with peers.

Chapter 3, "What's in a Person?" asks students to write a character sketch, focusing on the unique qualities of a person they have known or observed carefully. Students work inductively to develop a checklist of criteria for a character sketch by using as examples five student-written essays. After reading and rating the essays, students work in groups to develop the criteria. They then write their own drafts, and exchange them with other students. The criteria are applied as they read and respond to each other's work.

Chapter 4 provides students with a workshop opportunity. The material draws students' attention to the importance of paragraph structure with particular emphasis on focus, unity, evidence, and coherence. The chapter also provides an explanation of paragraph hooks, introductions, and conclusions. Students use drafts of papers from the second and third chapters for practice in these areas.

Chapter 5, "How Does That Happen?" focuses students' attention on developing an explanation with a process emphasis. Students engage in dialoguing, a prewriting strategy, and use written commentary to respond to each other's drafts.

Chapter 6, "What's Your Perspective?" calls for students to examine a topic from varying perspectives. A basic comparison/contrast approach structures the writing situation. Students examine several sample essays, use a modified listing prewriting technique, and engage in a spot-light response activity for reacting to each other's drafts.

Chapter 7, "What Do You Want to Write About?" introduces the prewriting strategy of cubing, which is a way of examining a subject from six angles to inventory its potential for writing. Students select their own topic, focus, audience, and purpose. The essays they produce illustrate applications of various techniques learned in the previous chapters.

Chapter 8 offers another workshop opportunity in which students look back at earlier writing efforts. This time they pay attention to sentence types and sentence variety, with suggestions about sentence combining and levels of generality. Students use their own writing, of course, for practice in these areas.

Chapter 9, "What Other Sources Are There?" moves students to consult resources beyond immediate personal experience. The general focus of the assignment is a comparison/contrast piece of writing using newspapers or magazines. The student selects a newspaper or magazine published on or near his birth date and an issue of the same publication published near the time of the assignment. Students then identify a focus for the paper and use evidence from the reading to build a case and make a point.

Chapter 10, "How Do You Analyze," focuses on a particular essay, "Surveyor in the Woods" by Kenneth Andler, where students encounter the use of marginal annotation. After practice involving the Andler essay students develop a critical response essay about a piece of writing, using either a sample essay in the text or an essay they locate themselves.

In Chapter 11, "What's Out There?" students get the opportunity to bring together the skills learned in the earlier sections of the text. They go outside the classroom, selecting a place and person to focus on for an on-site interview in a working environment. The assignment emphasizes asking effective questions, absorbing and recording details and information, capturing dialogue, and developing a point of view. Students write an essay incorporating the results of their investigation.

Writing Through Sequence: A Process Approach thus introduces students to a writing process model flexible enough to be adapted to many different writing tasks. Initially students draw upon what they know best—their own experience—and build upon that as they begin to integrate new materials and observations beyond their immediate experience. With each chapter of the text the student writers gain a bit more confidence as they encounter slightly more challenging writing experiences. Each chapter also offers new prewriting strategies to be tried in an actual writing assignment, ways of obtaining useful response from peers throughout the writing process, and numerous ways to self-evaluate the process as it occurs. The text does not ask students to memorize terminology or to go through extensive drills. From the beginning students work with their own writing and refine process skills while moving through the sequence of assignments.

Writing Through Sequence: A Process Approach contains little of the rhetorical apparatus found in many composition texts nor does it include the traditional handbook section. Although the text offers specific assignments, the material remains flexible enough that instructors may use it in several ways. The workshop sections on writing techniques may be used at any time, and instructors who want to use a reader or handbook may do so without great difficulty. An instructor's manual offers practical suggestions for organizing a course based on the text, outlines procedures for handling the paper load in a course where reformulation is stressed, and makes suggestions about arriving at grades for writing achievements. The manual also provides teaching suggestions for each chapter.

ACKNOWLEDGMENTS

No book develops in isolation. In this case, I have had the good fortune to teach writing for a number of years during which the material in this text went through extensive classroom experimentation. In fact, I was apprehensive about committing to a book much of this material for fear that it might cease to be as flexible as it has been. I have also been fortunate to have had a number of productive conversations with colleagues over the years about writing. Among those who have been instrumental in helping me arrive at the approach reflected in *Writing Through Sequence* are Donald Murray, University of New Hampshire, Gerald Zinfon, Plymouth State College, Lee Odell, Rensselaer Polytechnic Institute, William Strong, Utah State University, Roy Helton, Murray State University, Harry Brent, Baruch College, Kenneth Bruffee, Brooklyn College, Eugene Hammond, University of Maryland, and M. Beverly Swan, University of Rhode Island.

I also am most grateful to the teachers at all levels who have participated under my direction in the West Kentucky Writing Project, a part of the National Writing Project, and to the graduate teaching assistants at Murray State University. Their willingness to test the various writing assignments that appear in this text and their responses about the classroom effectiveness of both the approach and the materials have been helpful. But the most valuable population has been the students in my classes who have not hesitated to let me know what works and what doesn't about my teaching. Without their responses, this book would never have happened.

Finally, I want to thank Teresa Loveridge and Jamie Helton whose patience and skill in translating my left-handed scrawl to neatly typed pages greatly helped my own rewriting, revising, and editing.

Contents

CHAPTER **3**

What's in a Person?   37

CHAPTER **4**

Workshop: Constructing Effective Paragraphs   60

CHAPTER **5**

How Does That Happen?   *81*

CHAPTER **6**

What's Your Perspective?   *103*

CHAPTER **7**

What Do You Want to Write About?   *126*

CHAPTER **8**

Workshop: Writing Effective Sentences   144

CHAPTER **9**

What Other Sources Are There?   163

CHAPTER 1

Making Sense of the Writing Process

Some people approach writing with considerable caution, as if it might cause them to self-destruct at any moment. Naturally no one wants to get caught up in an explosion, but sometimes the physical feelings that go along with writing make a person feel explosive. Much of that frustration or tension stems more from a person's not being fully aware of what is involved in writing than from the writing itself. In your past experiences with writing, particularly those in a school situation, you may have been asked to write on a particular subject about which you knew little, complete the writing in a class period, pass it in, and have it graded; then, if you were lucky, it was returned the next day. You probably looked at the grade, perhaps made some attempt to figure out what all the red marks meant, and then went on about your business still not fully comprehending what had happened.

That kind of experience repeated over a number of years is bound to have had some effect on your feelings about writing. Consider also that when you read something—again let's say in a classroom—it usually is a finished product. You may marvel at how well the words fit together, how the style of the sentences is varied, and how pleasant such writing is to read. What you never see, of course, are all the drafts that led to the final product: the cross-outs, the scribbled notes, the crazy arrows meandering over the page. All you see is the clean white page with crisp black letters marching to a rhythm that may sound quite different from your own efforts. Little wonder, then, that writing seems a mystery to most people and that they assume there must be magic involved that some people have and others don't. It's important to acknowledge that some people may write better than others just as some people play the piano, paint, repair a car, sew, or sell products better than others. But the real point to keep in mind is that you can write with some degree of skill and ability or you wouldn't be here, reading this book and taking the course related to it.

CHARACTERISTICS OF THE EFFECTIVE WRITER

How does a person become an effective writer? To begin, let's consider some of the characteristics of an effective writer.

1. *Effective writers don't count on inspiration—that bolt out of the blue—to get them through the act of writing.* They write whether they feel like it or not, and usually they write on some kind of schedule. Most write until they've produced a specific amount of material. Without some regular pattern of writing, it is too easy to put off until tomorrow what should be done today. For you, this course will provide a schedule and a regular writing plan that will help you produce a certain amount of writing, perhaps more than you have ever thought possible.

2. *Effective writers meet their deadlines.* When you start your assignments in this course, you may find yourself taking more notes than necessary so you can postpone getting down to writing those notes in some other form. Or you may discover that your room needs cleaning and you can't possibly write until that task is done; you'll recognize this symptom when your friends start commenting on how clean your room looks and asking if you're feeling okay. Because most effective writers don't write unless they're facing a deadline—publication, performance, or request for information—deadlines will become a regular part of your schedule in this writing course. You will need to set some of the deadlines for yourself so you can meet those established by your instructor.

3. *Effective writers have to learn not to be impatient.* You'll have to expect to run into writing blocks, at which times nothing seems to make any sense or all words seem to leave your mind completely. Effective writers learn to recognize the signs of a writing block and to develop methods for dealing with it. Some writers become really

ingenious: They find that playing a vigorous game of tennis or having a karate workout may relax the block and allow them to get started again. Other writers simply skip the section of their writing that seems to be giving them trouble and move on to another part, or they go back and rework an earlier section. All writers encounter blocks at various times, but effective writers find ways to get around, over, and under blocks by experimenting and by observing their actions when blocks occur.

4. *Effective writers tend to work in stages.* They seldom plan to finish a piece of writing in one sitting, unless a deadline dictates that a piece be done that way. Although effective writers make some plans before they write, they're fully aware that the plans have to be flexible because writing is also discovering; that is, new ideas and insights occur throughout the writing process. This means that writers usually work slowly; some may write a first draft quickly, but then they spend considerable time rewriting it. Others may write only one or two drafts but they do so painstakingly, making changes as they go. This text is designed to help you identify the various stages and provide suggestions for working in each one.

5. *Effective writers reread and rewrite a piece often.* Effective writers continually reread what they have written to keep themselves on track and to encourage themselves to keep writing. Much revision usually occurs during the writing process as the writer considers word choices, arrangement of ideas, placement of paragraphs, suitable introductions and conclusions, and the right details and evidence. All of this cannot be done at once, which the effective writer knows even before starting to write. With that knowledge and an awareness of the writing situation—the audience, length and form of the piece of writing, and deadline—a writer can allow time for revising a piece of writing until it meets an acceptable standard for the writer and the audience. You'll find many suggestions in this text for dealing with the revision process.

6. *Effective writers quickly discover the importance of response to their writing.* Response may come from a friend, from an editor, from a teacher, or from a group of fellow writers. Because writing tends to be a solitary activity, many writers welcome opportunities to talk about their ideas, to share what seems to be happening in the stage where they are, and to seek additional ideas and suggestions to strengthen their writing. Throughout this text you'll encounter many response situations designed to give you feedback at the various stages of the writing process. Rather than waiting until your

work has been completed, you can identify your strengths and weaknesses early and make adjustments before your piece of writing is evaluated formally by others.

Effective writers, then, readily admit that they often have some difficulty starting to write but that the real satisfaction occurs when they've completed their writing and know they have communicated exactly what they wanted to say. But what if you think you're not an effective writer or you don't have the slightest idea how to go about writing well? After all, reading about effective writers may be interesting, but it doesn't show you how to become one. That's what this book and this course are all about. By the time you complete this text and the writing it requires, you should have a much better understanding of how effective writing is produced.

THE WRITING PROCESS

Let's consider what you will encounter in the pages ahead. Throughout the text, you will engage in what we call the "writing process." Usually the writing process contains three broad stages or steps: the *prewriting stage*, the *writing stage*, and the *postwriting stage*. Each stage has recognizable features, and writers pass through all three with varying degrees of speed. Once you become familiar with the different activities called for in each stage, you'll undoubtedly find yourself developing more efficient ways to move your writing to completion. Let's look at each stage in detail.

The Prewriting Stage

Many weak writers, after they obtain only a general sense of the writing situation, plunge in and write what they assume will be a final draft. The results of this approach usually are not good; such writers find that haste really does make waste. Effective writers, before they plunge into their writing, try to accumulate as much information about the writing situation as possible: the audience, the length, the restrictions on form—essay, poem, short story, memo, report, play, letter—and time for completion. This information will be easy for you to obtain in this course because either your text will specify these things or your instructor will provide the information.

Effective writers engage in a search for ideas in the prewriting stage.

Using a variety of prewriting techniques, which you will encounter throughout this text, writers cast about for material and ideas that seem to fit the writing situation. Sometimes there may be no more than a feeling, a general sense of direction that pushes the writer along; at other times, things seem to drop into sharp focus almost immediately and a specific purpose emerges along with the general shape of what will take place in the writing.

At some point in this prewriting stage, writers may discover a need for more information than they possess and they investigate other sources: people, books, and objects. Notes begin to pile up and a system for keeping track of the material becomes necessary—a rough outline jotted down or a more formal outline, if that seems appropriate. Depending on the amount of time, the length of the paper, the audience, and the purpose, this preliminary search for material may take several hours or days or it may be completed in a few minutes. Throughout the activity of prewriting, a writer may do some informal writing but only in rough form and never with a great concern for correctness of mechanics. All the writer's attention focuses on the development of raw material from which direction, shape, and communication will come.

The Writing Stage

Although some writing may have occurred in the prewriting stage, it is not of the concentrated kind that occurs in the writing stage. With material collected and somewhat organized in the prewriting stage, some writers like to rush through the first draft, their pens or typewriters churning out words as fast as possible to capture all the raw material. They want to get it down on paper with an uninterrupted flow of thought. You might compare this activity to "being on a roll," an expression that describes a time when everything is going in your favor; in writing, it's as if there were a direct circuit between brain and paper. With the words coming so fast and the mind tearing along at such a rate, writers make no effort to stop and correct their work. If a certain word doesn't come to mind immediately, they leave a blank to be filled in later; if their spelling is shaky, they guess and charge right on, knowing that such problems can be addressed later, in the postwriting stage. The rough drafts that emerge at the writing stage are truly that—rough working papers from which writers gradually shape a polished piece. Not everyone, of course, uses the pell-mell technique; other writers write their first draft more slowly, perhaps with some rereading and minor changes as the draft unfolds. Their concentration remains just as intense; their flow of thought is just a bit slower. A few writers handle the writing and rewriting at the same time, but this takes considerable practice and excellent control of the subject matter. Trying too hard to rewrite at this stage can stifle the flow of thought, frustrate the writer, and lead to a stiff, unimaginative piece of writing that reads more like the work of an unidentifiable committee than that of an individual.

The Postwriting Stage

With a draft from the writing stage, writers must spend some time determining what happened in that first writing. The draft must be reread several times; if it is not too rough, the writer may share the draft with other readers for suggestions. At this point, a writer looks for a sharp focus, a sense of shape or organization, and the amount of evidence in the paper. What the writer finds in this "re-viewing" of the draft will determine whether rewriting, revising, or editing will occur next. These terms can cause some confusion, however, unless the writer knows that each suggests a slightly different activity.

Rewriting

After some reviewing of the draft, the writer—and also perhaps some readers—may decide that the main idea has yet to come into focus. No one, including the writer, seems quite certain of what the piece is supposed to do. At this point the writer may decide to rewrite. That means the writer returns to the prewriting stage, attempts to explore the subject in more depth or selects a new subject, and then writes a new draft. Some of the original draft may appear in the new one but the writer does not rely solely on the first effort. *Rewrite*, then, means to go back to the beginning. Most writers, of course, dread the idea of going back and find a million reasons why they shouldn't. If, however, they can convince themselves that writing a new draft is just that—another draft— then the return may not loom so large. Better to discover the need for a new draft early in the process than to wait until you've handed in your paper only to discover that your audience can't understand what you have to offer.

Revising

A rereading of the rough draft may indicate that the general structure and the particular focus come through fairly well. In that case, revising is called for. Other readers can provide useful feedback at this stage and can raise questions about the material that need to be answered before the piece reaches its audience. Some paragraphs may not connect with others; details may need clarification; the introduction and conclusion may need strengthening. In other words, the general content is workable but the writer must pay considerable attention to different parts of it. The writer knows that a good amount of tinkering will be necessary to get the piece running smoothly, but the chassis is there and all the fundamental parts seem sound.

Most drafts call for some amount of revising, and some writers spend as much time at this level as others spend in rewriting; the only difference is that in rewriting the writer goes back to the beginning, while the reviser continues to work with what appeared in the rough draft.

Editing

Once the rough draft produced in the writing stage has gone through several concentrated efforts at revision, the writer reaches the point where the draft is ready for cosmetic touch-up. The writer may have shared drafts of the piece with small groups, and now a final version is almost ready for release to a larger audience. At this point, the writer has to acknowledge that control of the meaning of the piece will be gone when it is released to this larger group of readers. *Editing* requires attention to the surface details: spelling, punctuation, capitalization, neatness, and overall format. Just as most of us dress for the situation in which we expect to find ourselves, the effective writer polishes the final draft to be sure readers will not be distracted from the real message. Although we might agree that people and ideas should not be judged entirely on the basis of their appearance, why run the risk of having a solid presentation ruined because the audience simply could not get by the surface problems to see the real value beneath?

All these stages suggest that an acceptable piece of writing does not just happen. Instead, it is the result of time, thought, preparation, and, if possible, several drafts. Sometimes, of course, writers have to work rapidly to meet deadlines, whether on the job or in a classroom test situation. The only element that changes is that the writing process must be compressed because of time limitations. Prewriting, for instance, may occur mentally instead of on paper. Introductions and conclusions are more direct and possibly less inventive, and the luxury of extensive rewriting and editing usually disappears. The basic approach, however, remains a useful method for dealing with such writing situations. Once you understand the process and what you can do within it, you should feel far more comfortable approaching the many varied writing tasks that will occur in your life.

In addition to understanding the writing process, you will gradually understand some basic questions that writers keep in mind and try to answer before they complete a finished draft. These questions are similar to those that instructors may ask students in writing conferences or by written comments on drafts. Writers should begin using these questions as a guide after a first draft has been written. During the postwriting stage, effective writers work their way through the questions, determining if they can answer each one clearly and positively by pointing to specific evidence in the draft to support their answers. If the answers are positive, the chances are good the writer has an acceptable draft ready for submission to an audience. If not all the answers are positive, the writer should make the necessary changes before submitting the draft. In this way, the writer minimizes the chances that a draft will be returned or misunderstood. There's no real mystery to producing an acceptable paper; it simply involves preparation, care, and pride in the quality of the work. Here are the basic questions:

1. *What have I promised the reader that I will deliver in this piece of writing? How have I kept that promise?*
   A writer promises to do something: inform, argue, describe, analyze. It is not enough, of course, merely to state to readers what you're going to do; you actually have to show throughout the piece of writing that you are delivering what you promised; if the evidence is not there, then the writing does not work acceptably.

2. *How effectively have I organized my feelings, ideas, and evidence in this piece?*
   People become upset when they receive directions on how to do something or how to obtain something but can't use the information because it is unclear. Readers also get irritated when a piece of writing does not make sense and they have to work hard at discovering where the writer is taking them. By studying a draft carefully, you should be able to determine if you have presented a consistent pattern or order throughout the entire piece of writing. Making certain the order is clear will save time and spare you the frustration of having to go back and explain how your ideas relate to each other.

3. *What key details or pieces of information have I placed in this draft to increase my readers' understanding of my subject? Do I have enough of them?*
   One of the major differences between effective and ineffective writing is the presence of precise details and examples to support the main points; without detailed information, readers cannot become involved fully with your material and see it as you do. Even a simple

phrase like "an old coat" can be made more informative for the reader through revision: "The brown tweed coat, its buttons hanging from loose threads, the collar and cuffs frayed, looked as if he didn't know that dry cleaning had been invented."

4. *How have I controlled my subject for the reader through effective use of paragraphs?*
Most writing should not be a puzzle; readers like to know the exact purpose of each chunk of material they read and how it relates to what went before and what is coming next. Clear transitions are important here, and a sharp focus or purpose for each paragraph is essential.

5. *How effectively and consistently have I demonstrated my control of sentence construction and use?*
Most people don't care for monotony in speech; readers don't care for it in writing either. Effective writing has a smooth flow to it; readers are able to move along the lines of print easily because writers have made certain that the subject of each sentence works correctly with its verb, that modifiers do their job effectively, and that the length and type of sentences vary.

6. *How do I show that I have my language under control?*
At some time in our lives we probably have used a term or word incorrectly at an inappropriate time. The resulting embarrassment is not something we would like to repeat. You should have the same concern in your writing. If you know the words you are using and adjust your language for your audience and purpose, the language will work effectively because it is appropriate for the occasion. The best language use is that which calls the least attention to itself. A dictionary and a thesaurus are essential resources here.

7. *How effectively have I handled the spelling, punctuation, capitalization, and the general appearance of my draft?*
No one should expect a first draft to be clean; cross-outs, arrows, and blank spaces are all part of the effort to get things down on paper where you can look at them and decide what you need to do to make the information interesting, clear, and effective. But when the rough drafts are turning into a polished draft, one you are ready to share with an audience, it's time to get out the magnifying glass and examine the draft carefully for any signs of carelessness. Presenting readers with "finished" manuscripts that contain numerous mechanical errors is a bit like presenting a picture of yourself with "ring around the collar," "denture stains," and an "itchy scalp." Just as people take pride in their physical appearance, so

too should you as a writer take pride in the appearance of your writing. Time spent carefully proofreading reduces the chances that a manuscript will be returned for a cosmetic touch-up.

There we have it: the writing process. Perhaps it's still a bit of a mystery to you, but at least you now have a general framework in mind. In the following chapters this process will be divided into small steps, leading you from the start to the finish of a piece of writing. This entire text focuses on making you aware of the writing process and the various techniques you may use during it. The ultimate goal, of course, is to leave you with this process firmly in mind so that as you encounter future writing tasks you will not have to resort to magic, explosions, or procrastination. Instead you will feel confident in approaching the task, analyzing it, adapting the writing process to it, and then achieving your purpose.

CHAPTER 2

Writing: How Do You Feel About It?

Because you are enrolled in a writing course, you may associate writing with school more than with anything else. But academic writing provides only a small part of the writing experience you will have during your life. Even in an age when television, radio, movies, and computers supply us with so much information and entertainment, it's impossible to avoid writing. In fact, most professional people use writing daily to communicate with others in their profession. Anyone unable to write simply loses a vital means of communication. Consider the following list, which certainly isn't complete, of some writing experiences people may face.

letters	congratulations	inaugural speech
recommendation	order	promotional brochure
resignation	dispatcher's report	for town, school, in-
application	poetry	dividual, business
inquiry	obituary	psychiatrist's notes
protest	sermon	minutes of meetings
sympathy	caption	résumé
farewell	prayer	announcements:
to the editor	ship's log	birth, marriage,
advice	skits	death
warning	affidavit	war communiqué
invitation	telegram	time-capsule list
complaint	nominating speech	confession
pen pal	introduction	public notice
apology	eulogy	wanted poster

advertisement	suicide note	placards
list	diary	mottoes
epitaph	journal	undercover report
parody	dictionary entry	expense account,
news story	last will and	itemized and
human-interest story	testament	defended
legal brief	job specification	petition
editorial	contest entry	ultimatum
TV script	(25 words or less)	memo
graffiti	blurb for yearbook	report
slogans	picture	transcript
public statement	bumper stickers	

Whether we like to admit it or not, writing is a part of our lives. But where did all our experiences with writing begin and why should we care about them? If we recognize our past experiences with writing, we can better understand our present attitudes and our present ap-

---

WRITING QUESTIONNAIRE

Below are a series of statements about writing. There are no right or wrong answers to these statements. Please indicate the degree to which each statement applies to you by circling whether you (1) strongly agree, (2) agree, (3) are uncertain, (4) disagree, or (5) strongly disagree with the statement. While some of these statements may seem repetitious, take your time and try to be as honest as possible.

1. I avoid writing.	1 2 3 4 5
2. I have no fear of my writing being evaluated.	1 2 3 4 5
3. I look forward to writing down my ideas.	1 2 3 4 5
4. I am afraid of writing compositions when I know they will be evaluated.	1 2 3 4 5
5. Taking a composition course is a very frightening experience.	1 2 3 4 5
6. Handing in a composition makes me feel good.	1 2 3 4 5
7. My mind seems to go blank when I start work on a composition.	1 2 3 4 5
8. Expressing ideas through writing seems to be a waste of time.	1 2 3 4 5
9. I would enjoy submitting my writing to magazines for evaluation and publication.	1 2 3 4 5
10. I like to write my ideas down.	1 2 3 4 5
11. I feel confident in my ability to clearly express my ideas in writing.	1 2 3 4 5

proaches to writing; knowing what happened in the past helps us understand what we need to do to develop our skills further and, if necessary, change some of our attitudes. One of the purposes of a writing course is to make writing a more comfortable activity in your life; writing may never replace jogging or other favorite pastimes, but at least with some understanding of where you are now and how you got there, your progress in writing may be easier and bring more benefits in the future.

Let's begin by considering how you feel about the different activities involved in writing. Take a moment to fill out the questionnaire below. Many of the statements may help you recall some feelings from your past writing experiences. The final tally of your responses to this questionnaire will indicate how relaxed or anxious you are about writing. If possible, share responses with classmates; you may discover that considerable agreement exists among you about certain feelings and approaches.

---

12. I like to have my friends read what I have written.   1 2 3 4 5

13. I'm nervous about writing.   1 2 3 4 5

14. People seem to enjoy what I write.   1 2 3 4 5

15. I enjoy writing.   1 2 3 4 5

16. I never seem to be able to write down my ideas clearly.   1 2 3 4 5

17. Writing is a lot of fun.   1 2 3 4 5

18. I expect to do poorly in composition classes even before I enter them.   1 2 3 4 5

19. I like seeing my thoughts on paper.   1 2 3 4 5

20. Discussing my writing with others is an enjoyable experience.   1 2 3 4 5

21. I have a terrible time organizing my ideas in a composition course.   1 2 3 4 5

22. When I hand in a composition I know I'm going to do poorly.   1 2 3 4 5

23. It's easy for me to write good compositions.   1 2 3 4 5

24. I don't think I write as well as most other people.   1 2 3 4 5

25. I don't like my compositions to be evaluated.   1 2 3 4 5

26. I'm no good at writing.   1 2 3 4 5

Source: "Writing Apprehension Survey" from John A. Daly, "The Empirical Development of an Instrument to Measure Writing Apprehension," *Research in the Teaching of English*, Winter 1975. Reprinted by permission of the author.

That agreement may continue as you take the next step toward developing a writing autobiography, the subject for your first full writing assignment. Try recalling some of your early experiences with writing. Probably that will be like trying to remember when you took your first step as you learned to walk; you know it must have happened but you don't recall when or where. For some of us, the same might be said about our start as writers—if we have done a good deal of writing while growing up. But you may claim that a difference exists between walking and writing. Right you are. We can walk without any difficulty because we've done it every day, a kind of automatic practice. But writing—we haven't necessarily done that every day so we don't have the same degree of skill, smoothness, and comfort with it. Without frequent writing, anyone will feel awkward; the pen doesn't seem to move easily across the page, and words and ideas fade away even before they get to paper. In short, writing may or may not be a relatively easy task for you right now, depending on your early experiences.

Perhaps your first moment of "writing" came when you discovered crayons and how beautifully they marked clean walls or how the colors blended with the wallpaper designs. The results of such first efforts probably brought you immediate attention, but not necessarily praise. You might even have come to associate some pain with writing. Or perhaps you remember your first writing experiences as being linked with handwriting—penmanship lessons, copying of letters. One student recalls:

> In Mrs. B's third grade my writing woes truly began. Cursive writing was justly named—it certainly was to be a curse on me. My printing in first and second grades was not noticeably worse than that of my peers. I had not given any indications that I was going to grow up to have handwriting that would look as if a drunken chicken with its feet dipped in ink had staggered across my paper, but in the third grade all the signs were there.

As you grew older, you had other experiences with writing, some good, some bad. Occasionally, you may have had some attitude problems, either directly tied to writing or to school in general. How did these change? In some cases it may have been a combination of factors, as in one student's experience:

> There were still plenty of things about the writing process that I hated with a passion: finding a workable yet interesting topic, searching for sources, writing bibliography cards, and wasting Thanksgiving vacation filling out over sixty required note cards. Like all the other students, I continually put off the torturous job of actually writing the

paper. When I could procrastinate no more and finally fell to the task, I made an amazing discovery: the endless job of revising and polishing was a challenge in order to reach the reader and make him not only see, but feel, my point of view, and I was almost enjoying myself! When the tedious final typing was done, I actually felt good about my paper, as though I'd really accomplished something. But it was when Sharon "The Witch" Sorenson stamped it with her official seal of approval, the only A/A in the class, that the effort somehow all seemed worthwhile.

Some writers, of course, began ambitious projects even when they were very young; often these had nothing to do with school. For example, Norman Mailer, a well-known novelist, recalls a project he began at the age of seven. He describes it as a science fiction novel patterned after the adventures of Buck Rogers. But what Mailer remembers most about the novel is not its plot but the notebooks he wrote the story in and some little habits he seemed to have developed:

> This novel filled two and a half paper notebooks . . . about seven by ten. They had soft shiny blue covers and they were . . . only ten cents in those days or a nickel. They ran to perhaps a hundred pages each, and I used to write on both sides. My writing was remarkable for the way I hyphenated words. I loved hyphenating, so I would hyphenate "the" and make it "th-e" if it came at the end of the line. Or "they" would become "the-y."
>
> —*Writers at Work: The Paris Review Interviews*

By now a few memories ought to be coming back to you about those early days of learning to write. That means you're ready to begin collecting the information. Before collecting information, a writer always needs to establish both a purpose and an audience if the writing is to succeed in communicating. For this assignment, the purpose and the audience are identified for you; in some later assignments you identify them yourself.

ASSIGNMENT:
THE WRITING AUTOBIOGRAPHY

Purpose

In this essay you should identify and explain some of the most important influences that have shaped your attitudes and approaches to writing.

Audience

Readers of this essay will be English teachers who are just starting to teach writing at various levels. They need to know as much as possible about how students view the writing process and what kinds of techniques, activities, and situations help and hinder students.

Prewriting

Probably the easiest way to approach this assignment is to develop the material for the writing autobiography in two sections. In the first section you will recall incidents, people, places, and times related to your own strong feelings, positive or negative, about writing. In the second section you will describe your actual process of writing: what you do when you write and why. Together, these two sections will show the relationships between your past experiences and your present attitudes and approaches toward writing.

Listing

To begin, try the technique of listing. Take a blank sheet of paper and for at least five minutes—longer if possible—try to recall as much as you can about your early writing experiences. Jot down the details as they come, simply listing them without too much concern for order, although you may discover an order emerging. Your first jottings, or prewriting list, might look like the following:

Topic: A Writing Autobiography

Purpose: To explain how my present attitude toward writing was shaped

3rd grade
penmanship lessons
copybooks
formation of letters
use of symbols to reward good writing
time spent on lettering
Sister Teresa's attitude
lined paper
pencil
sounds made during lesson
inability to satisfy teacher
punishment
10th grade
Monday essays

in-class themes
topic selection
teacher comments on papers
class attitude
no explanation for writing
no chance to do over

Mrs. Simmons
careful assignments
workshops in class
extra time outside class
publication of newspaper article
prize-winning essay
vocabulary work

Lists of this type usually will help you identify some possible areas for exploration and development. Three items or areas have emerged from the sample prewriting list: third-grade penmanship, tenth-grade essays, and Mrs. Simmons. If these three areas definitely influenced the writer's attitudes, the writer has to flesh out the list with as many specific details as possible in each area. Let's see what happened when the writer took this next step with the area of third-grade penmanship.

3rd grade
St. Mary's School in Bingham, N.Y.
small classes—15 students
very disciplined—had to complete all our work by certain time; great emphasis on neatness, margins, etc. I was a very messy worker—always managed to smudge my papers, couldn't stay on the lines and hated deadlines
copybook—blue cover, blue-lined paper, 40 pages in a book; couldn't lose it—punished if we did by staying in after school and doing all the lost work over
wrote with No. 2 pencils that said "God Is Love"
symbols used to record progress—baby Jesus, angels, Wise Men— depended on quality of work as to which sticker was put on the page; I never got more than a baby Jesus; others in class got the whole manger scene
Sister Teresa—very stern, rarely smiled; whacked you across the knuckles if you didn't hold your pencil right; spent most of our class time making us form letters; I never got the idea that writing was anything more than putting *i*'s and *e*'s in neat rows with just the right amount of space between them
spent a good amount of time during recess, noon hours, and after school doing my copybook over and over

day's lesson always began the same; first, Sister put the letter for the day on the blackboard—green board, white chalk, the light made it hard to see; then we had to make a single row of the letter on a page in the copybook; when we finished the row, she would check it; if it was okay, we made three more rows; she checked these; if they were okay, then we "reviewed" by taking the previous day's letter and doing it for five rows; I don't recall when we got to put the letters together—I assume we did but all I can remember is the business of the letters in the rows, fearing Sister's disapproval and knowing that at least part of each week I was going to miss out on recess and other times because I couldn't please her

At this point in prewriting, some details and some directions usually emerge. When the ideas and details in one area of your list start to dry up, switch to another. Do this until you've put "flesh" on each of the areas. With this accomplished, you've identified some important information about your attitudes toward writing.

Response   Now you need some reaction to your material. You need somebody to raise additional questions, to point out areas and items that need more explanation, and to listen to you explain what seems to be emerging from the prewriting and how it can be developed.

Select a partner to work with you. "Walk" your partner through the information you have developed so far; that is, explain to your partner what each item on your list means and how it relates to other items. Encourage your partner to question any detail, any part of the material that seems unclear and not detailed enough. As new ideas or corrections occur to you, make adjustments in your list. Then provide the same kind of response for your partner on his or her list.

Clustering

The next step in developing material for your writing autobiography is to examine how you write. What do you do, physically and mentally, when you sit down to write. Your audience of new English teachers wants to know how you approach a writing task. Most writers follow some kind of process, and it may help if you examine your writing with that in mind. To assist yourself in keeping track of the information you will discover, try "clustering," a prewriting technique that simply calls for you to cluster your information around several small topics that relate to the larger topic, in this case the writing process. Study Figure 2.1 to see what clusters look like and then build your own as you proceed through the rest of this section.

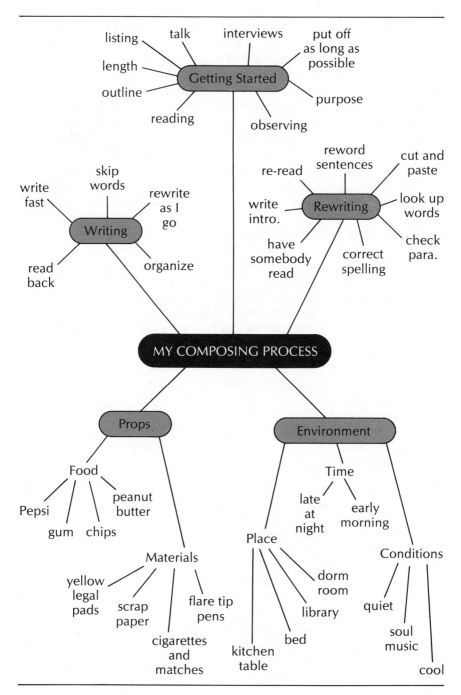

Figure 2.1 Clustering Diagram.

Props   The most logical place to begin clustering is with some of the factors that affect your writing. All writers, professional and amateur, have their *props*, objects that seem to make the writing process easier. For some writers, props are certain kinds of writing materials; for others they are simply items that make the writers more comfortable although contributing nothing of direct value to the writing. Some writers, for instance, seem unable to write easily unless they have a particular type of paper; many favor yellow legal pads; some like to do their preliminary writing in old-fashioned grammar school copybooks with lined pages and red-lined margins. Others write rough drafts only on wastepaper. Such writers claim they are thrifty because they know that much of the preliminary writing will be scratched out, even thrown away; working on paper already condemned to the wastebasket helps them feel more comfortable in revising than if they were working on crisp, clean, expensive sheets of bond paper.

Some writers can get superstitious about their props. Truman Capote, a fiction and nonfiction writer as well as a dramatist, claims he can't write if there are yellow roses near him—even though they're his favorite flower; and he can't allow three cigarette butts in the same ashtray. Now you're probably not as fanatic about props as Capote is, but you may have some props that you have never thought about before. Consider the following questions.

Do you find yourself eating while writing? What do you eat or drink?
Do you write better with some music or other sounds in the background? What are they and why do you like them?
Do you prefer a certain kind of pen or pencil? Why?
Do you find it easier to write in one kind of clothes rather than another?

Your audience of English teachers needs to know these things so they can understand why you respond as you do to different writing situations. Add notes in your cluster about props. Make the notes as specific as you can; name brands, recordings, colors of ink and paper, and so on.

Environment   Getting started can be difficult. Just the thought of having to write creates problems for some people. Some writers develop specific routines that get them into a writing mood; often these routines occur at a certain time of day. James Jones, author of *From Here to Eternity*, admitted that it usually took him an hour and a half of "fiddling around" before he could get started. During that time he might smoke half a pack of cigarettes and drink numerous cups of coffee before finally getting down to actual writing. What time of day do you prefer to write? Early morning seems to be a good time for many writers; something about the coolness and quiet of early morning works well for concentration. Other writers prefer the late evening hours; their other work is done and most people will leave them alone. Of course, you can't always pick the times in which you write. In test and work situations, writing often has to be produced regardless of whether the time is best for you. But in those cases when you have some time flexibility, you may have developed some preferences for when you write. Your audience will be interested in learning about this; add that information to your cluster about environment.

Time is not the only aspect of environment that may affect a writer; place may be equally important. Comedienne Joan Rivers says, "A great place to think of lines is in the tub. Every writer I know gets great ideas in water. I keep paper next to the tub. I guess it all goes back to floating in your mummy's tummy. I get my funniest comedy lines soaking in the tub. David Brenner [the comedian] says the most hysterical thoughts come to him in the shower" ("The Wacky Writing World of Joan Rivers"). Some students find writing in their dorm rooms impossible so they go to the library and find a corner where they can write undisturbed. Other students are content to write anywhere—in the middle of the cafeteria, riding in a car, sitting at a bar, during a ball game. Often writers seek out a special place where for some reason the writing seems to come more easily. Some professional writers actually construct a room or a separate building for that purpose. The following is a description of Ernest Hemingway's "writing place."

> The room is divided into two alcoves by a pair of chest-high bookcases that stand out into the room at right angles from opposite walls. A large and low double bed dominates one section, oversized slippers and loafers neatly arranged at the foot, the two bedside tables at the head piled seven-high with books. In the other alcove stands a massive flat-top desk with a chair at either side, its surface an ordered clutter of papers and mementos. Beyond it, at the far end of the room, is an armoire with a leopard skin draped across the top. The other walls are lined with white-painted bookcases from which books overflow to the floor, and are piled on top among old newspapers, bullfight journals, and stacks of letters bound together by rubber bands.
>
> It is on the top of one of these cluttered bookcases—the one against the wall by the east window and three feet or so from his bed— that Hemingway has his "work desk"—a square foot of cramped area hemmed in by books on one side and on the other by a newspaper-covered heap of papers, manuscripts, and pamphlets. There is just enough space left on top of the bookcase for a typewriter surmounted by a wooden reading board, five or six pencils, and a chunk of copper ore to weigh down papers when the wind blows in from the east window.
>
> —*Writers at Work: The Paris Review Interviews*

Your Writing Process   Now that you've considered the importance of props and environment and have made notes in your clusters about those aspects of your writing, you are ready to consider the actual writing. You may have to watch yourself for a while to detect what it is you actually do; after all, you are not accustomed to studying your habits that closely as a natural part of your writing. The following questions may help trigger some material for you to add to your clusters.

How do you begin? Do you just jump in and figure things out as you go along or do you carefully collect information, outline it, write a careful introduction, and then develop the paper?

Do you write the whole paper at one sitting or do you write it in stages? Do you like to write a draft of a paper and then leave it for a day or two before coming back to work on it? If you have used both methods, which one seems to give you the best results? Why?

Do you ever stop and read aloud what you have written?

Do you consult others while you are writing a paper? Do you let others read your rough drafts or only a finished copy? Why?

Do you try to correct obvious errors as you write the first draft or do you have some other way of handling such errors? What effect does this have on your progress?

Rewriting   One aspect of writing often overlooked by students is rewriting. Professional writers frequently spend more time on rewriting than on any other part of the writing process. Some writers keep rewriting even after their work has been published. James Thurber revised his stories by simply rewriting them from the beginning, again and again. One story he claimed to have "rewritten fifteen complete times. There must have been close to two hundred and forty thousand words in all the manuscripts put together, and I must have spent two thousand hours working on it. Yet the finished story can't be more than twenty thousand words" (*Writers at Work: The Paris Review Interviews*). Nobody is going to expect that you put in that kind of effort, but rewriting is usually vital to the success of a piece of writing, so consider the following questions and add your responses to your clusters.

How do you view rewriting? Do you rewrite as you go, changing words, sentences, maybe even whole paragraphs, or do you wait until you finish a draft and then return to these things?

What tells you something ought to be revised?

Do you rewrite sentences to get a better sound or rhythm?

Do you write several introductions and conclusions before selecting one?

Do you prefer to write or type your final copy? Do you continue to change things even while making the final copy?

Response   Now that you've accumulated considerable detail in your clusters, take a few minutes and, with the same partner you had for reviewing your earlier lists, "walk" your partner through your writing process; start with the props and then the environment; explain why each detail is significant in your writing approach; encourage your partner to ask questions about each cluster; move on to the act of writing, again explaining as you go along. When you have completed your discussion, reverse roles with your partner and follow his or her explanation. Be a curious partner and press for as much specific information as you can get. Encourage each other to add material as it emerges in your discussions.

The First Draft

Now that you've had an opportunity to locate some information about your writing experiences and your writing process, you're ready to write a rough draft of your writing autobiography. First you need to recall your *audience*—new English teachers who need to know specific information about your writing experiences and process so that they can teach their students effectively; and your *purpose*—to identify and explain what has shaped your attitudes and approaches toward writing up to the present. The following steps will help you get started on a rough draft.

1. Start looking at your first prewriting lists for common groupings of information; you may find the information falls into natural groupings that suggest a time scheme, such as from earliest experiences to most recent; in the example used in the text, the time frame seems to be third grade, then tenth grade; the writer, of course, knows if Mrs. Simmons fits with either of these or will have to be worked in somewhere else. If your material does not suggest a time sense, try arranging the items according to general areas or topics; for example, influences in the home, influences in school, influences on the job might be working categories. Don't be reluctant to explore several different ways of putting the material together, always remembering, of course, that the pattern must make sense not only to you but also to your readers, who may not know you very well.

2. Your prewriting clusters already contain groupings: your writing process broken down according to props, environment, writing, and rewriting. Now it's only a matter of seeing that you develop

them as fully as possible and of deciding the best sequence for presenting the details in each cluster or category.

After a preliminary identification of how you think your material should be presented, number the items in your lists and clusters to remind yourself of the sequence for introducing them into the paper.

The following are three options you have for writing your draft. From having examined your own writing process, you should be aware now of which option may work best for you.

> *Option 1:* Write an introductory paragraph that clearly sets the focus for your paper and indicates the order or direction you'll be taking as the essay develops. Remember your audience and their need to know why you are writing the essay. Write a draft that reflects this opening paragraph.
>
> *Option 2:* Perhaps you're not "all together" yet, so Option 1 isn't for you. If that's the case, try taking each general area you've identified and write short drafts for each, a bit like writing a mini-essay for each section. Then decide on the best way to organize the sections and finally how to introduce them and tie the mini-essays to one another to form one whole piece.
>
> *Option 3:* Simply start writing with the material you have and write yourself out; this might be called the "I-don't-know-what's-going-to-happen-but-here-goes" approach. Once you've written yourself out, examine the material to see how well it comes together and fits your original purpose. Move parts around, add and take away as seems appropriate until you have a version that focuses clearly.

Any of these options or combinations of them should eventually lead you to your destination: a reasonably clear rough draft of your essay. This draft can be refined, added to, subtracted from, and polished, depending on the amount of time you have before your deadline. The time you spent in prewriting (the lists and clusters) should have made it easier for you to produce a full piece of writing and should also save you time in revising. Whatever approach you have used at this stage—and you might try several before one works—remember that good writing takes time and that an important part of any writing is discovering what you want to say, why you want to say it, and how to say it. Approaching your writing in this way, you need not be too upset if a piece does not work out immediately. Be patient, take the time to think about what you have written, be willing to make changes, even to start over, and a workable draft will emerge.

Response

You have already had some response to your material. Now that you have finished a draft of your essay, you'll find it helpful to receive more reaction. In a group formed by you and your classmates or by your instructor, follow the approach outlined below. Once you've received response from that group and considered it carefully, move on to the revision stage.

SEEKING RESPONSE

Writer of the Paper

1. Avoid any preliminary apologies and commentary about your paper.
2. Read your paper aloud to the group, taking your time and speaking loudly and clearly enough for the group to hear.
3. Pause for a minute after your reading is completed; do not say anything.
4. If there is time, reread the paper aloud, remembering not to rush. (Your instructor will indicate whether you have time for a second reading.)

Listeners

1. After the reader completes the first reading, jot down words, phrases, and sentences that linger in your mind; perhaps the expressions seem unusually fresh or interesting to you, creating sharp images in your mind, making you stop and think about the experiences being described; or possibly there are some phrases you heard that strike you as being empty, vague, or repetitive; jot those down as well.
2. Listen carefully to the second reading and add to the list you started after the first reading.
3. After the second reading, group members should take turns doing the following:
   a. Tell quickly what seem to be the main points: specific events, feelings, people, and the like. (Don't hesitate to repeat a point even if someone else has mentioned it, but try to mention some new ones as well.)
   b. Summarize the main idea of the essay in one sentence, with each group member offering a version.
4. If time permits after everyone has had an opportunity to read and respond, talk about the papers in more depth, seeking more information, suggesting other examples, facts, and so on.

Writer

1. As you receive response from the group about your paper, don't hesitate to ask questions; if their responses are not clear, ask for clarification; if they make suggestions, discuss them.
2. Make notes on your paper as different aspects of your writing are discussed; don't trust your memory to recall responses after you have left the group.

Re-Viewing

With the comments of the group fresh in your mind, return to your draft with the purpose of making it even better. Consider the group's comments—what did they seem to grasp quickly, what did they seem unsure about or uninterested in? As you listened to others read their papers, what additional thoughts did you have about your own essay? Frequently when you hear or see what others have done, their work triggers memories and ideas in you and you can add or change things in your writing based on those discoveries. You may also find it useful at this point to read some of the writing autobiographies at the end of this chapter; these were written both by students and by teachers; the approaches reflect the individual experiences of each writer. As you read these essays, you may find it useful to keep the following questions in mind.

1. What are the key influences that the writer feels affected his or her writing?
2. What specific details or examples help you most to identify and understand these influences?
3. What process does the writer seem to follow in writing?
4. How clear is the connection between the writer's process and his or her experiences with writing?
5. What additional information or explanation would you have liked the writer to have supplied?

As you return to your own writing autobiography, keep in mind your reactions to the essays you have read. In addition to the preceding questions, you may find it helpful to consider the following in revising your work.

1. How have I kept my audience in mind throughout the essay? Where might I add or change details, examples, or facts to further increase the audience's interest and knowledge?
2. How well have I focused the essay so my readers have a clear idea of

why they should read it? How well is the focus shown in the introduction?

3. How well have I ordered my material? Might a reader become confused at any point about time, place, or sequence of events? Are paragraphs full of related information yet divided in such a way that the reader can easily see the development of thought?
4. How well have I avoided talking in general, vague ways about important aspects of my writing experience and process?
5. How much have I tried to use anecdotes and colorful details to let my readers know that a real person is behind this essay?
6. How well does my draft read? Have I taken care of spelling and grammar mistakes? Is the punctuation appropriate?
7. Can I honestly say that I have spent the necessary time on this piece of writing and that I see nothing more to do to it?

Response

If you can answer the preceding questions positively, then you are ready for a last response from a partner or a group of readers. Have your partner or readers note any places where possible confusion or incorrectness might make your draft less than successful. Do the same for their essays. If after such scrutiny your essay seems ready for submission, follow the procedures your instructor has indicated for handling essays at this point in the process.

SAMPLE AUTOBIOGRAPHICAL ESSAYS

Writing Habits and Influences

My first recollections of writing are hard to distinguish from those of reading. I was blessed with parents who read to me from Dr. Seuss storybooks before I had completely mastered the fine art of crawling. Stories of *Green Eggs and Ham* and *The Cat in the Hat* echoed throughout our house for years. I can recall tearfully copying the words: "this, that, these, and those" over and over again. Since they all started with the same letters, I would just guess at which words went with the rest of the sentence, thinking I could fool Mom and Dad into believing I could tell them apart. Having learned to read early made school more enjoyable than it would have been otherwise.

Just when I felt I knew it all, along came second grade at St. Francis de Sales. I had everyone's favorite teacher, Sister Mary Elizabeth; Sister kept a stack of green lined paper on a table beside her desk. We were allowed one sheet of paper at a time, and the main idea, as I saw it, was not to erase a hole in the paper. I had an overwhelming fear of going back for yet another sheet of paper and being told I had used my share of paper and was obviously a hopeless failure. After discovering we were allowed an unlimited supply of paper, thus relieving most of the pressure, I went on to the task of making sure my small letters touched the dotted line. I came to enjoy the challenge of handing Sister a perfect paper, and by the end of the year I had acquired quite a collection of holy cards and Madonna statues.

The third and fourth grades shared a room at St. Francis, because of their small size. Naturally, since my older brother was a fourth grader, I had to give a book report to the class that year. I wrote about *Beauty and the Beast*, and Sister Mary Dominic, a noted ruler-rapper, praised my report in front of the classes. I spoke up a lot more in class after that incident.

During all this time I kept a diary, which I still keep to a less personal degree in the form of a journal. This was probably the only writing outside of required school lessons I partook in until the eighth grade when I was assigned to a class taught by Mrs. Duprey. This wonderful lady was known to all as the "worst" English teacher you could get. She also doubled as my catechism teacher after class, where I finally found that teachers are people too. I began writing short stories and poems about that time, and I'd show them to her after class. I never felt patronized by her, though she was always quick on the draw with her red pen. Mrs. Duprey was the first teacher I had who gave two grades, to differentiate between the acceptability of subject matter, and grammar and punctuation. This way, you knew where the problem was, and could be proud of one aspect of your grade even if the other was deplorable. It kept me from losing all hope when I saw I had, at least partially, the right idea.

By the age of twelve, I had discovered that music had words. I was obsessed with copying lyrics to all the songs that seemed to pertain to my life. I was obviously an extremely vulnerable teenager, for I eventually copied over four hundred pages of lyrics. To this day I envy those song-writers for being able to convey what I felt and couldn't find the words to say. My parents discouraged my habit, on the grounds that it took too much time away from my studies. It was about this same time that they discovered my journal. Their disapproval at my undoubtedly "shocking" teenage viewpoints caused me to censor my writing to a great extent. To this day I take precautions not to write anything that would leave me open to criticism, a habit I've found to be a handicap. It's hard to write freely while trying to please someone else.

I always did my writing with a black, fine-point pen and college-ruled paper. If all I could find was a black, medium-point pen and a legal pad, I'd wait until later to do the writing. Total silence was the best background for thinking of ideas for required writing. Unfortunately, I generally had to resort to a bedroom to find complete silence, which inevitably led to propping myself in bed and falling asleep. Old albums turned down low always brought back memories, and never failed to put me in a thoughtful, melancholy mood, good for at least an hour of sentimental scribbling.

For the better part of my adolescent years, the majority of the conversations I had with my mother were on paper. Mom would leave notes on the kitchen table for me to read after school, and I would leave my side of the story in its place before I left the next morning. Several times our "notes" turned into pages. Since we couldn't yell at one another on paper, we underlined a lot instead.

At age fifteen, I was reading everything I could lay my hands on; Erma Bombeck, who writes mainly about middle-class, suburban life, was my idol. She made the tiniest details work for her to draw a hilarious picture of an otherwise dreary situation. Mrs. Bombeck has a way of using sarcasm without offending anyone, and her columns and books have something to say to nearly everyone of any age.

Rod McKuen's *Listen to the Warm*, given to me by a friend, was another type of writing that made an enormous impression on me. Until then, most of the poetry I had been exposed to was the rhyming kind. I couldn't find Mr. McKuen's books in my high school library, or public library, so I asked my English teacher to direct me to another source. She referred me to another English teacher, Mrs. Cardwell.

Rachel Cardwell had the strongest influence on my writing habits of any one person. She, too, was a fan of Mr. McKuen's, and let me borrow his books, as she had the entire collection. More than anything, she never made me feel as though I was imposing on her time. If anything, she encouraged me to stop by and talk over problems, even when I was not in any of her classes. Mrs. Cardwell was another of those teachers I was told to avoid because her classes were more difficult than most others. She shamed me out of a level-one class and into college prep, one semester. She also allowed me to sit in on her journalism class, whenever I had a chance, so I wouldn't have to choose between journalism and poetry.

Knowing this teacher was willing to go out of her way in my behalf made me want to prove to her and myself both, that I could excel in her class. Sometimes it takes knowing someone else believes in you before you can begin to believe in yourself.

Writing Autobiography

My earliest memories of writing are filled with negative impressions, most of which come from the eventful grade-school years. Following those years, my writing career was like a persistent, annoying habit as I progressed through the various high school courses, which brought me to the conclusion that writing is a necessary evil.

Writing seemed distasteful from the very beginning. In second grade we never got to write anything original: it was all either copying down what the teacher had written on the board or what was written in the copybook. I didn't like that book much. The "stories" we had to copy were only about two or three lines long. How can you justify the Grand Canyon in a story only three lines long? Being a rather advanced reader for a second grader, I wasn't enthused about those little stories or, at this point, about writing either.

The most prominent thing about writing in the third grade was an essay contest for little kids sponsored by the governor's office. The topic wasn't very original: "I like living in Indiana because . . . ." Some of the teachers thought that I should enter, so after a short and very persuasive talk, they entered me. I wrote some dumb little thing that sounded bad even to me since it was chock-full of generalities and meaningless niceties about how great our state was, but they sent it in. It surprised me that they would send in anything that bad without helping me make it any better. I thought teachers were supposed to tell you what was wrong with things like that and show you how to correct those problems, but they didn't. They never even said if they liked my paper or not, and I wondered if they'd even read it. At this point I didn't like writing very much.

As time passed, things continued in about the same manner. In sixth grade somehow I was coerced into another essay contest, this one sponsored by the Daughters of the American Revolution, and it was supposed to be about a character from the Revolution. This contest bore an amazing similarity to the first in that I wasn't interested, resented doing the paper, and didn't do a very good job. Writing was fast becoming something I did only on command.

By the eighth grade we were finally getting constructive criticism for our work and becoming more creative in our writing, but it didn't matter to me anymore. We saw slides one by one, writing down everything that came to mind; later we were to pick one and expand the notes into a descriptive paragraph. It wasn't a bad idea, but it came too late, for I was convinced that I hated writing and deeply resented the time it took to do a really good job. The problem was, being an achiever and a perfectionist, it was almost a moral duty with me to do a really good job. So I did. The papers turned out well, sounded right even to me, and got good grades. And I continued to hate writing.

Then it was my freshman year in high school, and I was taking English 11-C much against my will. Primarily a composition course, it was required for the better students. The teacher was privately known as Joyful Joyce. Basically she was a nice lady. She was polite to her students and talked about interesting things she'd read or unusual places she'd seen, but Joyful Joyce was an incessant smiler. I didn't care for the way she could twist the class's collective arm using a huge grin iced over with plenty of smooth talk. Unfortunately, she seemed to be able to read my mind and my entire past as well, for on the first day of class, when she didn't even know my name yet, she aimed that famous smile straight at me and gushed, "I can tell that you'll do very well in here!" Suddenly I was embarrassed about my writing and even more embarrassed for hating it, yet nothing was to change. By the end of the course I'd chalked up a few more A papers to my credit, but my negative attitude toward writing was exactly the same.

The next year I was guided into a course called Descriptive Writing; "guided" by the fact that it was the only English course that fit into my schedule. The class wasn't too bad, however, for a number of reasons. One reason was that behind me sat a really cute guy, and we got acquainted working on partner-type assignments and comparing finished papers and the grades we'd received. Another reason was the teacher. Her name was Selma Bubenzer, Miss B. for short. She must have been the original space cadet, because we were never quite sure where her thoughts were; nonetheless, she was a good teacher, for she taught me to tolerate writing by helping me to manipulate words to fit what my mind's eye saw and thus appeal to the emotions. Writing was slowly improving for me, but my fierce resentment of its demands on my time remained solidly unchanged.

Much as I may have despised writing, it seemed that I could never escape it. Finally I had reached the famed senior year, but I found myself quite inevitably in Advanced Expository Writing and scared to death, for now I had to face the feared Mrs. Sorenson. Not only behind her back, but in front of her face too, she was nicknamed "The Witch" and certain other rhyming terms. In a way the names had been earned: she was a demanding teacher and her classes were hard, the terror and downfall of more than one hopeful straight-A student. I felt the old fears of losing time and failing my goals creeping up once more. It was Mrs. Sorenson herself, however, who helped me. She proved to be a truly great teacher, and a great person in general. She showed a real interest in who I was, what I did, and what I liked: I found myself telling my audience of one all about things like my sewing, 4-H fashion shows, and bike trips as if I were talking to a close friend instead of the head of the English department. Then she taught me to write more effectively about those things that I liked, suggesting more precise phrases and coldly cutting out entire sections that were weak or unnecessary. Indeed, she demanded much effort, but only when she felt the student was able to meet those high standards for success. Mrs. Sorenson gave of herself, also, never failing to take the time to discuss problems with a student who needed her advice, even if it meant staying after school or missing her lunch hour. Her unusual concern, ability, and, most of all, her support for her students provided tremendous motivation for me. She was the most significant factor in my gradual acceptance of writing.

Then came the ultimate in high school writing courses, Mrs. Sorenson's Research Techniques class. There were still plenty of things about the writing process that I hated with a passion: finding a workable yet interesting topic, searching for sources, writing bibliography cards, and wasting Thanksgiving vacation filling out over sixty required note cards. Like all the other students, I continually put off the torturous job of actually writing the paper. When I could procrastinate no more and finally fell to the task, I made an amazing discovery: the endless job of revising and polishing was a challenge in order to reach the reader and make him not only see, but feel, my point of view, and I was almost enjoying myself! When the tedious final typing was done, I actually felt good about my paper, as though I'd really accomplished something. But it was when Sharon "The Witch" Sorenson stamped it with her official seal of approval, the only A/A in the class, that the effort somehow all seemed worthwhile.

Even today I don't enjoy writing, and I selfishly resent the time it takes from the many things I'd rather be doing. I also still feel the pressure, an inner pressure to excel and accomplish to my fullest potential. I've learned to handle it, though, and every technique that I use came from Mrs. Sorenson's wise advice and years of professional writing experience. I go off by myself where there's little interruption, just a bit of soft music, and preferably no people; once there, I hack out exactly what I'm thinking—and "seeing"—on a typewriter and cheap paper. I've learned to double- or even triple-space the lines; doing that leaves room to write in better phrases when I scribble out the old as new inspiration strikes. I've also learned that almost no sentence or paragraph, regardless of how good I thought it was, is completely immune to change or even total removal. Sometimes I'll take scissors and chop away an entire section, adding new sheets or just reconnecting the originals, until my drafts shine with yards of sticky cellophane tape.

Most important, though, I've learned not to give up, but to stay with a problem until it's worked out properly. And that lesson has helped me in more places than just writing class.

Why I Don't Write

The thought of writing triggers a specific sensory memory for me—the taste of the excessive cigarettes and coffee that I force on my system when writing. I pretend, when I'm writing, that the caffeine is responsible for the knot in my stomach and the shakiness of my hands, but it's clear that my symptoms are panic-related.

I feel a moment of sheer terror when I know that no one is going to give me a topic, that I'm on my own. I become impatient with myself as I sort through and reject ideas, and my uncertainty about the validity or interest of what I finally choose lasts until the damn thing is laid face-down on the teacher's desk, the destination of all my writing.

The ritual of getting ready to write has always been a mechanical, calming one of gathering together the props—ashtray, cigarettes (newly opened pack), matches, cup of coffee—and settling down to work in bed. Writing the thesis required for my M.A. degree confirmed and expanded the ritual. I would gather my aids and shuffle papers for a few minutes, blindly staring at words previously written, realize finally the passage of time, get a fresh cup of coffee, and begin to work. I wrote in notebooks or in the margins of the latest revision, copying from other scraps of paper. I spent a great deal of time looking for the right notebook, the desired scrap of paper.

At the beginning of a work session, I always wrote carefully, even trying to be neat. I composed sentence by sentence. I usually got impatient with the futility of that approach after a couple of hours, realizing that it would all probably be changed later, and I would end the work session by slopping words onto the pages, apparently almost randomly.

When I had several pages, I typed it. It always looked like it said more when it was typed, like running it through the typewriter lent more weight to my ideas. I did little revising, but proofread it and changed a few minor words. Then I sent it to my thesis adviser, trying first to dab up any spilled coffee from the sheets.

I haven't written anything—not even a grocery list—since I finished the thesis (*the* thesis—I don't even say "my"). It confirmed more than my prewriting ritual—it proved to me that I couldn't understand or appreciate the joys of revision or even the words used to talk about revision.

I had to return to NTSU to complete the thesis, leaving behind in Kentucky my husband, a job, and an interview for a possible teaching career. Working through the mail hadn't gone well; my thesis director and I are both procrastinators, so I resigned myself to several weeks at the university to finish.

The first day I waited in the café across the street from the language building. I sat in a booth looking through the plate-glass windows at people walking to class in the hot afternoon sun. I thumbed through the papers I held—the best I could do on Chapter One. I drank coffee and watched people, looking for familiar faces. She was late—she was always late. I fiddled with a pencil, slid the ashtray back and forth across the table, and drummed with my fingers on the polished wood. I got up to get a refill and almost without thinking bought cigarettes. Three months of abstinence down the drain.

I lit a cigarette and looked through Chapter One, admiring my examples, the clear argument, the fact that it *had* a thesis (unlike many on the shelves of the university library). I sat and smoked, waiting and wondering how long I'd be here dealing with the trifles we had left.

She whirled in, finally, in her perpetual hurry. "Ay, chica, how are you?" she had time to say, searching through her purse for coffee money. She got her coffee, lit a cigarette, and settled down to business. "Well, Debra, what've we got?" She read it slowly, thoughtfully, staring into space at intervals. With nothing else to do, I could focus on my nervousness; my body, already irritated by the unaccustomed cigarettes, encouraged uneasiness. I eavesdropped on conversations at neighboring tables and tried not to think about the possibility of never finishing a thesis. But I always ended up watching her read. She smoked, squinting her eyes against the smoke, pausing to drink coffee, light a cigarette, and hook her hair behind her ear. She marked little—just typos—but didn't look at me.

Finally finished, she thumbed through the pages again for a minute as I snapped to attention. "This is really going to be strong," she said. My intense relief almost blocked out the rest—"Let's go through it again." Nothing but total approval meant anything from her. In literature courses the worst she said—no matter how ridiculous the comment—was "All right. Anyone have anything to add?" So I was afraid she was just being gentle.

The fear that she was going to tell me tactfully to start over persisted as I listened to her. She inserted, restructured, "livened up," strengthened, and reworded, with minimal help from me. I never was sure which page we were on. After two hours she declared herself satisfied and we left the table—cluttered with cigarette wrappers, plastic cream containers, empty coffee cups, and overflowing ashtrays. Her final remark was "Once you make those changes I think things will be clarified—we'll be able to see what we need to do."

The excitement of getting down to serious work was gone. What I had considered final polishing was, apparently, preliminary. And indeed we did the same thing to that chapter three more times, before starting to revise another of the four chapters. She made me crazy, saying "Can you punch this up a little? Make it clearer just how horrible this guy is?" "How about—could you say his need . . . I don't know—is intrinsic or something?" and "What's another way to say this?" Finally after weeks of not understanding, I let my temper flare. "If I could think of another way to say it, I would write it down. That's the only way I can think of to say that." So she thought alone, staring ahead of her, apparently not perturbed by my defection. She loved polishing. I wanted to go home. Magically, the day my temper showed itself was the day we finished with the first chapter. I wondered if she had known I was about to leave.

I've never felt so completely at a loss as I did during that time. She would try to use me as a thesaurus, without telling me the nuances she was seeking. She "restructured" so freely I was afraid I wouldn't recognize my work after I typed it again. Alone with her, with that incredible energy trained on my work, I felt pushed without knowing how to move. I didn't know what she wanted, but I knew I had to do it before I could leave.

It doesn't seem now, thinking back on it, as if she personally did anything terrible to me, although I think of that time with her as the reason for my intimidation about writing. I doubt if she realized how intensely inadequate I was feeling. After I finished the thesis defense (where I smugly noticed that they asked me to return to my original wording in some cases), she assured me, as we celebrated over a beer, that she had done no more for my thesis than her thesis director had for hers. "They were just stylistic changes, Debbie." But I *had* expected to feel part of the process—or at least to learn how to do it myself—and despite her assurances I hadn't the least notion of how my work had been revised.

So even though she may not have contributed directly and personally to my fears about writing, I still built those fears, and I don't think it's amazing that I cry every time I have to write.

CHAPTER 3

What's in a Person?

Most of us will admit to being people watchers; give us some waiting time in a doctor's office, in a bus terminal, or in an airport, and inevitably we fall to watching the people around us. Usually we form impressions about the people we watch; perhaps we go so far as to guess individuals' occupations, their personalities, and their status in society; if we have enough time, we may create whole stories about what we imagine these people are like.

But along with being people watchers, we are people conscious. Our lives are affected by the people to whom we are related, by the people with whom we work, and by the people with whom we choose to spend our free time; and that does not begin to account for all the others who pass through our lives at various times. Frequently none of the people we encounter are famous; outside their immediate environment, they may not even be known to exist, but each person we meet makes a contribution, large or small, to our lives.

Writing about people becomes a way of sharpening our powers of observation while examining some of our perceptions about human behavior. We can learn about ourselves as well as others; we can come to understand how environment affects a person; we can come to appreciate people's contributions in a way we never considered before.

Often we've heard the expression "I know that person like a book," or we have predicted how an individual will react in a certain situation: "She would never do that; she's too shy." When we say these things, we're relying on what we know about the past behavior of a person. This information may come from our knowledge of the individual's physical or mental abilities, from our understanding of the person's emotional nature, or from having observed the person many times. At other times we may draw upon information provided directly by what the person says; and infrequently we rely on what others have told us about an individual. In spite of all this information, however, we occasionally may find ourselves surprised and have to change our view because we discover some new facet of a person.

Dominant impressions run throughout our perceptions of the people we know well. That is, we connect all the information we have to certain basic traits of these individuals. Unless we do this, we merely have a collection of unrelated facts and impressions that never provide us with a clear picture. Dominant impressions become particularly important when we write about people. Since readers frequently are not familiar with the person we are describing in our writing, we have to bring together various pieces of information and weave them into a profile that shows the dominant traits or impressions.

ANALYZING CHARACTER SKETCHES

Consider the following sketch of an old man written by a student. Read the entire sketch without pausing so you grasp the whole picture and the flavor of the piece. Then return to the beginning and look at how the sketch is developed, using the questions following the sketch as a guide.

The Old Man

1   I knew an old man once who drank beer all the time and who used an expression I'm not even allowed to *say*, never mind write down on paper. He'd been old for longer than I've been alive but he could still remember all the things he did when he was young. Sometimes he and I sat on the walk in front of his house and he told me stories all about how he used to live.

2   He wore white suits then with a vest that had big brass buttons running up and down the front, and a panama hat that laid low over one eye. He told me he used to smoke long, thin cigars too, but I didn't believe that at first because he always had short, flattened butts in his mouth when I knew him. But once he told me that the only way to tell a good cigar was to smell it from end to end right under your nose. That's when I knew he wasn't making up stories because his mustache

was burnt all srigley yellow from all the smelling and smoking he must have done in his lifetime. Besides, I got to thinking and I figured that since he'd never lied to me about anything before, he wouldn't lie about some stupid cigars.

3   He had even driven a carriage with monstrous black horses and he courted a lady in it. She had little, tiny ankles, he said, and he bought her all kinds of fancy shoes to make them look even tinier. I think he married her so he could look at her ankles because he didn't really love her. He loved a whore. (My mother doesn't like me saying that word either.) She used to drink beer with him and I guess she was just about as bad as he was. You could tell he really loved her because even the wrinkles around his water-colored blue eyes crinkled up whenever he talked about her. He'd look down the walk and mumble that expression I was telling you about at the beginning of all this.

4   One summer I helped him dig a garden and he grew rhubarb in it till it was old and tough. In the front yard we planted snowy white gardenias in little neat rows up and down the cement, but he planted the gardenias every year. They made his house look pretty and nice on the outside but the inside was always a mess the way he lived. Beer cans cluttered the coffee tables and the steps going upstairs but he never threw any beer cans on the walk where the gardenias grew. The same with butts. He'd sit on the front steps and puff and puff till I thought the smoke would come out the hairs in his ears but he never put a butt out on the walk. I asked him if the cigars were for him and the walk was for the lady but he just threw his head back and laughed and laughed at me. Then he told me I was . . . well, he called me that expression of his. He called everybody that, though, so I wasn't insulted or anything.

5   He used to say he was a man of hell: full of hell and determined to go there. I knew him and had no doubts about it myself. But for all his hell he would never let me lose more than four hands of poker in a row when we played on the walk. He never cheated once either, except when it was my turn to win and then his gnarled old hands fumbled with the cards and he'd pick up a beer to hide it. He told me he used to gamble a lot when he was young but I could always catch on to his tricks. He'd wink at me and tell me if I was so smart how come he always won four times out of five? I couldn't answer that and he'd say I was—his favorite expression which I'm dying to tell but I can't.

6   He was my friend for all that he gambled and drank beer and my mother didn't care, but I suppose that was because he gave her free rhubarb. She might not have let me be his friend if she knew I gambled too and sometimes had a can of beer myself. He said drinking beer

was a good part of life and I ought to get to know the good parts while I was still young enough to enjoy them. That's what he'd always done and anyone who didn't go along with that was . . . well, was what he always said.

7   My mother said he probably didn't go to hell at all when he died but met his lady and went to heaven. I don't think so. I think he went straight to hell and drank beer with his whore. He would have been a lot happier in hell, I know that, and anyone who doesn't think so is . . . what he always said!

Analyzing Development

Return to the beginning of the sketch and, using the following questions, examine its development. Jot down your answers to the questions so you'll have a basis for discussion with your classmates.

1. What does the writer do in paragraph 1 to let you know about the focus of this piece?
2. What does the writer do for you as a reader in paragraph 2?
3. Of what help to the reader is the last sentence in paragraph 2?
4. In paragraph 3 what is the function of the story about the lady with tiny ankles?
5. Why does the writer tell us about the two gardens and the inside of the house?
6. What words and details in paragraph 5 *show* the old man, not simply tell us about him?
7. What is the point of including the detail about free rhubarb in paragraph 6?
8. What is the idea the writer tries to leave with you in the last paragraph?
9. What one detail is carried throughout the sketch? What effect does this have on you as a reader?
10. How does the writer make you aware of her attitude toward the old man?
11. In one clear sentence describe the overall impression you think the writer has created in this piece.

After completing these questions, develop an outline of the sketch that you believe shows how it is put together; make it an outline that you might use as a guide when you write your own sketch.

Reading for Evaluation

Now that you have read, analyzed, and discussed one sketch, you should have in mind some of the ingredients that make this kind of writing effective.

Now you are about to read five character sketches written by students. Each one focuses on a particular person. These people will be strangers to you, although they'll probably remind you of individuals you know. As a reader, however, you'll be able to "know" these people only through the information the writers have provided. The assignment that led to the writing of these papers is similar to the one you will do later in this chapter. The purpose of the assignment was to describe a person of importance to the writer—not necessarily to the world— and to do so as clearly and as concretely as possible. A reader like yourself, who has never met the person in the sketch, should come away with a dominant impression so vivid that if by chance you happened to meet the individual being described or heard of his or her actions you might well recognize the person. Not all the writers of these sketches approached their work in the same way or with the same degree of skill; because of this you have an opportunity to examine some of the strengths and weaknesses in a variety of approaches. Your task is to identify as many of the strengths and weaknesses as possible and to explain which essays seem to be the most effective in meeting the purpose of the assignment.

1. Read all of the essays in the order that they appear.
2. Reread them and rate the essays on a scale of 1 to 5, with 1 being highest and 5 being lowest or weakest; you may discover that more than one essay fits into a category; if so, double listings are permissible, but try to make the necessary discriminations.
3. Look carefully at the sketches you rated 1 and 2; what was it about those that made you give them a high rating? Jot down specific notes, referring to sections with exact words or notations, such as "paragraph 5—details about walk are unclear." Do anything that will help you recall during class discussion what you considered strong points. The sample work sheet on page 43 provides an example of a way to record notes about an essay.
4. Look carefully at the sketches you rated 4 and 5; what was it about these that made you rate them low? Again, use the same approach for indicating weak points as you did for strong points.
5. Study the notes you made on the strongest and weakest papers; then at the bottom or on the reverse side of your work sheet, write

in clear, concise language a list of characteristics you believe are necessary for a successful character sketch. Be prepared to discuss your list with classmates.

6. From what you and your classmates list as necessary ingredients, develop a checklist of characteristics for a successful character sketch. Use that checklist as a basis for writing your own character sketch.

CHARACTER SKETCH ANALYSIS WORK SHEET

Rating: 1
Title of Essay: "Mr. Heil, English Teacher"
Strengths

Writer identifies the trait that's going to be focused on: cleanliness
Uses several incidents to show Mr. Heil in action; avoids just telling he's unusual
One detail seems to lead naturally to another
Keeps in mind audience may not know Heil; tries to explain special details like the cleaning of the board, chapel service, and recess so we understand what they are and how they're unusual
Lets us know what her attitude is and how she got her information—didn't like him because he was too fussy; had him as a teacher

Weaknesses

Perhaps too many incidents; better to stay with just a few and develop them in detail; leave out the bit about his shirts—didn't see much connection with cleanliness
Maybe use some dialogue to let us hear him as well as see him; for example, letting us hear exactly what he said when he told the boys to go to the bathroom and clean their sneakers

Rating: 2
Title of Essay: "Dear Old Uncle Walter"
Strengths

Identifies several traits—hard worker, likes to talk, gives many orders; owns a farm and a store
Uses concrete details about appearance, tan, scarred work boots, white long johns
Shows what the writer's relationship is to the subject and where the information comes from

Weaknesses

Doesn't seem to have a real focus; maybe tries to cover too much ground; reader has tough time figuring out what's important
Doesn't really show Uncle Walter in action; just tells about him
Needs to concentrate on one or two incidents and develop them in detail
Confusing ending; don't know who the writer is talking to
Introduction seems to suggest one thing; paper talks about another
Doesn't seem to be any real organization; just a bunch of paragraphs stuck together

SAMPLE CHARACTER SKETCHES

Geneva

Have you ever met a person who rummages through trash cans? I have and she uses those "goodies" to decorate her house. In addition to her being stingy, Geneva Huffman, my next door neighbor is lonely and old fashioned.

Geneva is lonely. She lives in a one room shack by herself not depending on anyone or any item. Every once in awhile she gets so lonely that she goes to the general store and waits for a familiar person to come in. She asks "Ya gots any news to tell me today?" If she is told "no," she constantly questions him again and again until she finds out something or he tells her to leave him alone. She then slowly wanders back to her house to relax until she gets lonely again. Since I have known her, about eighteen years, she has made no new acquaintances, but remains friends with her old acquaintances. Obviously these friends are not enough because she is still lonely which drives her to being nosy.

Another of her characteristics is that, she seems a bit old fashioned. She once received a lump sum of money and had the chance to install indoor plumbing. She did not take the money and said that because she had always used outdoor plumbing, why should she change now. A second activity is that she washes her clothes with a washboard, which is an old-fashioned way of washing clothes. A male relative of hers offered to give her his old washing machine, but again she refused to accept it. To her this is just another inconvenience. Finally she walks wherever she wants to go. People offer her rides, but she replies, "No, Thank Ya, I prefer to walk." Geneva's outlook on life is that everyone should be able to make do with bare necessities, not with many extravagant things.

Her final outstanding characteristic is that she is very stingy. She appears on the door step with a short purple dress on with panty hose that have about six holes to each leg. She also wears a pair of black army boots which lace-up with red shoe strings. Over her dress she wears an old tattered, grey coat, which must be at least thirty-five years old. The lining of her coat is torn at the seams so that on a cold winter's day she can let the hem slip down to prevent her legs from getting too cold. To cover her stringy, black hair she wears a dark green sock hat. For a purse she carries a burlap sack. To provide variety she cuts out flowers of different colors and types and then tapes them on the sack. Astonished at the sight of her, I asked, "What are you doing here?"

She answered, "I was wondering if you have any extra newspapers."

I said, "No, but what do you want them for?"

She said, "The paint on my walls is chipping off and I want to wall-paper them."

She figures she can "Kill two birds with one stone." She can repair her walls and entertain guests at the same time, by letting her guests read the walls. She thinks that there is no use in paying money for wallpaper when the newspaper is lying there waiting for her to use it.

Geneva is a lonely person, who lives off bare necessities. If everyone would sometime in his life practice her philosophy of life he might end up better off.

The Way You Were

Somewhere in the distance a siren was wailing down a dark street. It was 8:05 p.m., February 5, 1979, and the moment I heard the shrill whistle, I knew something was wrong somewhere, but little did I know that the siren would bring a tragedy so close to me. My telephone rang at 8:25 p.m. My friend was dead.

Even as the sun sets today, I cannot fathom in my mind how God could remove you, a young man in the prime of life. Thinking of all the smiles and laughter we shared brings back so many reflections of the man you represented.

Just a good old country boy was the first impression you gave—hat in hand, standing in the door, eyes crinkling at the corners, and a big grin spread all over your face, the picture of the all-American good guy with a touch of country gentleness. You stood there smiling like the cat that swallowed the canary, not knowing whether to sit down or wait until you were asked. I think you were a little embarrassed by the clothing you wore; those striped, carpenter overalls had become a part of you. But you were a man that worked with your hands, the salt of the earth; a farmer, a car-penter, the back-bone of America, but also a professional in another right. Those hands that gripped the steering wheel of a tractor or a hammer could also grip a pair of drum sticks. Playing the drums was another part of you, separate and distinct in being but you never quite shook the country boy image when you played.

The farmer/carpenter was the man I remember most of the time. From head to toe you shouted "down home, hard-working, country boy;" worn-out cap with Cat Diesel Power emblazoned on the front pulled down low on your close-knit brows to keep the mop of hair from falling in your eyes; heavy blue denim overalls with well-worn knees and pockets that bulged with pencils, nails, and ruler; no shirt and a pair of crusty, tread-worn plow boots. That image spoke to me best on a late summer afternoon last year.

From the road I could see you hammering intently away on the sub-floor of your house. You raised your head to see who was coming to visit and then started to rise from the flooring. I turned and drove up the narrow gravel drive to reach the building site and by the time I reached the porch and got out of the car, you were standing there, hat pushed back on your head, and smiling from ear to ear. You pulled your cap off and wiped the sweat from your face with a tanned, lean arm. The sun glinted off your shiny brown hair but the sight was subdued by the replacement of the cap. Your face seemed more angular and rough-hewn that day, perhaps from the shadow cast over your face by the bill of the cap. The smile of your mouth created a brilliant white gash in your tawny face and your warm, brown eyes reflected the smile. You stood and spoke for awhile in proper country gentleman style and then turned to begin your diligent hammering once again.

With each resounding blow, the muscles rippled in your neck and arms and your lean lankiness seemed to be sharpened in the intensified late afternoon light. The sweat gleamed on your back and ran in tiny rivulets down the side of your face, and I noticed the long-fingered grace of those calloused, work-worn hands as you wiped the sweat from your chin. Your hands seemed poetry in motion with each simple task you performed. Every movement suggested a graceful, smooth rhythm flowing from inside you like electrical currents fluxing from a generator. You seemed to sense my interest in your hands and offered them for my inspection while explaining that they really weren't in shape for the night's drumming that lay ahead.

From where I sat in the club that night, I could see the nimble swiftness of your hands as each drum was released from the dark confinement of its case. Your fingers flew as each adjustment was made, and the glittering red drums soon were assembled with professional precision. After adjusting the stool and giving a few taps to each drum and a clink on the cow bell, you dismounted and casually strolled over to the table where I sat. "You think you're gonna like this place? I know it ain't much to look at but everybody here is real friendly most of the time and as long as I'm here, nobody's gonna get wise with ya', ya' know what I mean?"

I had to laugh because the last thing on my mind was worrying about somebody "gettin' wise." I looked at you and asked, "Why do you think anyone could come over here and bother me? Everyone can see that I'm with you."

"Well, just look around and tell me what you see and you'll understand why I worry about you. You're the purdiest girl here and not many of these hicks have any manners a'tall. I'd hate to have to whup somebody over you and risk causing a big fight. Besides, somebody might get real mad and smash my drums!" With that closing remark you had to leave. The lead guitarist was on stage striking a few chords, and the crowd had begun moving in to sit at the tables surrounding the dance floor. You sauntered a pace or two away from me, paused, turned, and said, "Smile, purdy girl, 'cause I'm playing this set for you." With a wink and a flashing boyish grin, you turned, took a few steps and mounted the stage.

Dressed in a western shirt, blue jeans, and a shiny pair of cowboy boots, behind those drums you sat, flexing your wrists, rolling up your shirt sleeves, and with feline movement, captured your sticks in hand. As the music began, you tipped your drum stick in my direction and began your night's work with a smooth rhythmic beat. The musical pace quickened and the beat of your body intensified with every pelt of your drum sticks. The blur of your hands moved to and fro as you worked your way from one drum to another and with each clash of the cymbal, the eyes squinted and the mouth clenched in a straight, tight line. All the muscles in your arms strained with throbbing energy as you put your whole being into the pulsing beat. And at the end of the set, with a final thump and flourish of your sticks, you brought the house down with thundering applause.

Back to the table you came, leaned over, picked up a towel and flung it around your neck, sat on a chair and planted your elbows with a resounding thump on the table. "What's wrong," I heard myself say; "Don't you feel good?"

"Yeah, I feel fine but my drums are sick. The humidity is so high in here it's causing my drum heads to stretch and that last number sounded bad."

"B.S., man, that's just your artistic temperament talkin' now. You did a great job. Everyone was screaming and clapping. What more do you want?"

"I'll tell you what I want," you smirked. In the heavy silence that followed, my face must have turned a thousand shades of red because your face reflected a charming boyish glee. "I want a glass of Coke. Had ya' worried, didn't I?" We both laughed, leaning back against the wall in our chairs to watch the huddled people in the room.

"What are you thinkin' about when you're playin' those drums?" I queried. "Your face is really intent but you act like your mind is a thousand miles away."

"Well, it is, but I can't tell you what I'm thinking about. Drummers are like magicians, they keep their secrets and nobody can take your tricks away when you keep them to yourself."

"I'm not talking about tricks of the trade, temperamental artist, I'm asking if you think about anything besides playing your drums while you're up there!"

"Oh, yeah, I think about a lot of things but I ain't tellin' what I think about. Go home and listen to the title cut of that Linda Ronstadt album I brought over to your house the other night. Maybe you'll understand." And with that, you up-righted the chair and plodded off, leaving me with only the cryptic words.

When I arrived home that night, I picked up the album and dropped it on the turntable. As the song "Simple Man, Simple Dream" flooded the quietness, the words rolled over in my mind and I began to understand.

> When people don't know what you mean
> They may laugh at you and call you green
> They'll say your words are stupid
> And your plans are always schemes
> Truth is simple
> But seldom ever seen
> Let nothing come between . . .
> Simple man, simple dream.

Gina

Gina is a very unique individual. She has many different characteristics but there are a few that stand out more than others. Such as her physical appearance, her moodiness and the fact that she has a nerve out of this world.

When people first see Gina the thing that they will notice is the way she looks. She is dark complected all year long and has high cheekbones. Her mother is from India so this accounts for Gina's appearance. If she is with one of her brothers or sisters, people cannot believe that they are really her brothers and sisters.

Sometimes, this upsets her badly; for example, one time some guys met her and already knew her sister Lynn, the guys called Gina liar when she told them that she really was Lynn's sister. Gina then gets really mad and tells them exactly where they can go.

Gina is also very moody. She can change from one mood to the next in a matter of minutes. One time Gina, her mother, Lynn and I were playing cards and her mother was just learning how to play this game. Gina's mother and Lynn were partners and Lynn kept yelling at her mother because she was making mistakes. Gina kept asking Lynn to stop yelling but she would not do it. Finally, Gina got so mad that she got up and threw the chair she was sitting in across the room, where her niece was standing, and almost hit her. This made Gina that much angrier. She then started yelling and hitting Lynn. Gina was kicking and throwing things. This all lasted for about an hour. When she finally calmed down, Gina, Lynn and I went out riding and you could have never told that thirty minutes ago they were almost ready to kill each other.

Gina also has a nerve out of this world. She will do almost anything. For example, one time she was standing in front of the McCracken County Jail yelling back and forth to this guy that was in there and the jailer came around the side of the jail and told her that if she didn't get away from there she would be in there with him so Gina looked over at him and said, "Well, whatever," and walked off; by the way, Gina's favorite word in the dictionary is whatever.

These things are what make Gina such a unique person. She may not be all of the finer things a person looks for in another person but she is herself and that is the best thing a person could possibly look for. Because of this she is the best friend I have or could ever hope to have.

Snoopy

There will probably always be a few lost people. They are lost because they never seem to turn up in a place where they are wanted. They lead a dry, lifeless existence like a lone, forgotten grain rattling about in an empty box, occasionally "bouncing off" the other beings in society, but never interacting. One of these lost, lonely souls is Snoopy.

Snoopy was a regular customer at the neighborhood supermarket where I worked, and he frequently came by my cash register. He rarely spoke, always seeming withdrawn into his own silent world, with a blank gaze and a straight, expressionless line for a mouth. We workers at the check-out lanes gave him his name one spring because of the outfit he regularly donned at the slightest hint of cool weather. It was almost a uniform in its changelessness: a gray-black overcoat made of rough tweed, a knitted muffler around his neck, and a black vinyl cap lined with fuzzy imitation fur. It was an aviator-style cap, the kind with ear flaps that turn down—and he always wore them turned down. It was that hat, along with the scarf and his long sad face, that created the startling resemblance to the well-known beagle of "Peanuts" fame. Thus, he was tagged with the nickname Snoopy.

He was a lonely-looking figure; tall and plainly dressed to an extreme, never even a colored shirt to break the dark monotony of his attire, he was easy to spot and could almost always be found somewhere along the sidewalk of the main avenue which passed near the supermarket. Snoopy's main pastime was walking. Slow yet determined, he must have covered miles each day along this road, never stopping to speak to a soul, constantly staring straight ahead.

Snoopy had made the supermarket a part of his daily rounds of the neighborhood, stopping in early each morning for a pack of cigarettes. Most of the "cigarettes only" customers hardly gave even their change a second thought, and simply forgot the receipt entirely. Not Snoopy. He was very precise about such things. He'd step right up to the register, so close that an involuntary shudder would run down my spine when I looked up to see him standing there silently, for his eerie lack of expression spooked me more than anything he could have said. He'd hold up his single pack of cigarettes, and with an affected flourish hand over the carefully counted change, correct to the penny. Then, instead of hurrying off, as most people would, he'd stand there, never saying a word. Hand held out, he'd patiently wait for the receipt, which he always ponderously checked for accuracy before carefully pocketing it.

As the weather turned hot and sticky, the overcoat, scarf, and hat disappeared. Snoopy's summer "uniform" was a plain white, slightly too snug T-Shirt and baggy black suit pants with the front pocket, the one which collected all the receipts, stretched out of shape. That pocket was another weirdly intriguing feature of this odd character. Occasionally, along with the cigarettes, he purchased a single orange, produced from this pocket and displayed with the pack for the cashier's benefit; after the items were paid for, the orange went right back into this same pocket, accompanied by the receipt, of course. He'd wordlessly walk away, the orange forming a curious bulge at his hip.

After a time I began to get used to this character, and although his eccentricities still bothered me a great deal, I thought I knew what to expect, and how to control my expressions, and not offend the man by unconsciously recoiling at the sight of him. My technique was to take a deep breath, keep my eyes looking down at the cash register, and force my voice to keep calm while saying the fewest words possible to complete the transaction.

I was using this method one summer day and all was going well. Then, just as he was walking off cigarettes in his hand, orange and receipt safely in his pocket, I thoughtlessly looked up. Instead of his usual hairstyle, held greasily in place with a generous amount of hair tonic, his scalp had been shaved to a slick, smooth finish! A shocked gasp escaped me, but if he heard he didn't respond; he just continued toward the door.

Watching him go, I felt a pang of compassion: he seemed so lonely and bitter. Didn't he have a family somewhere who loved him, quirks and all? But no, probably he was a hermit, a silent, desolate man passing his time walking slowly through a society that rejects "freaks," in a totally uncaring world.

Aunt Mamie

My Aunt Mamie lived in a quaint little brick house in downtown Hohenwald. I remember the "W" sculptured into the chimney with white bricks which must have stood for her last name, although I don't know what it was. Even though I never knew her last name, it doesn't matter, because this small, quiet lady has given me a perfect model for what I want old age to be. She never complained, always made the best of things and, best of all, she always smiled.

I remember the stories my mom has told me of Aunt Mamie's undaunted courage. She lived on a farm, always in Hohenwald, with ten or twelve children, as did most people of that time. She worked hard, doing all the chores that family life on the farm required, but she never complained. Even when her husband died, she kept going. She knew that she had a family to take care of and the only way to do it was by the life she had always known. Her unique philosophy on "potty training" her children always amused me. She would say, "Well, when they get old enough to be ashamed of wearing diapers, I guess they'll train themselves."

It seemed that her whole life abounded with hardships, although one would never know it by talking to her. When most of her children were small, her house and everything she owned, burned to the ground. One would expect a widow with lots of kids, not much money and only the charred remains of a house to give up. But not my Aunt Mamie. She just smiled and trudged on.

I recall actually talking to Aunt Mamie for the first time when I was about four or five. I had a big wart on my finger which I wanted to get rid of quite badly. My grandmother told me that Aunt Mamie could make it disappear if I truly wanted it gone. I did, but I was a little skeptical of the idea that one of my relatives had magical qualities. These doubts were soon dispelled, however, when Aunt Mamie took me by the hand and led me into a dark room where the "wart ritual" was to be performed. I guess the cheery little laugh characteristic of Aunt Mamie sounded as if it were a witch-like cackle to me. I was awestruck, if not a little scared.

Then the ceremony began. Aunt Mamie took a kernel of corn from a very special cob and showed it to me. She asked me if I really believed that she could make my wart disappear. I nodded. Then she took the kernel of corn and rubbed it on my wart, mumbling a few magic words. After this she wrote down my name and placed the kernel in a box, tying it with a ribbon. She then instructed me to throw the box out at a fork in the road, because whoever found the box and opened it would get my wart. Well, amazingly enough, my wart disappeared within a week.

Aunt Mamie died quietly, just a few years ago on her 88th birthday. She hadn't been ill for a long time; she just died. I will always remember her for the way she took everything in stride, never complaining. Her life was filled with hard work and bad luck, but still she smiled.

ASSIGNMENT:
WRITING A CHARACTER SKETCH

Having read and evaluated the students' character sketches, you should have formed some fairly clear ideas about what makes this kind of writing successful. You also have a checklist of some of the essential ingredients that you and your classmates agreed on after discussing your ratings of the sketches. This checklist can be a big help to you as you begin to work out your own material. Keep it handy and refer to it often.

Purpose

At this point, you're ready to develop the material for your own character sketch. As always, a clear sense of purpose can help you as you work. Here are two possible purposes; choose one of them or develop another of your own.

1. Describe someone close to you whom you have known since childhood but who is not an immediate family member; try to discover the person's dominant trait or the central impression and give specific illustrations of it.
2. Select an individual outside your family who has had a marked influence on you; show how you met that person and fell under that influence.

Audience

Readers of your sketch will not have had the advantage of meeting your subject, so your sketch will serve as a record of the existence of the individual. Ideally, upon completion of a reading of your essay your audience should clearly understand why the individual is important to you or to others who have had contact with the person.

Prewriting

Remember, the purpose of prewriting is to locate as much material as possible prior to writing and then to organize the specific information and details to develop a draft of the essay. Attention to this phase of the writing process will decrease the chances of your having to search for a new topic or do a complete revision of an existing one.

1. List four or five people that seem to fall into at least one of the categories suggested by the purpose of this assignment. Perhaps you had a boss who made a strong impression on you; possibly you have a friend who seems to have an influence in your family; or maybe it is a town character, the individual that everyone knows and yet really does not. Still another way to locate potential subjects is to think of events or places and try to associate people with your memories of those places or events.

2. Once you have a list of four or five potential subjects, select one that seems to make the strongest impression on you and try "cycling" some information about that person. Cycling calls for a form of free writing in which you attempt to pull from your memory all the various bits and pieces of information that might relate to your subject.

   Cycling

   The benefit of cycling is that it helps you produce an idea to write about. Because cycling occurs within a general subject area, the process helps you move toward a specific focus. If you stop after each cycle and read your notes, you'll soon see that your thoughts are angling toward a particular topic or idea; this might be called the "center of gravity," which can be expressed in a single statement. With each cycle and with each center of gravity statement, you're helping yourself focus on a narrower subject.

   a. Write for five minutes about the person you've selected as a possible subject for your sketch. Once you begin, don't stop writing; if you lose your train of thought, just keep writing whatever comes into your head but return to the original topic as soon as possible; don't concern yourself about correctness at this point; just write down as much as you can in whatever form seems comfortable to you.

b. Stop at the end of five minutes (if you are doing this alone, a kitchen timer can be a big help); read over your notes on the topic. Where did your thoughts about this person take you? What seems to be the center of your thoughts on the person? Write a sentence at the end of your five-minute cycle that summarizes the central focus of what you wrote.

c. Now try a ten-minute cycle, using the sentence from the last cycle as your starting point. Keep your pen moving; if you stray from the topic, just bring yourself back to the center of gravity and keep writing.

d. Stop at the end of the ten-minute cycle. Once more, find the center of gravity by reading over what you have just written. Express this new center of gravity in a clear sentence.

e. Go now for the last cycle on the topic. Start with the most recent center of gravity statement and write about it as long as you can; try for another ten minutes if possible.

f. Stop at the end of this last ten-minute cycle. Read what you have written and write a center of gravity statement about this last cycle.

g. Put your three center of gravity statements together and study them closely for signs of a narrowing focus and possible additional cycles. Do you have hold of an idea that you can develop with reasonable confidence? What does it appear to be? Write the idea in one clear sentence.

3. The cycling should produce some center of focus; from this center you will probably locate the dominant trait or impression of your subject that you want to convey to your readers. Study that trait or impression quite carefully and then ask yourself the following questions:

What incident or incidents or specific time frame will help make this trait clear to my readers?
What specific details—dress, speech, action, beliefs, work—will contribute to this dominant trait or impression?
How might I put the details into an incident or time span?

4. Having asked yourself these questions, review your cycling material and begin to extract the necessary information, forming rough lists of details, examples, incidents, and so on, until you seem to have exhausted the written material; then look over the material to see if you can make it more concrete. Pinpoint times, locations, actions, and speeches; jot down the exact details as best you can remember

them; keep your focus—the dominant trait or impression—in mind at all times as you select information; discard other material, interesting as it may be, which doesn't fit your focus.

5. Concern yourself with how the material can be organized. Look at your raw material; what kind of pattern does it seem to fall into? Can you organize your sketch according to time—the span of a day, several years, a few minutes? Are there several aspects of the dominant impression or trait that need to be revealed? If so, what are they and how do they relate to one another? Could you start with the least important aspect and work toward the most important one? It may be that you want to show your character in several locations because each setting reveals some important aspect of personality. If that is the case, you can use those settings as a means of ordering your presentation of material; for example, you may want to show your character at work and then at home to demonstrate how the qualities in one are either reflected or changed in the other. Or you may want to show the character in a series of incidents, each reflecting some aspect of the individual's personality, starting with the least significant and working up to the most important.

Response

Before you actually write a rough draft, you may find it helpful to talk over some of the material. Select a partner and spend some time talking about your subject and then about your partner's subject. Using your notes, explain to your partner what you think the dominant impression will be in the draft and how you intend to develop it; urge your partner to ask you as many questions as possible about the material; here the checklist that you and your classmates developed will come in handy. Use it as a guide for deciding if you and your partner have enough material and a clear enough purpose to write a rough draft.

The First Draft

Once you and your partner are satisfied that you have things under control as much as possible at this point in the process, begin to write your first draft. Draw on the preliminary pattern of organization, the details, and the examples you've developed. Don't worry if you discover some gaps in the development of the sketch. Your rough draft is not a finished product; it is only an attempt to see what you have at this stage. Make notes to yourself in the margin of the paper as thoughts occur to you about developing further material; you can then consult these notes when you've finished the first draft. Write yourself out; exhaust all the material you have.

Re-Viewing

With a draft of your sketch in front of you now, you can begin to see the possible shape the sketch will take. Return to the checklist that you and your classmates developed. Read your sketch and indicate on it exactly where you meet the characteristics in the checklist. When you complete the reading, review your findings. How well did you meet the list of characteristics? Be honest with yourself. Where might you strengthen your sketch? Take the time to add material where it might make a point clearer or bring the character more to life. Remember that your readers want to see your character as a real person, one they might encounter if they were in the right neighborhood at the right time.

In addition to using the checklist, you may want to take a close look at your use of dialogue. Although you may have elected to write your sketch without dialogue—"The Old Man" is an example of how that might be done—if you did use dialogue, you may want to refine it during this revision stage.

Dialogue

Occasionally confusion arises about how to use speech in writing. For direct speech, the character's exact words are used with quotation marks to indicate that they are the exact words used by the speaker.

He said, "I haven't any place for you to dump your trash."

Indirect speech is simply a summary of what was said.

He said that he didn't have any place to dump my trash.

Along with the marking of direct speech, the writer also has to deal with the problem of dialogue tags, indicators of who says what. Consider the following example.

> "Well, you're Mr. Gordon," *she said,* looking me over. "I've been dying to get a peek at you ever since you moved in. Have a seat." She scooped a pile of clothing from one of the chairs and dumped it onto the crowded sofa. "So you finally decided to visit your neighbors. Get you a drink?"
>
> "You're a painter," *I burbled,* for want of something to say. I was unnerved by the thought that any moment she would realize she was undressed and would scream and dash for the bedroom. I tried to keep my eyes moving, looking everywhere but at her.

"Beer or ale? Nothing else in the place right now except cooking sherry. You don't want cooking sherry, do you?"

"I can't stay," *I said,* getting hold of myself and fixing my gaze at the beauty mark on the left side of her chin. "I've locked myself out of my apartment. I wanted to go across the fire escape. It connects our windows." [Italics added]

—Daniel Keyes, *Flowers for Algernon*

Note how Keyes sets up a sequence in the dialogue to avoid always using the characters' names or a pronoun; we simply know, from the alternation of the prepared speeches, who is talking. The writer also uses details to suggest what is happening during the conversation. After all, people seldom sit absolutely still during a conversation; their eyes move, their bodies shift positions, and, of course, the person telling the story may have some thoughts in addition to what he or she says. Dialogue can be a valuable device to suggest action, character, and relationships. Some careful attention to punctuation and paragraphing will make dialogue effective for the reader. Study the excerpt from *Flowers for Algernon* and determine the answers to the following questions. Then review any use of dialogue you may have in your draft. If there is none, consider the effect of replacing a description of a conversation with the actual thing or of adding dialogue to certain sections to make a character come alive.

1. Where do commas and periods go when used with quotation marks in dialogue?
2. When and where are quotation marks used in dialogue?
3. What device is used to keep the speeches of various characters separated so we always know who is speaking?

Response

Find an audience for your draft; your teacher may designate a group or you may be free to select your own. Whatever the case, you should get a reading from several people. Be sure you have the checklist for character sketches with you during this response period and follow the procedure outlined here.

1. *Read the sketches.* If possible, everyone in the group should have a copy of one another's sketches. Decide on an order of reading within the group. Each person should read the draft in question silently, at least once, without comment. Then the author should read his or her draft aloud. One way to check the clarity of your

writing is to read it aloud. Listen for places where the reading seems to get a bit rough, or where you seem to almost run out of breath. Sharpen your ear for repetition—are some words and phrases used too often? If so, make a note to change the wording to eliminate the problem.

2. *Spoken feedback.* The group members should discuss the draft with the author. Refer to the checklist to identify good aspects and weak aspects in the sketch. Make your comments supportive by suggesting possible improvements and congratulating the writer on effective parts; there is really never anything "bad" about a piece of writing—only parts that do not make sense or sustain interest for the readers. Group members should see if they agree about their perceptions of a sketch; if there is disagreement, discuss why it exists and how it might be resolved. Always encourage the writer to speak, and listen carefully to what is said; the writer also may have doubts about certain parts of the piece. During this time, each group member should also make marginal notations for future reference.

3. *Written response.* Stop talking after you have spent approximately ten to fifteen minutes on each draft. The writer also needs a written record of all the comments made by each person in the group; each group member should expand marginal annotations and on the last page of the draft make some specific observations about the whole paper to help the writer. The readers' overall view of the paper will be more helpful to the writer than their checking of spelling and punctuation errors; group members can use the checklist to determine what to say about the draft. Each reader should sign his or her name to the comments so the writer can get more clarification from individuals later if necessary.

After you have met with the response group and received all the written and oral comments, review them carefully; check your readers' responses against your own understanding of what you did or did not say in the draft. Difficult as this step may be, you've got to be hard-nosed about this process if you hope to make valuable and effective changes. Do not consider anything on the page as sacred; whatever you have written in the draft can be changed, dropped, moved around, or added to. Your draft at this point is really a series of building blocks of various shapes and sizes; your job is to find the best fit, chiseling here for a smoother connection, tapping there for a test of soundness. Master craftspeople do this painstakingly; so should you for best results.

You should work hardest on several specific areas in this piece: the *focus*, or the development of the dominant traits or impressions; *organization*, the arrangement of the various parts of the sketch for a sensible order; and the *use of details* so specific that readers can tell you exactly what kind of person they meet through your words.

As you might suspect, you could spend your time on other areas as well. Openings and closings often give writers problems; sentence construction often needs more variation and sophistication. We address these problems and others as we continue to describe the experience of the writing process. For that reason, you and your instructor will view your writing as "work in progress," realizing that you may return to a draft to work on it further. Throughout this book you will find revision workshops that will give you an opportunity to stop and look at drafts you have developed; each workshop focuses your attention on specific writing problems that may have appeared in your drafts and suggests ways you may overcome such difficulties. The further you can take each assignment, however, the less you will have to do during the revision workshops.

CHAPTER **4**

Workshop: Constructing Effective Paragraphs

Now that you've completed at least two pieces of writing, it's time to take stock of what you've accomplished. Throughout this text, workshops such as this chapter will highlight particular aspects of writing you may need to look at more closely as you continue to write and as you revise papers you wrote earlier. Plan to return to these workshops as you work on new pieces.

ELEMENTS OF EFFECTIVE PARAGRAPHS

This workshop focuses on paragraphs, the building blocks of any essay. If your essays are not broken into paragraphs, your readers might have problems trying to decide what your point is. Before medieval times, writers simply wrote what they had to say without concern for dividing their thoughts into paragraphs or providing any signals to readers to suggest where one part of the communication stopped and the next began. In medieval times monks, who spent much of their lives copying manuscripts, realized that making some physical separation of thought made both the copying and the reading easier. Fortunately for us as readers, this practice caught on and now we're accustomed to seeing white space separating chunks of information and indentations showing where a shift in thought has occurred. This practice depends frequently on the purpose of the writing, the audience, and the format of the material. To see how varied the practice is, compare the paragraphing in a modern novel with that in a nineteenth-century novel; notice the difference in paragraph form between newspapers and some of your textbooks; compare the paragraphing in *Reader's Digest* and *The Atlantic*. What you'll discover is that paragraph divisions offer the writer a useful way to communicate to the reader a variety of changes: in subject, of time, of point of view, of tone, of place, of mood, of emphasis, of speaker, of style, and of pace. These uses of paragraphing do not explain what writers try to do within the paragraphs and that's where you must pay the most attention. Consider the following student paragraph.

> Sally Bates has brown hair, blue eyes, and stands about 5'4" tall. She wears dark-rimmed glasses and has a shiny gold chain around her neck. Her ears are small, her nose cute, and her mouth about average. She is wearing a light blue blouse, open at the neck, a large tan belt, and designer jeans. Her shoes have high, pointed heels and no back. There is a high school ring on her fourth finger of the right hand and a large topaz ring on the middle finger of her left hand.

The first thing we notice about this paragraph is the amount of detail the writer provides. We have some specific items by which we could recognize Sally. All we really have, however, is an inventory, the kind of recording of detail we might find in a police report. Although that kind of writing has its place, we wouldn't read much of it before we began to wonder: What's the point of all this? The paragraph has no particular focus or order that allows us to come away with a sense of which items are most important to the writer. Compare the preceding description with the following one.

> Hank Snead looks tired. The medium-length blond hair that covers his head is lifeless and thinning and looks as if it hasn't been combed for days. His blue eyes are only half open and his lower lids sag down beside his large pockmarked nose. His large mouth droops at the corners. As he sits at his desk, he props his head up with both hands while the rest of his body slouches low in the chair.

Focus

What is the difference between the two paragraphs? The writer of the second one identifies a single *focus* and then proceeds to develop it, using only material that supports the opening, focus statement: "Hank Snead looks tired." Here, then, is the first principle of effective paragraph construction:

Paragraphs need a sharp focus.

Focusing a paragraph can be compared to shooting a scene in a movie. The camera focuses on a particular part of a room or a particular movement or a particular person; everything else becomes secondary as the camera directs viewers' attention to what is significant at that moment in the movie. Paragraphs serve the writer in the same way. Just as a movie is composed of many focused, close-up shots, so too is an essay. Writers often announce the focus of a paragraph by stating it in the opening sentence. Although some paragraphs may not have an opening focus sentence, in most cases an effective paragraph has a stated or implied focus.

Unity

Writers have to be sure that each paragraph really has only one focus, and a tightly controlled one at that. Ideas can get out of writers' control, particularly in rough drafts. Like the director of a film, writers need to go back and check each "shot" so nothing becomes blurred beyond recognition. Consider a slightly different description of Hank Snead:

> Hank Snead looks tired. The medium-length blond hair that covers his head is lifeless and thinning and looks as if it hasn't been combed for days. His blue eyes are only half open and his lower lids sag down beside his large pockmarked nose. His large mouth droops at the corners. As he sits at his desk, he props his head up with both hands while the rest of his body slouches low in the chair. Hank is wearing scuffed brown boots, baggy jeans, and a faded red flannel shirt only partly tucked in.

Without looking back at the original, you should spot immediately the details that blur the focus of the paragraph. In this case, the description of the clothing adds nothing to our understanding of how tired Hank looks. Such additions distract readers. They are reading along smoothly, thinking they know where the writer is taking them, and then some material appears that doesn't fit the pattern. The whole reading process gets derailed. The second principle of effective paragraphing, then, is one of unity:

All material within a paragraph contributes only to its single focus.

When you're revising a piece of writing, be alert for stray details and ideas that may have crept in during the rough drafts. A good rule is to delete any sentence or detail that does not directly support the focus. If in doubt about the connection, leave it out.

One of the best ways to check a paragraph's focus and unity is to remove the paragraph from its associations with others around it and perform a "structure check" by charting the relationship of each sentence to the paragraph's focus. If you study the arrows in the following example, you will see that all the material moves back to support the opening statement. The writer built the evidence to support the focus. This paragraph is especially interesting because the writer supports minor statements as well as the major statement with examples. Not only does the paragraph focus on one idea and remain focused throughout, but the writer also employs details convincingly.

Main focus of the paragraph	In a way, of course, the subway is a living symbol of all that adds up to lack of status in New York.
One reason for lack of status	There is a sense of madness and disorientation at almost every express stop.
Specific examples of previous statement	The ceilings are low, the vistas long, there are no landmarks, the lighting is an eerie blend of fluorescent tubing, electric light bulbs, and neon advertising.
Another reason for absence of status	The whole place is a gross assault on the senses.
Evidence supporting previous statement	The noise of the trains stopping or rounding curves has a high-pitched harshness that is difficult to describe.
More evidence of assault on the senses	Your tactile sense takes a crucifying you never dreamed possible.
Example supporting previous statement	People feel no qualms about pushing when it becomes crowded.
Additional evidence of assault on the senses	The odors become unbearable when the weather is warm.
Specific examples of assaults on the senses	Between platforms, record shops broadcast 45 r.p.m. records with metallic tones and lunch counters serve the kind of hot dogs in which you bite through a tensile, rubbery surface and then hit a soft, oleaginous center like cottonseed meal, and the customers sit there with pastry and bread flakes caked around their mouths, belching to themselves so that their cheeks pop out flatulently now and then.

—Tom Wolfe, "The Subway"

Evidence

The preceding paragraph by Tom Wolfe illustrates another important feature of effective paragraphs: *evidence.* Focus and unity are not effective unless they are backed up with evidence: details, examples, definitions, incidents. The best kind of evidence in writing *shows* the reader instead of just *telling*. Look at Wolfe's paragraph again and note how he takes each one of the supporting statements and develops it further with concrete detail and example. The arrows show how each of the statements in the paragraph is related to the one before it.

In showing the reader, the writer tries to select the strongest evidence possible and let that speak for itself rather than constantly telling the reader what is important or what has happened. Paragraphs that merely tell tend to become boring quickly.

> Billboards interfere with my enjoyment of natural beauty. They block my view of scenery and animals from the road. They remind me of all the things I would like to get away from when I go for a drive.

Although we get a general sense of this writer's focus, we don't get the full impact because the writer doesn't *show* us what causes the opening statement. Perhaps the writer could have shared this view with readers.

> Billboards interfere with my enjoyment of natural beauty. Just outside my hometown a section of highway runs through what was one of the most beautiful sections of the county. On both sides of the road, rolling pastures that always seemed to stay green year round stretched as far as a driver could see. Through some wonderful quirk of nature, elm, maple, and oak trees had grown up in various parts of the pasture, offering a variety of shapes and a constantly changing variety of foliage colors. On one side of the road a farm pond always had white ducks floating on its surface. Cows frequently clustered around the pond on hot days, standing in the water to cool their hoofs and bellies, dipping their noses into the water and then raising their heads to stare at the passing cars. But billboards have changed all that. Now the same stretch of highway reveals nothing but slogans and products, the billboards seeming to march in a deliberate row to hide any sign of natural beauty. One billboard masks the pond, urging motorists to stay cool by smoking Kools; another shows a giant oil can dripping oil; the trees and grass disappear behind a billboard that makes impossible claims for the softness of toilet paper, and a fourth shows a little baby flashing his bare bottom as a reason for buying suntan oil. Even the speed of cars has increased along this section, as if drivers can't wait to get by what has become an unnatural place.

Few readers will have difficulty understanding the point the writer wishes to make. The bare statements of the original paragraph have been fleshed out to provide a far more complete picture. By showing us, the writer convinces us.

> *Effective paragraphs contain convincing evidence that supports the focus.*

Coherence

We now have three major keys to effective paragraphs—focus, unity, evidence—but there is one more that can't be ignored: *coherence*. The first three could be present in a paragraph and the reading might still be difficult. A writer needs some way to keep thoughts moving smoothly; without it, everything seems to jar us as we read, as though we're bumping across a number of very rough railroad crossings, hitting each rail each time we move from one sentence to the next. Consider some of the following options for making smooth connections in your paragraphs.

Synonyms and Recurring Terms

Careful writers know how to alert their readers to the relationships within paragraphs as well as throughout their essays. By using key terms and their synonyms, writers can focus the readers' attention and move the reading along smoothly. Notice how the writers of the following paragraph use the word *hat* and various synonyms to keep us moving:

> Non-running is the best time to wear a *hat* because *it* is then least likely to fall off. Some non-runners prefer a *homburg* because of its distinguished appearance. Others go for *propeller beanies* for an air of rakish insouciance. Politicians like *hats* for tossing when they tire of non-running. Calvin Coolidge, one of the greatest non-running presidents, enjoyed wearing Indian *headdresses. These* were considered old *hat* until Jimmy Carter revived the tradition. However, few considered wearing *one* a feather in his *cap.* [Italics added]
>
> —Vic Ziegel and Lewis Grossberger, *The Non-Runner's Book*

Transitions

Another useful device for making connections with the ideas and words in your paragraphs is transitions. These signals announce where the writer is going and how the reader should follow. Because transitions are common words, we often forget how useful they can be. But the signals not only indicate the relationships between sentences, they also help connect one sentence to the next. Note the italicized words in the following passage:

> A plain wood chair stood *against* the *other* wall *next* to an old lobster pot that was being used for a table, and *above* it several framed black and white photographs of boats my employer had previously owned were prominently displayed. *In the corner* stood a Franklin stove and *beside* it a neatly stacked pile of wood and kindling. The only light in the room came from a window on the *far* wall *opposite* the

door, providing a view of the small harbor dotted with several fishing boats and many skiffs. Because the room was not large, the one window provided ample light during the day and a kerosene lamp hanging *at the end* of the workbench provided illumination in the evening. A sturdy rocking chair with a soiled cushion on it stood *in front of* the window, facing the room. *Here* it was that the old man must sit for hours when not at sea, knitting nets or just relaxing.

Each of the italicized words helps readers keep track of where they are in the description and how items are related to one another by their location. Without these connections, the picture would seem quite disorganized. In addition to the words pointed out in the previous paragraph, many others can be used to help keep your prose together. The following is a sample list.

Signals of Addition
again, also, and, and then, besides, finally, first, further, furthermore, in addition, last, moreover, next, second, still another

Signals of Comparison
also, as, in comparison, likewise, similarly

Signals of Contrast
after all, although, and yet, but, in contrast, however, nevertheless, on the contrary, on the other hand, otherwise, still, yet

Signals for Summarizing
as I have said, as has been indicated, briefly, in short, on the whole, in conclusion, to summarize

Signals for Examples
as an illustration, for example, for instance, in fact, in other words, in particular, specifically, that is

Signals for Results
accordingly, as a result, consequently, hence, in short, then, therefore, thus

Signals for Time
afterward, at last, at length, immediately, suddenly, presently, shortly, since, soon, temporarily, until, while, lately

Signals for Concession
after all, at the same time, granted, I admit, naturally, of course

All these devices—synonyms, recurring terms, and transitions—help readers move through paragraphs easily and understand their focus. Therefore, our fourth principle of effective paragraphing is coherence:

Effective paragraphs use appropriate connecting words.

Analyzing Your Own Paragraph Development

Studying the principles of effective paragraph development is not the same thing as working with your own paragraphs. At this point, you need to turn to your own writing and do some careful analysis of your paragraphs to determine what works well and what needs strengthening.

Select one of the essays you have written and choose one or two paragraphs at random from the middle (for this assignment avoid paragraphs that contain substantial chunks of dialogue). Using these paragraphs, follow the steps below.

1. Identify a sentence or two in the paragraph that clearly states or implies the focus of the paragraph. Underlining it will help you keep the focus before you. See Example 1.
2. Chart each sentence in the paragraph to show how it supports the main focus, as is done in Example 1.
3. Underline all the synonyms or recurring terms and draw a line from each to the word or words with which each is connected. See Example 2.
4. Circle all the words in the paragraph that serve as the connectors that keep the paragraph together. See Example 3.

Repeat this analysis for several paragraphs until you have convincing proof that your paragraphs contain all the ingredients necessary to be effective. Scan the rest of your paragraphs within your essay and wherever there seems to be any blurring of the focus or bumpiness in the reading, check the paragraph carefully and make the necessary adjustments. After you have done this kind of structure check several times, you'll find that you will be much more conscious of how your ideas are going together as you write. Do not, however, focus on this aspect of your writing exclusively in the early drafts; ideas come first, then structure.

EXAMPLE 1

Our second-floor bedroom presented a different kind of challenge.
Far from the stove, it represented a nighttime temperature of 46 degrees.
My wife and I were ready to tough it out.
We had purchased several pairs of flannel sheets at $20 per.
Never mind that they felt like towels.
They spared us the initial immersion-in-ice agony of our regular linen.
We were well stocked with reading gloves.
We made our bed with seven quilts.
The mere thought of all the money we were saving kept us warm as toast.
But our pets couldn't take it.
One by one the cats stopped curling up beside us.
Then it was the dogs.
Our little Corgis used to sleep by our feet.
One night when I descended to stock up the stove for the hours ahead, I discovered them gathered around it in a semi-circle, dogs and cats together, warming their paws.
I suddenly realized how silent our bedroom had become.
It was the stillness of the Arctic.

—Paul D. Zimmerman, "How to Beat the Energy Crisis"

EXAMPLE 2

Our second-floor bedroom presented a different kind of challenge.
Far from the stove, it represented a nighttime temperature of 46 degrees.
My wife and I were ready to tough it out.
We had purchased several pairs of flannel sheets at $20 per.
Never mind that they felt like towels.
They spared us the initial immersion-in-ice agony of our regular linen.
We were well stocked with reading gloves.
We made our bed with seven quilts.
The mere thought of all the money we were saving kept us warm as toast.

But our pets couldn't take it.
One by one the cats stopped curling up beside us.
Then it was the dogs.
  Our little Corgis used to sleep by our feet.
One night when I descended to stock up the stove for the hours ahead, I discovered them gathered around it in a semi-circle, dogs and cats together, warming their paws.
    I suddenly realized how silent our bedroom had become.
      It was the stillness of the Arctic.

EXAMPLE 3

Our second-floor bedroom presented a different kind of challenge.
  Far from the stove, it represented a nighttime temperature of 46 degrees.
  My wife and I were ready to tough it out.
    We had purchased several pairs of flannel sheets at $20 per.
      Never mind that they felt like towels.
      They spared us the initial immersion-in-ice agony of our regular linen.
    We were well stocked with reading gloves.
    We made our bed with seven quilts.
    The mere thought of all the money we were saving kept us warm as toast.
  But our pets couldn't take it.
    One by one the cats stopped curling up beside us.
    Then it was the dogs.
      Our little Corgis used to sleep by our feet.
    One night when I descended to stock up the stove for the hours ahead, I discovered them gathered around it in a semi-circle, dogs and cats together, warming their paws.
      I suddenly realized how silent our bedroom had become.
        It was the stillness of the Arctic.

Paragraph Hooks

So far you have been looking at the interior of your paragraphs. Once you've determined that they are effective, your next concern is the movement from one paragraph to the next. Focusing on this concern is not difficult because it calls only for an extension of your use of transitions within the paragraph.

It might help at this point to consider an essay as being similar to a train. The locomotive provides the power for pulling any number of individual train cars, but the train cannot function without couplings that hook one car to the next. Without such hooking, the engine might go to Chicago and individual cars might end up in Duluth, Boston, and Miami. To put it another way, a group of railroad cars becomes a train only when the cars are hooked together; the same principle holds for an essay. Until the various paragraphs of an essay are hooked together, they don't take the reader anywhere.

In this part of the workshop, you will consider the hooks you can use to hold your paragraphs together. You are already working with single transitional words within your paragraphs. Paragraph hooks, though, have to carry a bit more weight, so they have to be built more strongly; they also have to work smoothly and not cause unusual interruptions as the reader moves from paragraph to paragraph.

We can use the three previous paragraphs of the text as examples of some of the options open to you in selecting appropriate paragraph hooks. Let's repeat the first paragraph:

> So far you have been looking at the interior of your paragraphs. Once you've determined that they are effective, your next concern is the movement from one paragraph to the next. Focusing on this concern is not difficult because it calls only for an extension of your use of transitions within the paragraph.

At the conclusion of this paragraph, we're ready to move to the next idea. As we write the opening sentence of the next paragraph, we might try a single word transition:

> However, let's look at an essay as being similar to a train.

The *however* helps the reader realize that a shift in focus is going to occur, but one word has a tough job carrying the entire relationship between the previous paragraph and the new one. A different approach can capture more of the sense of how the new paragraph will relate to the previous one:

> *It might help at this point* to consider an essay as being similar to a train.

The first part of the new sentence is an *idea hook* because it summarizes the focus of the previous paragraph while feeding that main idea into the focus of the new paragraph: how an essay is like a train.

Still another technique is to find a key word in the paragraph, preferably in the last sentence of the paragraph, to use as a connection with the next unit of thought. Consider the last sentence of the second paragraph in our example:

> To put it another way, a group of railroad cars becomes a train only when the cars are *hooked* together; the same principle holds for an

essay. Until the various paragraphs of an essay are *hooked* together, they don't take the reader anywhere.

Here's how the reader is guided into making the transition to the third paragraph:

> In this part of the workshop, you will consider the *hooks* holding your paragraphs together.

By seeing and hearing a familiar and key word from the previous paragraph, readers keep the previous idea in mind as the new one comes into view. This connecting makes readers comfortable as the ideas unfold in each succeeding paragraph. Everywhere readers look, they find clear signals of where they're going and where they've been. The result is a pleasant journey through a piece of writing and a safe arrival at the destination with a clear sense of how the journey was accomplished.

Occasionally you may find it useful to combine the standard transitions you use inside paragraphs with either the idea or key word hook. This combination gives you added flexibility, for no reader likes to encounter one device again and again. Vary the hooks and look for ways to make the connections more subtle but still clear. Remember that the chief purpose of paragraph hooks is to assist the reader in following your train of thought. Always make certain that a clear link connects your paragraphs and that the links are there on paper, not just in your head.

Analyzing Your Use of Paragraph Hooks

Examine your essays carefully for your use of paragraph hooks; look for any repetition in the kind of "hooking" you do and find ways to avoid it. Select several consecutive paragraphs and identify the precise hooks you use in each one. Make any necessary adjustments. Besides looking at your own writing, be alert as you read other materials to different authors' use of paragraph hooks. Experiment with new ways as you encounter them, but never lose sight of their key function: building safe bridges among ideas.

The basic principles that work together to produce effective paragraphs, then, are the following:

1. *Focus:* Paragraphs need a sharp, single focus.
2. *Unity:* All material in a paragraph contributes only to its single focus.
3. *Evidence:* Paragraphs must contain convincing evidence that supports the focus.

4. *Coherence:* Synonyms, recurring terms, and transitions provide connections to hold a paragraph together.

Now that you've had some time to work on paragraph structure and to assess the effectiveness of your transitions between paragraphs, turn your attention to two other important aspects of the essay: the introduction and conclusion. Both require your growing skill in developing paragraphs. The only difference between the main paragraphs in your essays and the introduction and conclusion is that one introduces and the other ends—simple enough. But some special characteristics of each need to be noted.

The Introduction

Because every piece of writing has to start somewhere, the first paragraph or two can be the most crucial. That's where readers make an important decision: Should we read on or not? That kind of a decision suggests you ought to spend much time on your opening before going any further. Surprisingly, though, most professional writers do not spend much time on their introductions for first drafts. They wait until they've decided what they want to say and then have said it. After that, they return to polish the introduction. This doesn't mean, of course, that such writers don't have some sense of how they might start a piece or where they want to go with their ideas. But agonizing over those first few sentences in a rough draft is not very productive. The main thing is to get started. When you write a rough draft, therefore, your primary concern is not necessarily to produce an introduction that will last through all your revisions. Instead, like professional writers, treat your opening as simply a place for getting started, knowing that you can usually return to change it if necessary.

The most important keys to writing effective introductions are your audience and your purpose. A comparison may be helpful at this point. Most of us have heard enough public speakers to know that they rarely jump into the middle of their speeches. Instead, they spend time establishing a "connection" with their audience, perhaps by a reference to the occasion prompting the speech, possibly by referring to background or a need that the speaker and audience share. Like the speaker, you as a writer need to develop an early connection that you can then use to construct a clear path to the main focus of your essay. If you take this approach, your audience will usually be pleased. You have acknowledged them and are offering some benefit from reading your essay such as additional information, a new way of looking at a subject, a promise of entertainment, or an insight into themselves or you. This early connection gives readers a sense of what is to come and how it may relate to them.

To explore the possibilities for developing this connection, draw on one of your best sources for information—yourself. Ask yourself some of the following questions:

1. How did I get interested in the topic? Would that prompt others' interest in the subject?
2. What personal connection do I have with the topic—an event, a book, a television program, a movie? Will some of my audience be likely to have had similar connections?
3. What subjects that many people already know about are related to my topic? Can I build on that relationship?
4. Am I looking at an old subject from a new angle? If so, how can I alert my audience to this?
5. Is my position on the topic likely to create opposition from my readers? If so, how can I be sure that my readers will give my side a fair hearing?

Connections also establish a promise from you the writer to your readers. In a sense, you say to your audience: Here is what I propose to do. If you have sufficiently interested your readers, they will read on to see if you live up to your promises.

On the surface, developing an effective introduction doesn't sound too hard and in reality it isn't. But you have to take your responsibility for good introductions seriously. Too often writers try to rush through an introduction by throwing out a one-liner and hoping the reader will go on. This approach seldom works, however. An opening such as "Playing basketball is interesting" won't light up the eyes of most readers, and if it is coupled with an "introduction ramble," you've created a song-and-dance routine that bores an audience quickly. Consider the following:

> Playing basketball is very interesting. Many people find that basketball can add interest to their lives. Many players have made a living out of basketball. Spectators like watching basketball. It is an interesting sport for all.

Readers who encounter an introduction like this are going to quit reading. They have little sense of where the piece is going or whether the piece has anything to offer because the writer has made no clear connection with them. All they are offered are some vague topics: playing basketball, a possible hint about making money playing basketball, and the fact that everyone is interested in basketball—a rather risky statement, unless the writer has canvassed the world's population carefully. The writer needs to narrow the focus of the introduction and create more of a connection with the audience, as in the following revision:

> Anyone who has watched NBA play-offs knows that basketball is a fast-moving, brutal sport that can turn ordinary people into raving lunatics. Watching these people can be almost as entertaining as the game itself.

By beginning this way, the writer quickly suggests a potential connection with people who watch basketball games as well as with people who might watch the fans. The writer also has identified an aspect of the game that he or she finds interesting. The last line establishes a focus for the writer to develop; readers will expect to find ample evidence of how watching some of the fans can be as entertaining as the game itself.

The introduction ramble, then, is not a route to follow, but neither is the introduction that completely forgets its audience. Consider the following:

> It is very difficult to know what the answer to this problem is.

What is the problem referred to in this statement? Why is it difficult to find an answer? Where do we, the readers, fit into all of this? Reading an opening of this type is like walking into the middle of a conversation and catching just part of what has been said. We have no reference points, so we have little sense of what the main topic of conversation is and we would be pretty confused if we tried to become part of such a conversation. The confusion that such an opening produces usually discourages readers from going any further.

We've identified some of the things not to do; what, then, can you do? Writers preparing to open an essay have to consider the purpose of their writing and the expectations of their audience. Those considerations usually lead to one of two choices: to produce a highly condensed introduction that clearly states the central idea of the essay or to hook readers while introducing the focus of the piece.

The highly condensed introduction is desirable for examinations or reports because readers of these are, for the most part, committed to reading what the writer has to say. Suppose you were taking a history exam and you were asked the following question: "Discuss three reasons why American resistance to British taxation was risky." Knowing that you have only a limited time in which to respond and little chance to revise, you might choose to open an essay answer this way: "American resistance to British taxation was risky because the Americans did not yet have a solid government, unanimous support among the colonists for resistance, or a clear sense of what might occur if resistance proved successful." Your history instructor probably would praise you for highlighting the major points of your answer in your lead sentence. Your audience in such a situation wants a demonstration of your knowledge as directly and concisely as possible.

An opening can be a bit more developed but still very direct. If you received the assignment "Explain the term *bias* as it pertains to television network news today," you might begin an essay response this way:

> *Bias* is used as a negative codeword by those politicians who feel the networks have been unfair in their coverage; other people who support the networks deny the existence of bias. *The main problem is that neither side seems able to define the term adequately.*
>
> In the few cases where network officials have attempted to define the concept of bias, the results have been disappointing. For example, Mike Wallace of CBS's "60 Minutes" said not long ago. . . .

This opening is a little longer only because the writer wants to suggest that the problem is fairly complex. But the writer moves quickly to isolate the main point (the italicized statement) and then in the next paragraph to begin the discussion directly. In this type of introduction, you assume your audience knows a great deal about the subject and wants to see if you do too; plunging into the heart of the matter is a good idea.

When your audience is more general and you can't be certain that they will be as dedicated to reading as your history instructor, you need to hook your readers while introducing your focus. You have to use more imagination and variety to write effective introductions for this kind of audience.

Each of the following examples suggests a possible strategy to create readers' interest in an essay on the general topic "teachers." Note how each introduction suggests a connection for the reader while identifying the particular point that will be developed in the essay. The bridge the writer uses to move from the introduction to the body of the essay is important as well.

Starting with a Question

A question in an opening can suggest direct communication between writer and reader, offering a personal connection with the subject matter; the question also can suggest an answer, providing a quick way for the writer to lead readers to the main discussion.

> How many of us have stopped to reflect on just how much teachers can influence our attitudes toward a subject or toward school? Maybe we've given the idea a fleeting thought now and then,

but the real impact of teachers' influence didn't hit me until I finished high school and discovered that I couldn't face the thought of going to school for four more years.

With high school graduation behind me I was ready for freedom, but. . . .

Starting with a Story or Incident

Most readers like a sense of action or story. A fictionlike opening creates a sense of timeliness and movement, but the writer must remember that a story for the story's sake is not enough; it must help the reader sense the importance of the main idea in the essay.

> I had stopped for a drink at a water fountain outside a classroom and was waiting for the student in front of me to finish getting his drink. I was surprised to see him swallow six different pills and then glance around hastily to see if anyone had observed him. As luck would have it, someone had—a teacher who had just come out of the classroom. Before the student could move, the teacher had him by the arm. "Got any more of those pills?" The student, his mouth still full of water, gargled an answer and then with an explosive spurt showered the teacher and me with water and ran off down the hall. Later I discovered this was not an isolated incident. Being a teacher today means, among other things, being an expert at spotting drug use among students, and getting sprayed with water is one of the less hazardous aspects of the job.
>
> Although teachers may not want this new responsibility, it has been thrust upon them because. . . .

Starting with Unusual Facts or Examples

Carefully selected facts or statistics can highlight the importance of a subject and suggest that the writer has done some research beyond his or her immediate experience. People like to believe the writer knows what he or she is talking about.

> Ten years ago, many bright students were electing education as a profession. Today, schools of education are trying everything they can to encourage students to major in education. However, only 1 out of 1,500 students now entering college will major in education. That represents a 200% decrease in the last ten years. The basic reasons for the decline appear to be a lack of employment opportunities and low pay after a person completes the necessary training. Experts are now predicting, however, that there will be a definite need for more teachers in the 1990s and these teachers will be better paid and better educated. To meet this new challenge, schools of education are making some unusual changes in their programs.
>
> One of the first changes has been. . . .

Starting with Selected Details

Sometimes by selecting key details the writer can set a mood and also suggest a position. Readers begin to sense the details building on top of one another until their significance is finally made clear.

> I was seeing the room in the late afternoon and the shadows made everything seem gloomy. The remnants of a few scarred desks were crowded into one corner, the heavily initialed desk tops coated with several inches of dust. The floor, badly worn from where desk chairs had scraped their marks forever into the faded floor boards, revealed here and there a broken board. Shafts of light from below coming through these broken places gave a crazy patchwork effect to the ceiling. Still hanging over the blackboard at the front of the room was a tattered American flag. The homeroom for the ninth grade wasn't as I remembered it. I couldn't help thinking as I stood in the room that sometimes progress may mean we lose something that was very important to us, for it was in this room as a ninth grader that I first discovered that education could be exciting.
>
> My introduction to Homeroom 252 was quite a shock. The first day I learned. . . .

You need to study your material, your audience, and your purpose before deciding which approach is most suitable for a particular piece of writing. At this point in your writing development, make a conscious effort to experiment with different types of introductions and get in the habit of looking closely at how other writers introduce their material. No matter what kind of introduction you use, however, it should always be influenced by your sense of your audience and what you want from them.

The Conclusion

Just as the function of an introduction helps readers understand where a piece of writing will lead them, a conclusion reminds readers of the point of the piece they have just read. Few people enjoy going to a movie that seems to have no beginning or ending. People leave such a movie muttering to one another, "Well, what happened? I didn't get it. Did they leave something out?" Certainly you don't want your readers to leave a piece you've written muttering such things. The function of a conclusion is to bring an essay to an end. You should neither stop in the middle of a thought nor drag on indefinitely trying to find a place to end. Readers expect writers to round off the writing, giving clear signals that the final point has been made.

The best way to consider a conclusion is to stop after completing the introduction and body of the essay and reread what you've written.

Reading aloud is a good idea because you might hear a kind of building effect, in which details and sentences all seem to march toward a rousing finale. This rereading also gives you a chance to view your work as a whole, something you may not have been able to do while involved in the writing. Often, after such a rereading, you will begin to see some possibilities for bringing the piece to a close. You want to create a sense of completion for readers, an understanding of your point and how you arrived at it.

Often a writer's first thought about ending a piece of writing is to provide a summary of the piece. This in itself is not a bad idea, but it can quickly become boring if it is used too frequently or with no consideration for the audience or the material. An essay that develops only one or two major points does not need much summarizing. The conclusion is the last thing the reader encounters, and so it is one section of the paper likely to have a strong impact. Just as a minister wants to make sure the congregation carries away the message of the day and therefore plants it in a strong, rousing conclusion to the sermon, you as a writer need to consider how to leave a strong impression with your readers.

You should avoid the following two pitfalls in developing conclusions.

1. *The single-sentence ending.* Just as effective writers do not use a one-sentence opening, most effective writers avoid resting the entire impact of their writing on one final sentence. A writer who does so is probably not certain that the material has done the job. A typical result goes like this: "I knew I never should have gotten up on that fateful morning." If the readers haven't figured out such a fact by the end of the paper, stating it in the ending is unnecessary because the writing has already failed.
2. *Introducing new subjects.* A conclusion is the end, not the beginning. Remember the main focus of your paper and stick with it to the end of the paper. If you have additional ideas to discuss, either you have not organized your paper properly or you moved away from your original focus. In either case, introducing new ideas will not help the reader get a sense of ending.

Although occasionally a piece of writing will seem to end on its own, writers usually have to give the same consideration to their endings as to their beginnings. The following sample conclusions suggest the range of possibilities for ending a piece of writing.

Ending with a Sense of Responsibility

Appealing to readers' sense of responsibility can create a feeling of sharing between readers and writer. Suggesting that "we're all in this together" can minimize any sense that the writer feels superior to the audience and may help readers take the writer's point seriously.

> ... The evidence is clear; a child's mind can be polluted and corrupted just as easily as his body can be poisoned by contaminants in the environment. Children are essentially powerless to deal with such problems. This means that the responsibilty for effecting change rests with every adult citizen. Meaning you. Meaning me. Meaning us.
>
> —Victor B. Cline, "How TV Violence Damages Your Children"

Ending with a Final Illustration

An illustration or anecdote at the end of an essay can be effective if the material emphasizes the writer's major point. Using a format for the anecdote that is different from the main style of the essay helps highlight the ending and attracts extra attention from the reader.

> ... New York is a city in which large, cliff-dwelling hawks cling to skyscrapers and occasionally zoom to snatch a pigeon over Central Park or Wall Street, or the Hudson River. Bird watchers have seen these peregrine falcons circling lazily over the city. They have seen them perched atop tall buildings, even around Times Square. About twelve of these hawks patrol the city, sometimes with a wingspan of thirty-five inches. They have buzzed women on the roof of the St. Regis Hotel, have attacked repairmen on smokestacks, and, in August, 1947, two hawks jumped women residents in the recreation yard of the Home of the New York Guild for the Jewish Blind. Maintenance men at the Riverside Church have seen hawks dining on pigeons in the bell tower. The hawks remain there for only a little while. And then they fly out to the river, leaving pigeons' heads for the Riverside maintenance men to clean up. When the hawks return, they fly in quietly—*unnoticed,* like the cats, the headless men, the ants, the ladies' masseur, the doorman with three bullets in his head, and most of the other offbeat wonders in this town without time.
>
> —Gay Talese, "New York"

Ending with a Prediction

Occasionally writers want to place their ideas in a time frame. The purpose of the essay may be to point out a future problem or to suggest a direction that future events will take.

> ... No matter who eventually wins the battle for Conoco, the whirl of mergers in the oil industry is likely to continue. The losers of the current campaign will still be left with billions in cash or bank credit to

buy up other companies, and natural-resource firms will probably be the first targets. The struggle for petropower has barely begun.

—Charles Alexander, "Reaching for Conoco's Riches"

Ending with a Quotation

Writers often use statements by another person if they want an emotional or unusually emphatic expression of the main idea.

> . . . With so much documentation, one would think that by now the mystery of Houdini would have been dispelled. But this is not the case. There are still many who do not accept the physical explanations of his feats. The fascination, the mystery, have never diminished. People find them too remarkable and ingenious. Indeed, if anything, the explanations have reinforced the conviction of those who believe that Houdini had supernatural powers. And who, after all, can say? Let Bess have the last word. Writing to Sir Arthur Conan Doyle on December 16, 1926, she stated: "He buried no secrets. Every conjurer knows how his tricks were done—with the exception of just where or how the various traps or mechanisms were hidden.
> "It was Houdini himself that was the secret."
>
> —Raymund FitzSimons,
> *Death and the Magician: The Mystery of Houdini*

As you have done with introductions, become aware of the endings of different things you read. Decide how effective different conclusions are, and if you come across some especially effective examples, copy them down for future reference.

Analyzing Your Introductions and Conclusions

Select one of your essays and examine your introduction carefully. Then write two other possible introductions, using completely different techniques. Show the original and your two new versions to a writing partner and ask the partner to select the one he or she finds most effective. Discuss the results. If a change in your essay seems appropriate, make it. Repeat the procedure with your conclusion.

Review other essays you have written to determine the effectiveness of your introductions and conclusions. Keep revising until you have a version that accurately leads the reader into the essay and out of it.

You should make every attempt in the revision stage of your writing to pay attention now to all the elements of an effective paragraph and essay: focus, unity, evidence, coherence, paragraph hooks, introduction, and conclusion. Return to this workshop frequently to review the principles discussed here. Your instructor and your readers expect you to practice what you've learned; don't let them down.

CHAPTER 5

How Does That Happen?

"How do you do that? I can't seem to get the hang of it." "How did you learn to do that? I never saw that done before." "Geez, I wish I'd known how to do that a long time ago." How many times have questions like these caused you to stop in the middle of what you're doing to ask yourself—Well, how do I do it? Whether it's learning how to flip pizza dough so it doesn't come down around our heads like a soggy blanket or finding a way to stretch hamburger so it feeds six instead of three, all of us at some time in our lives have probably discovered a successful way to do an activity. What we often don't realize is that our particular way of doing something may be useful to others.

THE PROCESS ESSAY

When the word *process* is mentioned, your mind probably turns to things like the making of cheese, the making of steel, or perhaps just tying a shoelace. If you stop and think for a moment, however, you'll discover that the idea of process governs much of everyday life. You don't have to limit yourself to practical things; often in the ways people relax, find entertainment, or even think about what is happening a process may be lurking. Suppose you can't afford to own a musical instrument but you are very much attuned to the noise around you. Maybe you can't even read a note of music, but you know what you like to hear. Should any of this stop you from creating your own music? It doesn't stop some people, if we believe the following account.

> I got started musically because I was sick and tired of all the honking and noise in the street. You walk around all day like I do, you got yourself a migraine by 10 A.M. So I decided to counteract all the racket and strike back, and I started making my own music as I went around. I usually have one free hand. I started with one of those little white plastic coffee spoons, and I'd whack stuff as I went by. Originally, sides of trucks, fire hydrants—things like that. I broke my first spoon on a yellow Ryder. Then I got and used a Flair pen. But when I went for a big note the top fell off, so I switched to a seventy-nine-cent ballpoint, without a top. It works fine; if my musical taste changes, I'll move up to something else.
>
> Currently, the music I play is one of two kinds: the simple pling-a-plink-a-plonk, where you hit everything you see as you walk along and you see if you like it, and the other kind, which is where you start with something like, say, an awning frame, or the metal alongside the plateglass window of a coffee shop. Ping! You got your first note. Then I select some song or tune that comes to mind, like "The World Is Waiting for the Sunrise," and I see if I can pick up the next note somewhere down the block. You have to keep the song firmly in mind. If you don't cheat, it might take twenty blocks. I usually give up, but it's a challenge. I once got all the way to the last "baby" before "now" in "Yes, Sir, That's My Baby," but I was in a very good area—lots of garbage cans.
>
> Some areas are lousy, like Fifth Avenue. You're very restricted—to hydrants, signs. No garbage cans. You have to know what you're do-ing—like there are two different kinds of "No Parking" signposts. There is your basic round one, which is hollow, and then you got your solid post, which is basically bent metal with holes in it. Now, these two types make an altogether different note. You learn these things. A nice big mailbox will give you a tremendous bass note, you probably think. It depends. Hit it at the bottom, you'll get a bass note, but hit it at the top, you'll get a tink. A streetlight will give you a tink, too. For reso-nance, go for a bus-stop sign, but give it a belt. If it's loose, you got something. Clang! You can get a nice arpeggio off a wire trash basket; concrete ones give nothing. The metal bars in those gratings in the sidewalk that make you sick when you look down and it's a thirty-foot drop under there? You can get music from them, but people are going to stare at you. Sometimes it's better to do without. A store that's closed and has a metal fence over it is good, especially if you do it at a dead run. Brnnnnng! The best time I ever had was a truck carrying bottled water. High, sweet notes. I just stood there about ten minutes and improvised.
>
> —"Music," *The New Yorker*

Perhaps not all of us are ready for such a musical career but we can discover a process in practically anything we do. The test of our understanding of a process may lie in our ability to communicate our understanding to someone unfamiliar with the procedure. Often we have to help others perform a task that we learned at an earlier time. As we teach people, our own knowledge is reinforced so that both of us, learner and teacher, come away with benefits.

Of course we're bound to encounter some peculiarities when we try to teach someone else a process we know very well. We're all familiar with the "pinch of this and dab of that" recipes that grandmothers like to pass on to their granddaughters; and the "well, my boy, you just take this here piece, see, slap it against this one, give her a few twists with the socket, and she'll be as good as new" advice that grandfathers offer to grandsons. Such instructions may work satisfactorily if the grandparents are around to correct the wrong dab or the wrong twist, but what if they aren't available? Certainly, we can ask them to write out the directions but sometimes that doesn't work because they're so accustomed to the procedure that they assume everyone else is too, and they may omit certain key details. When we're trying to follow such directions for a first effort, we can begin to appreciate the importance of careful explanation and an understanding of an audience's needs.

You've been practicing a process in all your work in this book. Throughout the various writing assignments, the word *process* has been stressed; assignments have taken the form of stages or steps that have led—we hope—to your producing a satisfactory piece of writing. Imagine instead what it would have been like to have the following directions as a basis for doing your writing:

Recipe

Joan Smith

Purdue University

Ingredients:

1–2 pounds of periods, drained
    (reserve ½ cup of commas, colons, etc.)
1 tablespoon nouns
1 tablespoon strong verbs
1 teaspoon verbs
1 tablespoon prepositions
6 telling facts
¼ teaspoon opposition
1 cup of sentence structure (good)
4 medium size inkpens or pencils
12 sheets of paper

5 pinches of tightening
dashes of liveliness
1 good dictionary
−2 hours of proofreading
Directions:

1. Place 4 inkpens or pencils, 12 sheets of paper, and erasers on a desk.
2. Sit back in a chair 5–10 minutes and think. Focus on plot and concentrate upon telling facts.
3. Slowly, pick up 1 inkpen or pencil, place in right or left hand, and begin writing.
4. Drain periods onto 1 sheet of paper in appropriate places. Blend in commas and colons.
5. Add nouns, verbs, strong verbs, and prepositions.
6. Spread a mixture of opposition and liveliness all over the paper.
7. When the paper fails because of spelling, look the words up in the dictionary.
8. Meanwhile, add in the pinches of tightening and good sentence structure.
9. Just before calling it quits, proofread for ENGFISH. Before turning the paper in to the teacher, proofread it again. Make lots of servings for reading.

Such a recipe provides little assistance to anyone unfamiliar with writing an essay. Fortunately in your case, you do not have to rely on such skimpy advice. This chapter emphasizes explanations about how particular tasks or activities are accomplished—or not accomplished (sometimes we can be more helpful by telling what not to do). The audience is a crucial factor in this kind of writing; the process has to be clear enough to your readers so that if they have not seen or done the procedure, they will at least comprehend what the steps are and what the outcome may be. Most people would consider the making of a peanut butter and jelly sandwich to be a simple task. But let's assume that someone who has never seen a peanut butter and jelly sandwich needs to know how one is made. Asked to provide directions for this task, a careless person might produce these steps:

1. You need two slices of bread, peanut butter and jelly.
2. Spread peanut butter on each slice of bread.
3. Put the jelly on top of the peanut butter on one slice of bread.
4. Place the other slice of bread on top with the peanut butter inside.
5. Your sandwich will be combined as follows: bread, PB, jelly, PB, bread.

Looking at these directions, you may be inclined to say, Well, it's all there. But wait a moment; consider some of the following questions that an inexperienced sandwich maker might ask:

1. What do I use to spread the peanut butter? You haven't told me anything about the utensils I'll need.
2. How much peanut butter should I put on? How much jelly?
3. Do I spread the peanut butter on both sides of the bread?
4. Do all kinds of jelly and peanut butter work equally well?
5. In step 4 do you mean that the slice I put on top has the peanut butter inside or is it the other slice I have to put that way?

Oh, c'mon, you're saying; anyone can figure out how to make a peanut butter and jelly sandwich—stop nitpicking. Maybe so, but if seemingly simple tasks like making a sandwich can be questioned this way, imagine what your readers might think if you used the same approach in explaining how to do something they had never heard of.

Recipe writing is one type of process that fulfills a definite need. When readers are trying to follow a recipe for molasses cookies, they're not in the mood for anything but the bare facts. In many other instances, however, your readers are not going to be standing in a kitchen with all the ingredients spread around, waiting to pop the product into an oven, or hunched on their knees at midnight on Christmas Eve trying to glue the last piece to a "hot wheels" kit car for their brother. Instead, your readers might want to understand how something happens without their actually doing it. At such times, the human factor is essential; that is, you need to let your readers know there's a real human being involved in the explanation. This approach calls for anecdotes, conversation, actions—techniques that will entertain as well as inform.

ASSIGNMENT:
WRITING A PROCESS ESSAY

Purpose

By now you've probably begun asking yourself, What do I do well enough or know enough about that would be of value to a group of readers? Fortunately the answer should not be long in coming. In fact, the subject for this piece of writing may well turn out to be the easiest to find of all your topics so far. The purpose of a process essay or how-to piece is to provide information of some value to the readers. The subject should be potentially interesting to a group of people and should not be simply a restatement of what they already know. How to knot a tie or tie a pair of jogging shoes probably won't hook many readers. How to vacuum a house, sharpen a pencil, or do a load of laundry may not be of much interest unless you can find some very specific benefit that may not have occurred to people involved in such everyday activities.

A further consideration in selecting a topic is to remember that you are the expert; that is, you must be so well versed in how the procedure works that you can anticipate and answer most of the questions potential readers might be likely to ask. Writing about something that other people know as well as you do can be a waste of everyone's time, so try to pick a subject about which many readers know little if anything. Throughout the essay, you should sound confident and you should leave readers feeling they have benefited from reading your explanation.

Prewriting

Dialoguing

With this piece of writing, you're going to add another technique, called *dialoguing*, to your collection of prewriting strategies. Dialoguing should not be unfamiliar to you; you probably have been doing it mentally for a long time for a variety of purposes. Consider, for instance, your mental preparation for an important job interview; inside your head you might run through a question-and-answer scenario something like the following.

Voice 1: Okay, so you've got an appointment for an interview. Now what?

Voice 2: Well, it probably wouldn't hurt to think about some of the topics I'll need to talk about.

Voice 1: Good thinking—so what are some?

Voice 2: I've got to be able to talk about my education, my previous work, skills, stuff like that.

Voice 1: Yes, background is essential—better review the résumé. Then what?

Voice 2: I've got to know something about the company and the job itself.

Voice 1: Great—where do you get that information?

Voice 2: Jerry works there—he's been there two years, I'll ask him to fill me in. . . .

And so the dialogue continues until you're satisfied that you've explored all that you can; the actual process may take only a short time or it may continue for several days. Like everyone, you switch these dialogues on and off without thinking about it; if you're so good at it mentally, there's little reason to think you can't do it on paper. Here's how to get started.

1. At the top of a blank piece of paper write "What do I know how to do that someone else might like to know how to do?"
2. Start your dialogue with a sentence such as "Well, I can do—" and continue writing things you can do for five minutes or until you run out of ideas.
3. Stop and look at your efforts. Then write "Which one of these do I know the most about or find the most interesting?" Respond to that question, writing as long as you can without worrying about anything but getting information down.
4. When you slow down, write another question: "What are the steps involved in the process?" Then write those out.
5. Now start letting your "voices" take over. It might help to imagine a tough stranger in your head who keeps pestering you with questions about the material you have so far; write out your answers. Whenever you find yourself running down, bring the stranger to life again to ask you another question. Try to carry on this dialogue for at least fifteen minutes; if you're like most people in dialogue, you'll begin to anticipate the questions and keep the information coming.
6. Eventually your voices are going to stop and you'll know that, for now at least, you've written yourself out. Take a rest and then move on to the next step, listing.

In a sense what you have done with the dialoguing is to inventory the possible areas for this assignment. You undoubtedly avoided getting into a discussion of broad processes such as the making of automobiles or the production of gasoline because they're too complex; unless you are a design or petrochemical engineer, such processes lie beyond your scope at this time and probably outside the immediate interest of your audience. That's not to say, of course, that no audiences exist for such topics, but such readers tend to be quite informed and your lack of expertise in those areas would make it hard for you to be useful to your audience. You might, however, have some experience in a small part of a larger process. Perhaps you worked in a steel mill. You might be able to describe the process of your specific job without having to get into an explanation of the whole steel-making process. Although the previous examples have been of jobs, don't overlook the possibility that your area of expertise is with a hobby or other leisure-time activity. Most of us have taught ourselves or been taught by someone how to enjoy our leisure time. Topics in such areas are appropriate too.

Listing

With some information in front of you now as a result of dialoguing, you're ready to move on to identifying the material for your essay. Here you can use a technique that should be quite familiar by now. In fact, this technique should have become such a natural part of your writing activity that if someone yells "list" at you as you're walking across campus, you'll know that person has been attending the same kind of writing class you have—or else you're walking peculiarly. Don't rush the listing step, for you have to do two things at this point.

The first is to identify all the steps in the process you'll be explaining:

1. Separate the process into specific stages or steps.
2. If the process contains a number of steps, cluster the steps into categories such as "preparation," "making," "applying."
3. Be certain all steps are presented in clear sequence.

Once you've clearly established the steps by writing them out and leaving a good deal of space under each one, move on to filling in under each step all the details you can recall that might help explain that part of the process. Your dialoguing material will come in handy here; pull out details, incidents, and examples, placing them under the appropriate steps. Remember that in most cases you'll be addressing an uninformed reader, so the more complex your subject is, the more careful you will need to be in explaining everything thoroughly. As in all of your writing, being specific at this stage in the prewriting process makes your work easier as you proceed with the first draft.

Response

After you have put your material into a rough sequence, take a few minutes to discuss it with a writing partner; talk to your partner about what you plan to explain and invite questions and suggestions. If your partner is familiar with the process, check your understanding against his or hers. If your partner knows nothing about the process, invite many "dumb" questions to see if you're anticipating the problems your readers might have. Make notes carefully and pay particular attention to the need for adding a step or moving a step. The sequence in a process essay can be of vital importance to the audience's grasp of the material.

When you have finished your discussion, stop for a moment to relax your writer's cramp and take stock of the situation. Did you and your partner agree that you had enough information at all points in the process? Do you need to do some reading or perhaps discuss your material further with someone familiar with the subject? If everything has gone well, you should have quite a mountain of information to draw upon; that "mountain" testifies to what an expert you are.

Audience

Now you must decide how to shape all of your information into an understandable format for your readers. You have not yet identified your audience, a slight change from previous assignments where the audience has been identified before the prewriting stage. That omission was deliberate. You're now at the point where you can begin to make some decisions about your potential readers. Few people other than a writing instructor will want to read an essay just because it is an example of process explanation. Most people will read if they suspect they're going to discover something they didn't already know or to see how to approach a familiar topic in a new way. Do you want to persuade your readers of the usefulness of the process? Do you want to show them the extent to which you underwent all kinds of experiences in order to learn? Possibly you want your audience to have a better understanding of why a particular process or procedure exists so that even if they do not use the procedure, they will at least be tolerant, even supportive, of those who do.

The following questions may help you determine your audience.

1. Is the audience very experienced or inexperienced with this subject?
2. What kinds of interest in the subject might the audience have?
3. What is the age, occupation, and educational level of the audience?
4. Is the audience mostly male, mostly female, or mixed?
5. Do you suspect the audience will be friendly or hostile toward the subject?
6. Will the audience have any misconceptions about the subject?

Use these questions as a basis for building in your mind or on paper a working profile of your readers. Keep this picture firmly in mind throughout the drafting process and make your decisions about what to include and what to omit on the basis of this audience.

Organizing Strategies

With the assessment of your audience clearly fixed in your mind, you're ready to move on to some critical decisions about presentation. Two basic strategies are available: step by step and narrative.

Step by Step

Undoubtedly the most natural shaping strategy for process writing is presentation of the steps of the process in sequence. Although such "recipe" writing has its purpose—keeping the reader aware of sequence—unless writers humanize the steps by offering incidents, dialogue, or reactions, they run a real risk of presenting nothing but a recipe. This works well for cookbooks or how-to manuals, but you aren't writing for either at the moment. If you worked as a lifeguard at a pool, for example, a bare recitation of the rules and duties will do little to interest your readers and probably will do little to increase their understanding of what it's like to be in that position. On the other hand, if you use specific experiences to illustrate how the duties are carried out, your readers will have a deeper understanding and appreciation of the work you and other lifeguards do.

Narrative

Can you find a "once upon a time" focus (an hour, one day, one experience) within which you might demonstrate your procedure? Instead of writing about the process of checking groceries at a supermarket, for example, why not show in story form exactly how you learned the appropriate procedures or what your first day on the job was like? Why not put readers there with you as you learn the process—show the mistakes as well as the successes because both are informative and interesting. After all, even experts have had to go through early stages of learning both how to do things and how not to do them.

The techniques you use in both approaches will overlap, of course; that is, you'll have to follow the sequence of steps in a process no matter what format you use. But that is no reason to rely solely on the steps to get you through the writing. Remember that devices like dialogue, comparison, and descriptive detail—all of which you have used in earlier assignments—can be effective in this type of writing as well.

Sampling Other Writers' Presentations

Before you begin a draft, take some time to read the essays at the end of this chapter. Each suggests a slightly different way of presenting information about a process. As you read, keep in mind the following questions.

1. How do the writers show an awareness of their audience?
2. How do the writers add interest to what might otherwise be a fairly dull topic?
3. How do the writers avoid sounding as though they were giving orders to the reader throughout the essay ("you do this, then you do this . . .")?
4. How do the writers reveal the purpose of their essays? That is, do the writers have a particular reason for discussing the topics other than "I had to write a process paper so here is what I came up with"?

The First Draft

With the prewriting stage behind you, your material accumulated, and some sample reading of others' efforts with process writing, you're ready to begin a draft. One of the nice things about drafting this piece of writing is that you know pretty well before you begin where you have to finish. The trick, of course, is to get from the beginning to the end without losing your readers along the way. That calls for a clear identification of purpose: By now you have established a sense in your own mind of the potential audience for your explanation; along with that should have come a clear sense of why this audience might be interested or could benefit from your discussion.

In drafting this essay you'll quickly discover that it's easy to leave out small steps or details that are so obvious to you. Remember that you, not your audience, are the expert, so what seems insignificant to you may loom very large in their understanding of an explanation. If you suspect there's any danger of omission, keep playing the role of the curious onlooker who constantly asks, "Why or how do you do that?"

You may also discover the "stepping" problem in process writing. Words like *first, second, third,* have an alarming way of becoming repetitive in a process explanation. But in your rough draft don't worry too much about this; you can adjust the wording and use more subtle transition signals when you rewrite. In fact, these words may serve a useful function the first time through by helping you keep all the steps in proper sequence.

Another factor in writing a process paper is use of the word *you.* Some process essays end up sounding like drill sergeants conducting calisthenics for the readers: "You put this here; then you must remember to place the. . . ." A whole paper that keeps hitting the reader with orders even though the readers have no intention of rushing out to do the process quickly becomes like an Excedrin headache—it feels so good when it stops. The reader finds relief comes from quitting after the first paragraph. Remember that you're offering a process explanation so that readers can understand, though not necessarily duplicate, the process. Still another way to overcome the repetitive command tone is to switch pronouns. You can write a process explanation in the first person (I, we) or the third person (he, she, it, they), and you can make a choice between past or present tense, as shown below.

First Person	*Third Person*
Present	*Present*
Once I have the screw threaded into the hole, I take the screwdriver and with a firm grip begin to. . . . (This form suggests that the writer is explaining a process that he or she follows frequently.)	The disc jockey places the record on the turntable with one thumb in the center of the record, lifts the thumb, and the record spins freely. (A habitual process performed by someone other than the writer.)
Past	*Past*
I knew that putting the board over the puddle would not work well, so I reached for my coat and started to absorb the water with it. (A process done in the past by the writer.)	The kiln was fired and then he placed the clay pot inside, once the temperature had reached the appropriate degree of heat. (Process performed in the past by someone other than the writer.)

The easiest way to handle pronouns is to stay with an account of how *you* learned a particular procedure or with the steps *you* follow habitually in completing a task. Although at this point such advice may not seem important, as the writing continues you'll probably feel relieved if you don't have to sound like a driver's manual or a Betty Crocker cookbook. Relax, take the readers along, let them see you in action, and let the process explanation flow naturally from that vantage point.

Re-Viewing

With a rough draft completed, put a skeptical eye to your material, particularly in the following areas.

1. *Focus:* Have I tried to cover too much or too little territory in the process? Do my stages or steps look "skinny," like a basic grocery

list? Have I produced only a "how to make a phone call" type draft that provides merely a skeleton of the process?

You can find some evidence of problems in focus by looking carefully at the visual effect of the paper; many skinny, short paragraphs could suggest the grocery list effect; on the other hand, perhaps the paper has become too technical or detailed and it bulges in various places. In the first case you'll need to develop your discussion more or review your purpose to determine if it is still suitable. If your paper has become too "fat," it's time to step in and impose a diet; check to see if all the material is directly relevant to your purpose; if not, trim the excess.

2. *Organization:* Have I followed the process carefully step by step without omitting any crucial stages? How do I help the reader keep track of the shift from one step to the next and how do I show the relationship of one phase to another?

   Although the general organizational structure of a process explanation is fairly well defined by the nature of the subject, you can't afford to assume that the sequence is automatically clear. Go back to your prewriting and the outline of steps; check off each step in the draft to be certain all steps are present. Paragraphs usually correspond to major divisions in the process, although more than one paragraph may be used to discuss a step. Transitions such as "after this," "before," "next," "then," "along with," and "when I have finished" help readers keep track of the sequence in the process. The key here, of course, is not to fall into a rut of repetition in which the transition words begin to strike the readers' consciousness with regularity. Be alert for opportunities to substitute for repeated words and to vary sentence structure so the words do not always appear in the same position.

3. *Support:* Have I offered ample explanation for each step? Have I taken the necessary time to explain the "why" as well as the "what"? Do I include examples, incidents, and details that explain as well as provide interest? Do I include examples of what not to do or what might happen if a step is not followed properly, if such information is appropriate? Have I clarified all technical terms so readers unfamiliar with the topic will have little difficulty understanding the explanation?

4. *Introduction/Conclusion:* How have I made it apparent to readers that they can gain something from reading my explanation? How have I created interest in my opening and how effectively do I keep that interest sustained throughout the draft? What does my conclu-

sion do for the focus of the essay? Does my conclusion once again support my purpose for the benefit of readers? Does my conclusion take in the whole essay and not just the last step of the process?

Rewriting/Revising/Editing

Having reviewed the draft in relation to the points listed above, you can now move on to rewriting or revising the draft. Pay particular attention to any comments from the readers of your work at this stage. Remember to play the role of the curious but uninformed reader throughout your revision, constantly asking "Have I explained this as interestingly and as clearly as possible?" "What questions might I ask as a reader of this process explanation? What would I like to know if this is the first time I have met this particular process?"

Move on to "housekeeping" details after you have taken care of any major problems. Look back at drafts of earlier essays to see what seemed to be the major difficulties there. Although the subjects differed, some of the basic writing procedures and concerns have appeared in each assignment. Check the present draft to see if any of the previous problems may have sneaked in again to haunt you. Once you have satisfied yourself and at least one other reader that the revised draft now stands as a solid piece of process explanation, you are ready to submit the polished draft for evaluation.

SAMPLE PROCESS ESSAYS

Scan-Scan-Bag

"Anita—telephone!" my mom yelled from the back door.

I dropped my badminton racket and ran in the house to answer the phone. I picked up the receiver and was astonished to hear the voice at the other end say, "You've got the job. When can you start?"

For a minute I just stood there, unbelieving, wanting to jump up and down. Two days before, I had turned sixteen, the minimum age in my county to apply for work, and already I had a job. Somehow I managed to sound calm as I answered my future boss, "Anytime, sir, it's up to you."

"All right, then, I'll see you tomorrow morning at ten o'clock. Looking forward to working with you."

As soon as I was dead sure that he had hung up his end of the phone, I let out the loudest whoop ever heard. I had my very first job. I was going to be a cashier for one of the largest supermarket chains in the South.

My first two days on the job were merely four-hour training sessions. At first I read books, watched films, and answered questions on checking and bagging techniques and store policies. After I had finished that, I could begin training on the scanning terminal.

From the books I learned the basics of operating manual IBM terminals, most commonly known as the cash register. The machine is set up similar to a typewriter, but with only number keys ranging from zero to nine, arranged in three rows of three with a space bar–like key, which is zero, underneath. There are also three department keys: grocery, produce, and meat. These departments are represented on grocery items by different-color price stickers and the right key must be keyed in after the cost of the item. Keying in means simply to press the keys that record the cost of the item inside the terminal. After keying in all the items, I learned to press the total key to total the order and to press the cash-tendered key, which automatically figures out the correct amount of change to be given back to the customer. (See Diagram 1.)

Although the manual terminal played a large part in the checking process, our store had just begun a new way of checking, called *scanning*. Scanning is a relatively new way of computerized checking. The scanner is a window-like compartment that is built into the checkout counter. A conveyor belt moves the groceries to within an inch of the scanning device. Each grocery item is coded with what is called the Universal Product Code (see Diagram 2). A laser beam from inside the scanning "window" picks up this magnetic code, transmits it to the base com-

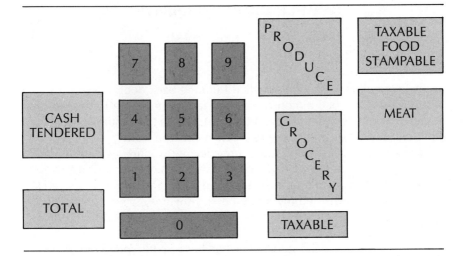

Diagram 1   Keys of an IBM cash-register terminal.

Diagram 2   Sample Universal Product Code.

puter which looks up the price, relays it back to the cashier's terminal, and flashes the price up on the register screen all in a fraction of a second.

The head cashier, my trainer, demonstrated to me the proper procedure of scanning groceries. She stood between the scanner and the set-aside counter. On the shelf right in front of her she placed two open grocery sacks, and then flipped a switch on the side of the terminal that started the conveyor belt moving.

"First," she explained to me, "reach with your right hand, get an item, and pass it over the scanner with the Universal Product Code facing down. If a green light on the side of the scanner comes on and you hear a beep, then reach with your left hand and do the same thing with another item. If a red light comes on, then rescan the item once. If the item will not scan, just key the price in the register manually. After you have scanned two items, bag them at the same time. That's our scanning slogan—scan-scan-bag." That slogan was drilled into my head for days to come, and I still can't walk into a grocery store without thinking scan-scan-bag to myself.

After practicing on my own for a while, I soon found out that the scan-scan part of checking was fairly easy. It was the bagging that was tricky. Often crushable, lightweight items that should be placed at the top of the bag reached the scanner before the heavy items that are needed to provide a solid base for the bag. When I came to an item that was to be saved for the top of the bag, I placed it behind me on the set-aside counter and bagged it later. Large, bulky items, such as cartons of soft drinks, gallon jugs, and laundry detergent, I placed directly into the shopping cart. By the end of the second day of training, I was ready to face the public. The head cashier set me up in a terminal next to hers just in case I had a few problems.

My first customer was Mr. McGillicutti, a little old man who was in the store every morning to buy a pack of cigarettes. Remember, I thought to myself, as I gave him a big grin, a smile is the store's most important asset. "Good morning. How are you?" I asked, but later I learned to avoid this question, because Mr. McGillicutti let off a string of ailments, aches, and pains three miles long. I hated to interrupt him to give him his total, "Forty-seven cents, please."

He handed me a dollar bill, but when I put my hand out to give him his change, he grabbed it and kissed it. Change went flying everywhere. Mr. McGillicutti just stood there chuckling to himself as I scrambled to pick up his fifty-three cents.

After he finally had left, the head cashier laughingly said to me, "Guess I should've warned you about him. He's one of those tinkers that likes to give new cashiers a hard time. You'll meet all kinds, so be prepared!"

"What's a tinker?" I dumbly asked.

"Oh, that's what we cashiers call customers who just come in and tinker around. Most of them are really picky. Mr. McGillicutti's one of the better ones."

I had never before realized what cashiers had to go through in dealing with the public. I vowed to myself from that moment on to be a more alert and considerate shopper. I didn't want anyone to call me a tinker.

I slowly turned to face my next customer. "Good morning," I said and smiled, making sure to greet the customer. When he grunted instead of answering, I knew this was going to be a tough one! I nervously began scanning his groceries.

"Hey, wait a minute," he yelled, "that's on sale!"

"Are you sure?" I asked him. Then I turned to the head cashier and asked, "Is this a sale item?" Sure enough, it was, so I punched the void key and the price that had scanned the first time and rerang the sale price by hand. "I'm sorry, sir. Usually sale prices scan automatically. Something must have gone wrong."

"Obviously. I can also see that you didn't study the sales ad in this morning's paper," he grumbled. "A good cashier always knows what's on sale."

I apologized again, practically in tears, and quickly totaled his grocery bill. When I told him the price, he shoved a check into my hand. I didn't notice the manager desperately looking my way as I asked, "Do you have a check-cashing courtesy card, sir? It's store policy to never accept a check without one."

"For your information, little lady, I am the supervisor of all cashiers in this store. I do not need a check-cashing card! Go ahead, ask your manager."

By that time my manager was beside me, looking about as nervous as I felt. He nodded his head for me to take the check, and I did. The supervisor walked away in a huff. I glanced over at the head cashier who was standing there flabbergasted. She said, "That's rule number one: Remember important faces."

"How could I forget," I said, "and the next time I see that face, I'm hiding under my counter!"

The day wore on, and things got a little easier. Finally, it was time to go home. First, I scrubbed down my checkout counter with soap and water, put up reshops—groceries customers don't buy and leave lying around—and swept around my terminal. Then I walked over to the time clock, trying not to look too anxious, and punched out.

When my mom came home from work that night, she found me sitting in the softest chair in the house, soaking my aching feet in warm, soapy water, chanting scan-scan-bag over and over.

She looked at me strangely and started to ask, "How was your—" Then for some reason, possibly the look on my face, she changed her mind.

If only everyone could spend a day working in a supermarket. . . .

Jogging

Everywhere you look, television, magazines, and newspapers, you discover people exercising and getting back into the good health they once

had. The most popular of these exercises is jogging. The activity was introduced to me when I was in grade school, but it never had a real meaning
until I jogged with some friends last summer. Getting up early and running
around the football field for a half hour or so at first seemed stupid; but
later I enjoyed it so that when I had to quit because of school starting and
the cold weather setting in, I really did miss it.

Some people ask me why I like to run. The answer is simple: Running
gives me a revived feeling to start the new day with and helps me to relax
by giving me time to think out my problems. Although these are the main
reasons I enjoy jogging, the fact that running tones up the muscles of the
legs, hips, and back, giving them more strength and me a better figure,
adds to the list of reasons. It also improves the digestion and circulation
systems by letting the blood flow more rapidly and easily through them.

Although running is considered a strenuous exercise, anyone in good
physical condition can start it but should see a doctor first. I have been
running for about two months steadily and have found that I enjoy it as
much now as I did in my P.E. classes at school. When the other kids were
angry about having to run laps around either the football field or basketball
court, I was just as willing to do this as any other exercise. Many over-
weight people begin jogging because it is a sport that requires no special
equipment or great skills to start. Jogging one mile will burn off approximately one hundred calories; this is another major reason for people to
jog. After getting used to running one mile, you can run longer distances
without getting any more exhausted than from just one mile. After six
months, the devoted runner can average about three miles a day more than
he started out doing.

Most runners have a favorite or set time for their daily jogs; for example, many enjoy starting their day off with a brisk run. This is a good
time to run during the summer because it enables the participant to beat
the heat. When I graduate from school in May, I am planning on getting up
early each day to jog. People say that once you get into this routine, you
will like this time better than any other. Some joggers might agree, but the
ones who like to run at night would probably reject the morning completely. They like the quietness of the night better than the business of the
morning. The possibility of running on the road instead of the sidewalk is
also an idea that attracts night runners. The blacktop of the road is a softer
substance than the concrete of the sidewalk, thus being easier on the feet.
Another good time to hit the pavement is right before lunch or dinner,
especially if you are on a diet. You will find that the exercise will help
decrease your appetite so you will tend to eat less at meals.

No matter what time you choose to run, wearing the right clothes is a
factor that should not be overlooked. Clothes should be very comfortable
and suited to the day's weather. Cotton is the most desirable fabric because

it absorbs perspiration and allows air to circulate freely around the body. Most runners wear blue-jean or cotton shorts and a T-shirt in the warm weather and sweat pants with a lightweight jacket in the cold weather. My running attire has been an old pair of jeans and a bulky sweatshirt of my brother's. This summer I will probably wear a pair of shorts and a cotton top or T-shirt. Because I run in the morning, I might also wear a lightweight jacket to keep from getting chilled. The shoes of a runner are also important. The majority of people wear tennis shoes for jogging; but some people, like myself, just hop into old sneakers from the summer before. The difference in the type of shoes is that the preferred running shoes have a built-up heel to reduce strain whereas the regular tennis shoe is flat-heeled and this causes the bottom of your feet to hit harder on the pavement.

Another measure that helps reduce the strain on the legs and feet is the way you run. I thought I would never learn to jog correctly because of the difference in the way you should run. After reading the dos and don'ts in my health book at school, I discovered that I was doing more of the don'ts than the dos. The first step is to run so the heels are the first parts to hit the ground instead of the toes. This can be achieved by lifting your leg from the thigh instead of the calf. Another rule is to keep your body straight with the head up and the shoulders in their natural position. Leaning slightly forward and keeping your mouth open makes it easier to take in as much air as you need. Breathing from your abdomen helps prevent the sharp pains that can develop in your side. After you finish running, you should always do some exercises, such as shaking your arms and hands vigorously, to help slow your body back down to its regular pace.

If you enjoy being out of doors and getting some exercise, you will probably like jogging. Training your mind and body to this sport-exercise takes time and effort, but many feel it is most rewarding. Good health is something to consider now; and with the shortage of gas getting more real all the time, jogging may be a very good solution.

My Problems Playing Golf

My problems playing golf are disastrous to my golf pro husband, outrageous to my friends, and totally frustrating to me. Golf is a wonderful game but there is more to it than hitting the golf ball.

One of my major problems deals with hitting the golf ball. I'm having a hard time since my husband insists I do everything just right. I didn't know there are certain ways of standing while I hit the golf ball. My legs have to be about shoulder length apart, my knees bent slightly. My eyes must be always on the ball, and my left arm must be kept completely straight when

I am swinging the club at the ball. By the time I've gotten my knees bent, I have forgotten to keep my left arm straight and then I have to start all over again. By some miracle, if I've remembered everything, I'll look away from the ball and miss it entirely. My husband becomes very annoyed if I haven't hit it after about three times, because generally golfers are waiting to play behind us.

Thinking that just hitting the ball is the major obstacle, I turn to the clubs. They are the woods and irons. Individual clubs are made to be used on different distances from the green. The woods are used in longer distances and the irons in the shorter distances. Generally, the woods are numbered one through four, with the number-one wood hitting the longest distance and number-four wood a shorter distance. Also, there are generally nine irons numbering one through nine. The same principle as the woods applies, with the lower-numbered iron hitting the longest distances and the higher-numbered irons the shorter distances. For example, if I have started on the tee, I would usually use my one wood (called the driver), and if I was about fifty feet away from the green I would use my nine iron. The player has the choice to make for the appropriate club, but I have trouble swinging any of them, much less having to worry about distances.

Another handicap happens when I finally get to where I can hit the ball, but it only rolls about twenty feet in front of me. There are just so many times I am supposed to hit the ball. For example, if one hole is a par four, that means I have to get the ball in the hole in four strokes. On an average par four there are about four hundred yards. So it sometimes takes me about twenty strokes from tee to green.

Real trouble happens when I finally hit a really good ball and it goes into the woods. This sometimes takes me a long time, because I have a terrible fear of snakes and because sometimes *I just can't find my ball.* If I do happen to find it, I have to try to hit the ball from the spot where it lies. In the woods there are trees, bushes, and underbrush which present obstacles that trap the ball. I have enough problems in the wide-open spaces, much less in the woods.

The real fun and anxiety of the game begin on the putting greens where I use my putter. With this club I don't hit the ball as hard as I can; I have to gently tap it and get it to roll. In the greens' construction there are little dips and hills, which are supposed to make the shots more difficult for the experienced golfer. These little obstacles make my shots almost impossible, because they make the ball go in crazy directions.

Many golf courses have water and sand traps that come into play on the course. My problem is if they are out there, my ball somehow always finds them. Ending up in the water usually means I can't hit my ball out. Removing the ball from the water and placing it where I can hit it means taking a penalty stroke, which makes my score go up. Sand traps are a little better because I do have a chance to hit the ball. My problem with sand is sometimes I bury the ball and that makes hitting it hard.

Another inconvenience is keeping score. I don't believe I've ever met a golfer that doesn't tamper a little with his or her score. I've tried tampering with mine, but when I've scored close to two hundred there isn't much anyone can do.

The most enjoyable thing is riding in the little golf carts the course offers. I've always had desires to be the next Richard Petty, and since I can't race in our private car on the streets, I try my best on the golf course. I take curves, hills, and dips at top speeds of fifteen miles per hour. Of course, this causes problems, especially if I have someone riding with me, because the passenger can become violently ill.

When I do play with a friend and we both hit a good shot, and the balls happen to land in about the same place, then we have to figure out which ball is which. I always try to go for the one that is a little further ahead than the other, because I need all the little advantages I can get. Sometimes this causes problems because my friend may also need an advantage. I usually work this out by moving both balls to the same spot.

It is pretty clear that playing golf may elude me for a long time. But golf is a very enjoyable activity and I get to be outdoors. So I'd encourage everyone to try playing. Even if you do as badly as me, you'll find yourself having a lot of fun.

CHAPTER 6

What's Your Perspective?

Stop and think. Eyewitness accounts of some event or place are the most reliable reports we can receive or make, right? Not according to police officers, who report that people frequently do not view things the same way even though they may be standing only a few feet apart at the same place. This point is quite evident in the following poem based on an old fable.

THE BLIND MEN AND THE ELEPHANT
John G. Saxe

It was six men of Indostan
   To learning much inclined,
Who went to see the Elephant
   (Though all of them were blind),
That each by observation
   Might satisfy his mind.

The First approached the Elephant,
   And happening to fall
Against his broad and sturdy side,
   At once began to bawl:
"God bless me! but the Elephant
   Is very like a wall!"

The Second, feeling of the tusk,
   Cried, "Ho! what have we here

So very round and smooth and sharp?
To me 'tis mighty clear
This wonder of an Elephant
Is very like a spear!"

The Third approached the animal,
And happening to take
The squirming trunk within his hands,
Thus boldly up and spake:
"I see," quoth he, "the Elephant
Is very like a snake!"

The Fourth reached out his eager hand,
And felt about the knee.
"What most this wondrous beast is like
Is mighty plain," quoth he;
" 'Tis clear enough the Elephant
Is very like a tree!"

The Fifth, who chanced to touch the ear
Said, "E'en the blindest man
Can tell what this resembles most;
Deny the fact who can,
This marvel of an Elephant
Is very like a fan!"

The Sixth no sooner had begun
About the beast to grope,
Than, seizing on the swinging tail
That fell within his scope,
"I see," quoth he, "the Elephant
Is very like a rope!"

And so these men of Indostan
Disputed loud and long,
Each in his own opinion
Exceeding stiff and strong.
Though each was partly in the right
And all were in the wrong!

Although the "witnesses" in the poem didn't have the advantage of sight, they were all using other senses that might have led them to similar conclusions but did not. Consider this problem another way. Suppose we look out the classroom window and see a tree. Now, it's only natural to assume that everyone sees the tree the same way. Imagine our surprise, then, when we discover that this is not the case. Let's say that a student majoring in art looks at the tree; what would such an individual see? The shape of the branches and limbs might suggest some other form than a tree; the texture of the bark might arouse sensations of touch; the silhouette of the dark limbs against a blue sky could remind the art student of the importance of color contrast; the movement of the branches and leaves could help the viewer recall other rhythmic movements in nature. If a forestry major looks at the same tree, does he or she see the same things? Possibly, but with a difference. The forestry major may classify the tree according to its type, remember certain facts about the species from reading and lectures, begin imagining how a forest of such trees might look, compare the growth rate of the tree to others around it, calculate the number of board feet, and determine if the tree looks diseased. And so it would go with one tree, until we might discover that although there is only one object to be seen, it can be viewed in different ways.

The ability to view your surroundings, events in your life, people, ideas, and objects from a variety of perspectives is a valuable one. It allows you to consider not only your own view but also that of others with whom you may have to communicate. Much of your perspective on your world is controlled by your purposes: what you need to know, what you want to share, what you consider important, and what will be most useful to your audience. You and your classmates have selected a college or university to attend. During that selection process, many of you read countless brochures, pored over college catalogues, and talked to many people. Undoubtedly you soon came to realize that these sources offered many different perspectives on the same subject. Consider the following excerpt from a college catalogue:

> Tuskegee Institute is a co-educational, privately controlled, professional, scientific, and technical institution, with regional accreditation from the Southern Association of Colleges and Schools, and with specialized approval for several of its programs—nursing, dietetics, veterinary medicine, and teacher education—from their respective national professional associations. This non-sectarian, independent institution—founded by Booker T. Washington in 1881—is located in Tuskegee Institute, Alabama, one mile west of the town of Tuskegee—which can be reached via three U.S. Highways, 80, 29, and Interstate 85. . . .
>
> Special features in Tuskegee's program include: The George Washington Carver Museum (named for the distinguished scientist who worked at Tuskegee) which preserved the tools and handiwork of Dr. Carver, as well as houses displayed on Tuskegee, Africa, and Negro life

in general; the George Washington Carver Research Foundation, center for a variety of research sponsored by government agencies and private industry; the fully accredited 160 bed John A. Andrew Hospital, which provides general health services for the community and specialized care for some patients from outlying areas; the Tuskegee Archives, a chief center for information on the problems and history of the Negro since 1896.

If we turned to a novelist for a description of the place described by the college catalogue, we might receive a different account, although some of the information is the same.

> It was a beautiful college. The buildings were old and covered with vines and the roads gracefully winding, lined with hedges and wild roses that dazzled the eyes in the summer sun. Honeysuckle and purple wisteria hung heavy from the trees and white magnolias mixed with their scents in the bee-humming air. I've recalled it often . . . : How the grass turned green in the springtime and how the mocking birds fluttered their tails and sang, how the moon shone down on the buildings, how the bell in the chapel tower rang out the precious short-lived hours; how the girls in bright summer dresses promenaded the grassy lawn. Many times . . . I've closed my eyes and walked along the forbidden road that winds past the girls' dormitories, past the hall with the clock in the tower, its windows warmly aglow, on down past the small white Home Economics practice cottage, whiter still in the moonlight, and on down the road with its sloping and turning, paralleling the black powerhouse with its engines droning earthshaking rhythms in the dark, its windows red from the glow of the furnace, on to where the road becomes a bridge over a dry riverbed, tangled with brush and clinging vines; the bridge of rustic logs, made for trysting, but virginal and untested by lovers; on up the road, past the buildings, with the southern verandas half-a-city-block long, to the sudden forking, barren of buildings, birds, or grass, where the road turned off to the insane asylum.
>
> —Ralph Ellison, *Invisible Man*

Are these really describing the same place? Of course, but each selection has a different perspective or way of seeing. Although these are two separate passages, perspectives often can be combined within the same passage or piece of writing to offer comparisons and contrasts. In fact, a person doesn't have to look far to realize that likenesses and differences often play a strong role in our perspectives. Two relatives may live in the same neighborhood and have the same kind of job but be quite different in their political beliefs. Two children can grow up in the same home but become quite different. Cities, sections of the country, customs, words, and ideas—all have their similarities and differences. Because of this, we can look at subjects in a variety of ways, sometimes emphasizing how things are alike, at other times how unlike they may be.

Look at the following essays to see the variety of perspectives available to you through comparison and contrast; each essay suggests a different approach. Read the essays carefully, considering the four key questions below as you read. Then answer the more specific questions that follow each essay.

1. What specific points in each essay are compared or contrasted?
2. What significance, if any, is there to the order in which the points are presented?
3. How does the writer assist you as a reader in keeping track of the movement from one point of comparison or contrast to another?
4. How effective are the openings and closings of the essay in helping you understand the purpose of the essay?

SAMPLE COMPARISON/CONTRAST ESSAYS

Two Views of a River

by Mark Twain

Now when I had mastered the language of this water and had come to know every trifling feature that bordered the great river as familiarly as I knew the letters of the alphabet, I had made a valuable acquisition. But I had lost something, too. I had lost something which could never be restored to me while I lived. All the grace, the beauty, the poetry, had gone out of the majestic river! I still kept in mind a certain wonderful sunset which I witnessed when steamboating was new to me. A broad expanse of the river was turned to blood; in the middle distance the red hue brightened into gold, through which a solitary log came floating, black and conspicuous; in one place a long, slanting mark lay sparkling upon the water; in another the surface was broken by boiling, tumbling rings, that were as many-tinted as an opal; where the ruddy flush was faintest, was a smooth spot that was covered with graceful circles and radiating lines, ever so delicately traced; the shore on our left was densely wooded and the somber shadow that fell from this forest was broken in one place by a long, ruffled trail that shone like silver; and high above the forest wall a clean-stemmed dead tree waved a single leafy bough that glowed like a flame in the unobstructed splendor that was flowing from the sun. There were graceful curves, reflected images, woody heights, soft distances, and over the whole scene, far and near, the dissolving lights drifted steadily, enriching it every passing moment with new marvels of coloring.

I stood like one bewitched. I drank it in, in a speechless rapture. The world was new to me and I had never seen anything like this at home. But as I have said, a day came when I began to cease from noting the glories and the charms which the moon and the sun and the twilight wrought upon the river's face; another day came when I ceased altogether to note them. Then, if that sunset scene had been repeated, I should have looked upon it without rapture, and should have commented upon it inwardly after this fashion: "This sun means that we are going to have wind tomorrow; that floating log means that the river is rising, small thanks to it; that slanting mark on the water refers to a bluff reef which is going to kill somebody's steamboat one of these nights, if it keeps on stretching out like that; those tumbling 'boils' show a dissolving bar and a changing channel there; the lines and circles in the slick water over yonder are a warning that that troublesome place is shoaling up dangerously; that silver streak in the shadow of the forest is the 'break' from a new snag and he has located himself in the very best place he could have found to fish for steamboats; that tall dead tree, with a single living branch, is not going to last long, and then how is a body ever going to get through this blind place at night without the friendly old landmark?''

No, the romance and beauty were all gone from the river. All the value any feature of it had for me now was the amount of usefulness it could furnish toward compassing the safe piloting of a steamboat. Since those days, I have pitied doctors from my heart. What does the lovely flush in a beauty's cheek mean to a doctor but a ''break'' that ripples above some deadly disease? Are not all her visible charms sown thick with what are to him the signs and symbols of hidden decay? Does he ever see her beauty at all, or doesn't he simply view her professionally and comment upon her unwholesome condition all to himself? And doesn't he sometimes wonder whether he has gained most or lost most by learning his trade?

Questions

1. What two main perspectives or ways of looking at the river does Twain offer?
2. What specific evidence supports the different perspectives Twain takes?
3. What items from paragraph 1 also are referred to in paragraph 2; what is the difference in how the items are presented?
4. Why does Twain contrast the rivers in this way?
5. What pattern or sense of order do you see emerging in this piece?

Death of a High School
by Anita Strange

The seventh and eighth grades of my high school years were a great deal of fun. Of course, the big jump from junior high to high school was an experience my friends and I had been anticipating excitedly for both of those years. We were all set to enter our first year of high school together, but something happened to change that freshman year: court-ordered desegregation. Little did we know that it would change our school so completely.

Durrett High School, before busing, had been one of the largest high schools in Louisville with an enrollment of over two thousand students. Despite its size of three hundred, our class had always been like one gigantic family. We had grown up together and were inseparable.

Our freshman year, the first year of court-ordered busing, was different. Instead of walking into a classroom full of smiling, familiar faces, we were thrust into a situation where many faces were those of complete strangers. Lifetime friends had moved to another county to avoid being bused, had enrolled in parochial schools for the same reason, or had been bused to a totally strange school on the opposite side of the city. All our high school dreams of proms, senior rings, and graduation had been trampled upon and destroyed by some powerful high court judges whose children and grandchildren probably had never been a part of the public schools system.

Because of busing, Durrett's enrollment, including its junior high, dropped to between one thousand and fifteen hundred students. Parents tried desperately to exempt their children from busing. The parochial school systems quickly filled to capacity. The population of neighboring counties which were excluded from court-ordered desegregation increased tremendously. The idea of being ordered to attend a school not of their choice was resented by almost everyone, but the majority of people just couldn't afford to pay the expensive tuitions charged by parochial schools or to move to other counties. Those of us that were left were forced to accept the situation, and we tried to make the best of it.

Try as we might, it never seemed to get any better. There was a strong sense of apathy about the school. No one seemed to care about anything. The students that had been bused to Durrett didn't feel as if they belonged and didn't seem to want to. Their real pride was directed toward their home school, the school they would normally have attended.

Pep rallies before busing had always been the high point of each week. Everyone jammed into the gymnasium, almost at the point of frenzy, ready to cheer the team on to victory. The bleachers shook from all the foot-stomping and hand-clapping, and the walls rumbled with excitement. We all left those pep rallies with ears ringing.

Pep rallies, after integration, were a whole different story. Attendance was low. We were lucky to have one full wall of bleachers filled. The cheerleaders chanted their chants, yelled their yells, and jumped their jumps, but to no avail. The crowd just sat there and looked blankly at them as if they were idiots, jumping around on the gymnasium floor for no reason at all. The new students just wouldn't cheer for a team their home school had rivaled for years and years before. The crowd would often become rude and unruly. Our once weekly pep rallies were soon cut to only three per season.

Durrett had always prided itself in its athletics and extracurricular activities. Practically every boy in the school played on the football, basketball, or baseball team; and those who didn't dreamed of someday being on one of those winning teams. The drill team and cheerleaders brought back first- and second-place trophies almost every time they entered a competition. Club memberships were high. There was hardly a student that didn't belong to at least one organization.

Again, busing changed everything. Because of the newly acquired expenses to cover transportation costs, athletic funds were cut drastically. Poor equipment and fewer coaches, however, were merely minor causes of athletic decline. Many former players were bused away. The athletes bused into our town school lived too far across town to come to the practices every day. Thus, turnout for team tryouts was lower than ever before, and each year our teams shrank tremendously in size. The drill team and cheerleaders quit bringing home those first- and second-place trophies. Eventually, they even quit participating in competitions altogether. Club memberships dropped so immensely that many had to disband. Last year for the first time in Durrett's entire twenty-five year history, there was no senior play. We could not arouse enough interest among the students to get them to join the Drama Club.

Court-ordered desegregation took the fun out of acquiring a high school education. Who could believe that class unity, school spirit, athletics, and extracurricular activities, once such an important part of those high school years, had deteriorated so much in such a short span of time; and the saddest part about it is that no one seemed to really care.

Questions

1. What is the focus of this essay?
2. What are the major points of contrast?
3. Where might the writer have offered more information to make the points clearer and more effective?
4. What is the writer's attitude about the changes? Point out specific places in the essay where this attitude becomes apparent.
5. How would you describe the order of presentation the writer follows?

In Florida: Jumping with the 82nd
by Don Sider

He feels the giddiness deep in his gut: an amalgam of excitement, anticipation and, he admits only to himself, a touch of fear. His unit has just been alerted for a mass jump. With each ritualistic step from now until he is back on the ground, the giddiness will return. That is part of all this, a part the Paratrooper likes best.

The largest U.S. parachute drop in peacetime wafted down onto the sandy scrubland of Florida's panhandle early one morning this month:

2,640 soldiers leaping from 20 huge C-141 jets, along with three more planeloads of Jeeps and other heavy equipment. They came from the XVIII Airborne Corps and the First Brigade of the 82nd Airborne Division at Fort Bragg, N.C. If war or the threat of war were to come in the Persian Gulf area, these paratroopers likely would be the U.S. spearhead.

He feels the inner electricity again during the intense hours of refresher training that precede every jump. The sessions are like a football team's pregame warmup, insurance that the jumpers are sharp and ready, that in an inherently risky venture, risk will be held to a minimum. They trigger his adrenaline.

The scenario for this exercise has a small friendly nation, "Granna," under attack by forces from two of its neighbors, "Holguin" and "Kupa." Granna requests assistance. The President sends U.S. troops.

Late in the afternoon, the Paratrooper is trucked with the others to barracks alongside the airfield at Fort Bragg. Here they will spend the night. But first their jumpmasters must check them in and assign them positions for the drop. It is a long, dull procedure, and the Paratrooper smiles when he thinks how much like a flock of sheep or a herd of cows they all are— passive, oblivious to the time and space they occupy, psychically removed. In their minds many of them are, like himself, already in the plane or stepping out of it. As one of the guys says: "When you see yourself going through the door, all the hassles disappear."

The paratroopers are to seize an airstrip 10 km from the jump site so that, in a real war, thousands more could fly in aboard transport planes. On the way, they will engage two companions of "Aggressors," played by other units from the 82nd Airborne and the Air Force.

The men are finally dismissed at 7:30 p.m. By 8 most are in bed: the day ahead will start at 4 a.m. The Paratrooper lies there thinking of what his brigade commander, Colonel Charles Ferguson, said that afternoon: "It's exciting. You get up for it. You have to do everything right. If you jump from 1,000 ft. and your parachute doesn't open, you hit the ground in eight seconds." The Paratrooper does not sleep well, and he suspects most of the others do not either.

If this had been the real thing, the First Brigade would have been in the air within 18 hours of the signal to go. The 82nd, two other Army divisions and one Marine division are the ground combat element of the Rapid Deployment Force. Because paratroopers are able to land anywhere with maximum speed and surprise, the 82nd is always at the ready.

At 6 a.m., the Paratrooper draws his chutes—the main, worn on the back, and the small reserve, which will ride on his chest. "Put 'em on," orders the jumpmaster, and the Paratrooper and a buddy help each other, threading the straps, snapping the hooks, fitting each item by the book. An officer pokes and tugs and checks every item, again by the book, then slaps the Paratrooper on the rump and says, "O.K." It is light now, and the Paratrooper stares with amusement at the troopers around him. Their faces, like his, are smeared with camouflage grease paint, blending with their mottled uniforms and helmet covers, as in some military minstrel show. The order to board the plane snaps him from his reverie. "The only way down now will be to jump," he says to himself, just as he has said to himself with every takeoff before every jump.

Lieut. General Thomas Tackaberry, commander of the XVIII Airborne Corps, was the first man out of the first C-141. Standing in the drop zone, he said the mass assault had a dual purpose. It tested how well the Army and Air Force could carry off such a huge troop movement (very well with a brigade, but a whole division is so much larger that there may be barely enough planes to deliver it across the sea). The exercise did something for the individual paratroopers as well. Said Tackaberry: "Psychologically, it helps a man to know he's part of a big unit." Every jump is a revalidation, a reassurance that the paratroopers are special.

Aboard the C-141, the Paratrooper, jammed among his equipment-laden buddies, drifts into and out of sleep. Twenty minutes from the drop zone, the final commands begin. Then he is out the door and into the clear sky, counting aloud, "One thousand, two thousand, three thousand, four thousand." His chute is snatched open by the rushing air, and he drifts toward the ground.

One V formation after another of C-141s lumbered 1,000 ft. overhead at 125 m.p.h., spewing parachutists from both sides, as escort planes darted above them. It was an explosion, an inundation, a blizzard of men from the sky, lasting less than five minutes.

The Paratrooper hits the ground and rolls into a proper landing fall. It is a good jump, a good landing. He looks up at the dense cloud of green parachutes, and he explodes with joy. "You are bea-u-ti-ful!" he screams. "Bea-u-ti-ful!"

Injuries had been expected to run as high as 1%, but the rate was less than half of that, only eleven in all; the most serious was a shoulder separation. All but 5% of the force landed on target and began moving out.

In the 92° Florida sun, the Paratrooper shoulders his 60-lb. rucksack and his M-16 rifle and joins his squad. The jump is a mere memory. Here on the ground, there is soldiering to do.

Questions

1. What adjustments does the reader have to make in reading an essay of this type?

2. What do you think the writer's purpose was in presenting the information this way?
3. Besides using the different type of print, how does the writer make the reader aware of the difference in the perspectives?
4. How effective is this approach to you as a reader?
5. How would you explain the order in which the information is presented?

Grant and Lee: A Study in Contrasts
by Bruce Catton

1   When Ulysses S. Grant and Robert E. Lee met in the parlor of a modest house at Appomattox Court House, Virginia, on April 9, 1865, to work out the terms for the surrender of Lee's Army of Northern Virginia, a great chapter in American life came to a close, and a great new chapter began.

2   These men were bringing the Civil War to its virtual finish. To be sure, other armies had yet to surrender, and for a few days the fugitive Confederate government would struggle desperately and vainly, trying to find some way to go on living now that its chief support was gone. But in effect it was all over when Grant and Lee signed the papers. And the little room where they wrote out the terms was the scene of one of the poignant, dramatic contrasts in American History.

3   They were two strong men, these oddly different generals, and they represented the strengths of two conflicting currents that, through them, had come into final collision.

4   Back of Robert E. Lee was the notion that the old aristocratic concept might somehow survive and be dominant in American life.

5   Lee was tidewater Virginia, and in his background were family, culture, and tradition . . . the age of chivalry transplanted to a New World which was making its own legends and its own myths. He embodied a way of life that had come down through the age of knighthood and the English country squire. America was a land that was beginning all over again, dedicated to nothing much more complicated than the rather hazy belief that all men had equal rights and should have an equal chance in the world. In such a land Lee stood for

the feeling that it was somehow of advantage to human society to have a pronounced inequality in the social structure. There should be a leisure class, backed by ownership of land; in turn, society itself should be keyed to the land as the chief source of wealth and influence. It would bring forth (according to this ideal) a class of men with a strong sense of obligation to the community; men who lived not to gain advantage for themselves, but to meet the solemn obligations which had been laid on them by the very fact they they were privileged. From them the country would get its leadership; to them it could look for the higher values—of thought, of conduct, of personal deportment—to give it strength and virtue.

6   Lee embodied the noblest elements of this aristocratic ideal. Through him, the landed nobility justified itself. For four years, the Southern states had fought a desperate war to uphold the ideals for which Lee stood. In the end, it almost seemed as if the Confederacy fought for Lee; as if he himself was the Confederacy . . . the best thing that the way of life for which the Confederacy stood could ever have to offer. He had passed into legend before Appomattox. Thousands of tired, underfed, poorly clothed Confederate soldiers, long since past the simple enthusiasm of the early days of the struggle, somehow considered Lee the symbol of everything for which they had been willing to die. But they could not quite put this feeling into words. If the Lost Cause, sanctified by so much heroism and so many deaths, had a living justification, its justification was General Lee.

7   Grant, the son of a tanner on the Western frontier, was everything Lee was not. He had come up the hard way and embodied nothing in particular except the eternal toughness and sinewy fiber of the men who grew up beyond the mountains. He was one of a body of men who owed reverence and obeisance to no one, who were self-reliant to a fault, who cared hardly anything for the past but who had a sharp eye for the future.

8   These frontier men were the precise opposites of the tidewater aristocrats. Back of them, in the great surge that had taken people over the Alleghenies and into the opening Western country, there was a deep, implicit dissatisfaction with a past that had settled into grooves. They stood for democracy, not from any reasoned conclusion about the proper ordering of human society, but simply because they had grown up in the middle of democracy and knew how it worked. Their society might have privileges, but they would be privileges each man had won for himself. Forms and patterns meant nothing. No man was born to anything, except perhaps to a chance to show how far he could rise. Life was competition.

9   Yet along with this feeling had come a deep sense of belonging to a national community. The Westerner who developed a farm, opened a shop, or set up in business as a trader, could hope to prosper only as his own community prospered—and his community ran from the Atlantic to the Pacific and from Canada to Mexico. If the land was settled, with towns and highways and accessible markets, he could better himself. He saw his fate in terms of the nation's own destiny. As its horizons expanded, so did his. He had, in other words, an acute dollars-and-cents stake in the continued growth and development of his country.

10   And that, perhaps, is where the contrast between Grant and Lee becomes most striking. The Virginia aristocrat, inevitably, saw himself in relation to his own region. He lived in a static society which could endure almost anything except change. Instinctively, his first loyalty would go to the locality in which that society existed. He would fight to the limit of endurance to defend it, because in defending it he was defending everything that gave his own life its deepest meaning.

11   The Westerner, on the other hand, would fight with an equal tenacity for the broader concept of society. He fought so because everything he lived by was tied to growth, expansion, and a constantly widening horizon. What he lived by would survive or fall with the nation itself. He could not possibly stand by unmoved in the face of an attempt to destroy the Union. He would combat it with everything he had, because he could only see it as an effort to cut the ground out from under his feet.

12   So Grant and Lee were in complete contrast, representing two diametrically opposed elements in American life. Grant was the modern man emerging; beyond him, ready to come on the stage, was the great age of steel and machinery, of crowded cities and a restless burgeoning vitality. Lee might have ridden down from the old age of chivalry, lance in land, silken banner fluttering over his head. Each man was the perfect champion of his cause, drawing both his strengths and his weaknesses from the people he led.

13   Yet it was not all contrast, after all. Different as they were—in background, in personality, in underlying aspiration—these two great soldiers had much in common. Under everything else, they were marvelous fighters. Furthermore, their fighting qualities were really very much alike.

14   Each man had, to begin with, the great virtue of utter tenacity and fidelity. Grant fought his way down the Mississippi Valley in spite of acute personal discouragement and profound military handicaps. Lee

hung on in the trenches at Petersburg after hope itself had died. (In each man there was an indomitable quality . . . the born fighter's refusal to give up as long as he can still remain on his feet and lift his two fists.)

15   Daring and resourcefulness they had, too; the ability to think faster and move faster than the enemy. These were the qualities which gave Lee the dazzling campaigns of Second Manassas and Chancellorsville and won Vicksburg for Grant.

16   Lastly, and perhaps greatest of all, there was the ability, at the end, to turn quickly from war to peace once the fighting was over. Out of the way these two men behaved at Appomattox came the possibility of a peace of reconciliation. It was a possibility not wholly realized, in the years to come, but which did, in the end, help the two sections to become one nation again . . . after a war whose bitterness might have seemed to make such a reunion wholly impossible. No part of either man's life became him more than the part he played in their brief meeting in the McLean house at Appomattox. Their behavior there put all succeeding generations of Americans in their debt. Two great Americans, Grant and Lee—very different, yet under everything very much alike. Their encounter at Appomattox was one of the great moments of American history.

Questions

1. List the paragraph numbers 3 to 16 on a sheet of paper. Then return to the essay and examine each paragraph; beside each number, indicate whether the focus of the paragraph is primarily on Lee or Grant or on both. Indicate as well exactly what characteristic or characteristics are being explained in each paragraph.

2. Study the results of your survey. What do they suggest about the following?
   a. The order in which Catton presents his information.
   b. The different ways comparison and contrast may be used.
   c. The signals given to the reader when change in the pattern occurs.

3. Examine the beginning of each paragraph. How does Catton make certain the reader sees a connection between that paragraph and the one before it?

4. Study the introduction and conclusion of the essay. How does Catton prepare the reader for what is to come and how is the reader left with a feeling of completion at the end?

ASSIGNMENT: WRITING A COMPARISON/CONTRAST ESSAY

Now that you've explored a number of examples demonstrating different perspectives, all of which used comparison/contrast as a basis for their organization, you're ready to begin work on your own comparison/contrast essay. In this essay, you will present at least two perspectives on the same topic, using, of course, comparison and/or contrast. Your perspectives may come from a passage of time, from a desire to show both sides of an issue, or from a question of needs—looking at a topic for one reason and then turning to look at it for another reason.

Audience

For this piece of writing, your audience won't be as clear as for some of your past assignments. Instead, you'll be writing to a curious but uninformed audience of peers. They'll rely on you to show them the importance of the material. Their basic question will be "Why are you sharing this information with us?" So the audience can answer that question, you'll need to provide a clearly defined focus, an easily followed plan of organization, and sufficient details for readers to understand what you're communicating.

Prewriting

Begin by making an inventory of your experience and knowledge for possible topics. This will take some time, of course, but you've already discovered that time spent thinking prior to writing saves frustration and delays later. Consider some of the following perspectives as possible starting points:

1. Have you moved a great deal during your life but occasionally returned to some of the places after you've been away for some time? What changes or lack of change did you notice? How do you account for these? How much of the change might be due to your own changed way of looking at things, how much just to the passage of time? What does all this suggest about the way human beings perceive things as they grow older?
2. How about your hometown—what would a native see in it that a casual visitor might not?

3. Consider adopting the perspective of two people of different ages toward a common subject: How might a child view something in contrast to or comparison with an adult's view?
4. Changing seasons tend to affect our perspectives. What place do you know where the changes affect your way or others' ways of looking at that location?
5. Look for news items that might be viewed from different perspectives; consider, for example, the view of a tenant and the view of a landlord toward the same piece of property.
6. Examine your own campus life for possible topics. What are the similarities and differences between the perspectives of the regular student and the handicapped student in terms of opportunities and facilities on campus?

Listing

Once you've identified a potential topic, spend some time using the listing technique you've already learned. This time, set up your list in a split fashion; that is, put one perspective on each side of your paper. Placing your material under those headings helps you keep track of the points you discover that you'll have to address from both sides. The following is a split list set up by a student who wanted to explore the difference in viewpoints between a child and an adult toward an old barn.

THE BARN

Adult View	*Child's View*
dilapidated, roof half off, leaning walls, weeds around it; holes in the floor where child could twist an ankle; boards with nails	off by itself—a hideout; can be a castle, a boat, a fort; holes in the walls become gun ports; the boards become material for making barriers or tepees; wood for making swords or guns
old hay bales could fall and smother a child; dust and chaff could be dangerous for allergies; climbing into the hayloft or on the large beams, a child could fall and not be discovered; there may be rodents and stray animals living in the hay and the barn	the hayloft makes a great lookout post; can be the upper deck of a ship; can play house in the loft, build tunnels with the hay, even create "hay showers"; the bales can double as furniture or as walls for a fort; a rope can be tied to the beams and swings can be taken; cats often make nests for their kittens in the hay

outside the barn is dangerous; long weeds and grass invite snakes, mosquitoes, chiggers, and ticks; weeds can cut and scratch a child; some weeds can cause allergic reactions

can make trails in the tall grass and weeds, play games of hide and seek; small animals may have their nests hidden in the weeds; great fun tracking the animals; maybe spending time trying to catch sight of animals coming out of their burrows; weed blooms make ideal bouquets to carry home

old machinery lying around is an invitation to cuts, to getting grease on clothing, for tearing clothes on gears and levers; some pieces of machinery might be tipped over by the child and pin the child or cause injury

old machines become test machines—airplanes, cars, tanks, tractors; they become jungle gyms, great for climbing exercises, follow-the-leader games; some become make-believe prisons or ships at sea; old tires can become swings or be used to throw stones through

junk pile, eyesore, hazardous area

an amusement park with no entrance fees; a stimulus for the imagination

Once you have done some preliminary listing and fleshed out your list with as much concrete information as possible, look for clusters of information. These clusters help you make preliminary decisions about the best way to organize your material. In the list about the old barn, two major clusters seem to emerge—the area immediately outside the barn and the inside of the building. Within these two large clusters are smaller ones; a diagram of these relationships might look like Figure 6.1.

Organizing

As you've seen in the essays you read earlier in this chapter, you have several options for organizing the material for your essay. Although you may not use any one of the options exclusively, you'll find it helpful to identify one of the approaches as your major organizing strategy. The basic choices are whole to whole, part to part, and combination.

Whole to Whole   In the whole-to-whole pattern, you focus the reader's attention on the whole of one perspective on the subject before moving to the other perspective. Mark Twain does this in "Two Views of a River." If you use this approach, you have to remember that the more points to be made, the harder the reader works to remember those points when you shift to the other perspective. The whole-to-whole approach works best for broad comparisons or short contrasts in which

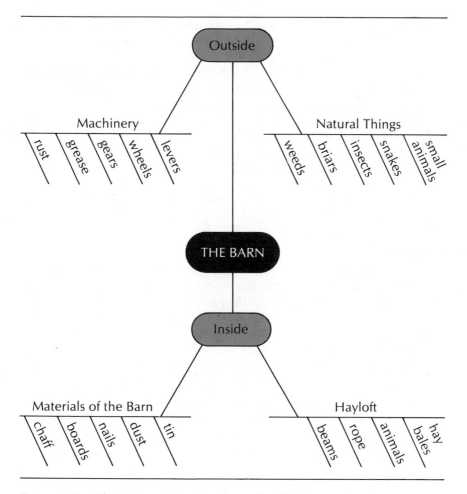

Figure 6.1 Clustering of Details About the Old Barn.

only a few points are examined. This option permits a tight focus and a clear arrangement of the points, two things your readers will appreciate.

Part to Part If you're going to develop numerous points, sometimes it helps your readers if you take one point at a time and develop it from both perspectives before moving to the next point. Readers can then keep track of the material being presented and get immediate reinforcement for both perspectives. Readers feel they're participating in collecting the evidence as the essay progresses. The approach can become choppy and distracting, though, almost like a grocery list, if you don't select broad enough points and develop them fully. You also must pay particular attention to connecting the points and to varying the sentence structure. Sections of "Grant and Lee" (especially paragraphs 10–15) and the essays "Death of a High School" and "Florida: Jumping with the 82nd" provide examples of this strategy.

Combination   Many writers find that a careful combination of the previous two options adds interest and effectiveness to their presentations. If you do this, be consistent in deciding where a part-to-part relationship is desirable and where a whole-to-whole arrangement works best. Bruce Catton's "Grant and Lee" offers clues about how combinations can work effectively. Compare the first part of the essay, paragraphs 4–9, with the last part, paragraphs 10–15.

Response

Just as in earlier prewriting preparations, you need to test your ideas on a reader. Doing this frequently during the writing process gives you a clearer sense of how you're progressing and if you're making appropriate decisions. After listing as much detail as you can about your topic and after deciding what your main point is and how you will present it, find a writing partner and discuss your ideas. You'll want to ask each other specific questions, such as the following.

1. What is the point you're hoping to make in this piece?
   Remember that simply comparing or contrasting two things isn't enough; we do that every day without really thinking about it. What main idea or purpose do you have for bringing your perspective to the reader? You might want to write this idea out where you can refer to it later.
2. How have you balanced your perspectives?
   Sometimes you may find yourself getting carried away with one side of a presentation, forgetting to give equal time to the other. If this happens, you may need to reexamine your material to see if what you have is really worth comparing or contrasting.
3. What plan of organization are you going to use?
   Although you might change your mind after the rough draft, making an early decision about the order you'll use to present your points will help you get started on the draft. You might be contrasting a particular place as it is seen during two different seasons, and your topics might be familiar landmarks, climatic changes, and activities. Which of these should come first? Which should you end with? These questions may raise another one: What is the relative

importance of each point? You might be discussing the differences in your school before and after football was adopted as a major sport. A fairly common approach is to present the least important items first and then work up to the most significant, giving readers a sense of direction and increasing emphasis.

During the discussion with your partner, be sure to obtain as much help as possible, take notes, and add details; return the favor, of course.

The First Draft

Once you have completed the discussions with your partner and you are satisfied that the plan and the material are adequate for beginning, you're ready to write a rough draft. As usual, try to write yourself out. Don't worry about correctness in this first attempt. Get your words down on paper where you can look at them and begin to evaluate their effectiveness. By now you know that no one can determine just how well a draft will turn out until the words are on the paper. During your writing if you discover that you have too little material, put down what you have and make some notes in the margin of the paper to remind yourself what else you may need. When the draft is finished, review the notes as you reread and decide then if the notes are still appropriate. If they are, search for more material before working on the draft any further. Trying to write something about nothing is a waste of time.

Re-Viewing

With the rough draft in front of you, begin to examine the elements listed below.

1. *Focus:* Does the draft have a narrow enough focus so the reader can tell without a struggle exactly what your purpose is? Do you present a clear enough situation so the reader will understand what's going on? Have you shown the comparisons and/or contrasts rather than simply telling the reader they exist? Consider again how Mark Twain focuses on only one specific section of the Mississippi River and for a very clear purpose; note how the *Time* article deals with only one parachute jump to make its point. One helpful clue at this point is the "eyeball test." Take a close look at your paragraphs: Are they all about the same length? If they're all short, check to see if there's a lot of fast movement from one point to the next. If so, this may be a tip-off that you haven't provided enough information and detail. On the other hand, if you discover mostly long paragraphs,

check for both balance and focus: Have you spent more time on one point than another? Have you possibly combined too many items into too few paragraphs, making it difficult for the reader to know what you're focusing on?

2. *Organization:* Although you've tried to set up a clear pattern of organization, check it again. What choice did you make and did you use it consistently? What clues have you offered about the relative importance of each point? Perhaps all the points are of equal importance: How do you make that clear?

3. *Introduction and Conclusion:* You might not have paid too much attention yet to your introduction and conclusion. That's not surprising, since an effective opening and closing are difficult to develop in a first draft. Yet each is crucial to the success of a piece of writing. What have you done to interest the readers, to convince them that they can benefit from your discussion? Review the sections about introductions and conclusions in Chapter 4 as well as the sample essays in this chapter for possible ideas on how to strengthen your openings and closings.

Rewriting/Revising

After you have focused your attention on specific areas of the rough draft, you can decide how much rewriting will be necessary. Does your essay need just some cosmetic touch-up or is major surgery required? Whatever your decision, allow yourself the time to polish the draft, adding and deleting where necessary, rewriting whole sections for stronger emphasis and more information if necessary.

Response

With this assignment, you will experience a different way of receiving response to your writing and of responding to others' writing. Previously you worked with a partner or in a small group. With this assignment, you will read several other essays and you will focus on only one aspect of each paper and devote your comments to that aspect. Your instructor will tell you which question to use in your assessment and how the rotation of papers will occur within a group or the whole class. Try to remember that your assessment of each writer's paper should be as helpful as possible; the adage "Do unto others as you would have them do unto you" is appropriate only if you remember to be as specific and constructive as possible in your comments. The following are the questions you and your classmates will consider.

1. What is the main idea of the essay?

   Write the main idea in one sentence and then identify several places in the essay where you think the writer has made this idea unusually clear. If you're unable to identify the main idea or places where it appears, explain why and suggest a focus the writer might develop.

2. What is the pattern of organization in the essay?

   The writer may have used one or more patterns; select the appropriate label to describe it and identify several places in the essay that clearly demonstrate the pattern. If you're unable to determine the pattern, say so and make suggestions for how improvements might be made.

3. What details, examples, and incidents used in the paper are effective?

   Select several good items and explain their effectiveness. If you feel the essay would be stronger with more evidence, indicate where the additions could be made and suggest some possibilities for the writer to follow up. If there is too much evidence, suggest where cuts could be made and why.

4. Why are the introduction and conclusion effective or ineffective?

   Comment on the strengths and weaknesses of each; suggest ways for improvement if appropriate. Indicate what creates interest for you and what does not; what helps set the focus and what does not; and whether or not you have a sense of closing.

The Final Draft

When your rough draft comes back, you'll receive with it a number of responses from your classmates about each of the four questions. Study the responses carefully. If you have a chance to talk to any of your classmates about their responses, do so; ask them for clarification wherever necessary. Turn your classmates' comments over in your mind for a time; sift through them, not just picking out the ones that make you feel good but considering the negative ones too. Decide how you might answer some of the questions about your draft. Work on the sections that your readers suggested need improvement. Then put the whole thing together and write a polished draft. Check carefully for any mechanical errors and then submit it to your instructor for evaluation.

What Do You Want to Write About?

ASSIGNMENT: YOUR CHOICE

Up to this point, you have not had too much choice in the kind of writing you do or in the topic you write about. In fact, you're probably wondering if you'll ever get a chance to strike off on your own and focus on a topic that is entirely yours and that reflects your personality. Your assignment in this chapter is to do just that.

Choosing a Topic

Some people, of course, prefer to have the topic, purpose, and audience outlined for them. You have had enough experience in previous chapters so that the thought of selecting, focusing, and developing a topic shouldn't present too many problems. The rewarding aspect of writing is how much there is to write about that can be shared with other people. Even a hobby or an activity that is not well known can be the subject of an interesting discussion; or perhaps an incident that occurred in your life has led you to see something in a new way or to come to a better understanding of yourself and others. You may have even experienced a situation that develops into an amusing commentary on yourself or other people. Before you pursue your own ideas any further, you might want to stop and read the essays at the end of this chapter. Note how the writers drew on things they knew well and how each essay gives readers a sense of the person behind the words.

When you face this kind of open-ended assignment, at first you might draw a blank; nothing comes to mind. You look aimlessly out the window, especially if it's a classroom window; you might go to the movies, watch a game, read a book or magazine—you might do just about anything in the hope that divine inspiration will occur. By now you should be able to recognize these dodges for what they are: classic symptoms of procrastination. You know that writing never gets done by avoiding it.

So, to begin, you might read through the following list of topics and respond to each one by writing in the appropriate letter:

A   What is this? Never heard of it.
B   Hey, I know a little about this.
C   Okay, now this I really know.
D   That sounds interesting—I'd like to know more.

____	1. acting	____	28. ceramics
____	2. acupuncture	____	29. chemistry
____	3. advertising	____	30. chess
____	4. animal training	____	31. clamming
____	5. antiques	____	32. coins
____	6. antiquing	____	33. collecting coupons
____	7. archeology	____	34. collecting mushrooms
____	8. archery	____	35. comic books
____	9. armadillo racing	____	36. computers
____	10. astrology	____	37. cooking
____	11. astronomy	____	38. decoupage
____	12. backgammon	____	39. deep-sea diving
____	13. backpacking	____	40. deep-sea fishing
____	14. ballet	____	41. dirt biking
____	15. baseball	____	42. Disney World
____	16. batiking	____	43. diving
____	17. boating	____	44. electronics
____	18. bobsledding	____	45. embroidery or crewel
____	19. bowling	____	46. energy saving
____	20. busing	____	47. falconry
____	21. cameras and photography	____	48. family trees
____	22. camping	____	49. fashions
____	23. candle making	____	50. films
____	24. canoeing	____	51. fly tying
____	25. car engines	____	52. flying
____	26. carpentry	____	53. folk art
____	27. caterpillars and insects	____	54. folk medicine
		____	55. football

_____ 56. foraging
_____ 57. Frisbee throwing
_____ 58. frog-gigging
_____ 59. funerals
_____ 60. gardening
_____ 61. gerbils
_____ 62. go-cart racing
_____ 63. grading
_____ 64. gumball machines
_____ 65. gymnastics
_____ 66. haircutting
_____ 67. hang gliding
_____ 68. hog calling
_____ 69. homemade ice cream
_____ 70. horse racing
_____ 71. horses
_____ 72. humor
_____ 73. hunting
_____ 74. ice fishing
_____ 75. indoor plants
_____ 76. intramurals
_____ 77. impersonations
_____ 78. jogging
_____ 79. journalism
_____ 80. judo
_____ 81. jug and bottle bands
_____ 82. karate
_____ 83. kazoos
_____ 84. kite construction
_____ 85. kite flying
_____ 86. knife collecting
_____ 87. knitting and crocheting
_____ 88. kung fu
_____ 89. lacrosse
_____ 90. landscaping
_____ 91. leatherwork
_____ 92. lifesaving
_____ 93. lobstering
_____ 94. macrame
_____ 95. Mah-Jongg
_____ 96. maple syruping
_____ 97. marriages
_____ 98. model construction
_____ 99. modeling (clothes)
_____ 100. Monopoly

_____ 101. moonshine
_____ 102. moviemaking
_____ 103. musseling
_____ 104. national parks
_____ 105. needlepoint
_____ 106. numerology
_____ 107. oil painting
_____ 108. origami
_____ 109. paper plane construction
_____ 110. Parchessi
_____ 111. pastels
_____ 112. pen-and-ink drawing
_____ 113. pinball machines
_____ 114. playing a musical instrument
_____ 115. poetry
_____ 116. politics
_____ 117. polo
_____ 118. poltergeists
_____ 119. pool
_____ 120. pop music
_____ 121. prejudice
_____ 122. puppetry
_____ 123. prestidigitation
_____ 124. quilting
_____ 125. railroads
_____ 126. reading
_____ 127. rock climbing
_____ 128. rock hounding
_____ 129. rocketry
_____ 130. rodeos
_____ 131. sailing
_____ 132. script writing
_____ 133. scuba diving
_____ 134. sewing
_____ 135. sign language
_____ 136. silversmithing
_____ 137. skateboards
_____ 138. singing
_____ 139. skating
_____ 140. ski jumping
_____ 141. skiing
_____ 142. sky gliding
_____ 143. small engines
_____ 144. snowmobiling

____	145. soap-box derby	____	158. trains
____	146. soccer	____	159. trapping
____	147. softball	____	160. Transcendental
____	148. spelunking		Meditation
____	149. sports cars	____	161. traveling
____	150. squash	____	162. trivia
____	151. surfing	____	163. tropical fish
____	152. stamps	____	164. watercolors
____	153. swimming	____	165. weaving
____	154. taffy pulls	____	166. weight lifting
____	155. tarot cards	____	167. wildflowers
____	156. teachers	____	168. wood carving
____	157. track and field	____	169. writing

Take a look at your results. How many items did you mark *C*? How many *D*? Chances are good that in 169 items you found at least one or two you could label in those categories, and you might have been able to use *B* a fair number of times. See, things are not as bleak as they might seem. If you have even a few *B*, *C*, and *D* answers, you're ready for the prewriting stage.

Prewriting

By now you're familiar with a variety of prewriting techniques—listing, clustering, dialoguing, cycling—that you can use to begin to focus on a subject. Another approach, one that may open up even more territory for you as a writer, is *cubing*.

Cubing

You're accustomed to looking at a subject from at least two perspectives. But there is no need to stop with just two perspectives; let's go for six. The best way to visualize how this might be done is to think of a cube, a six-sided figure you may have encountered in geometry class. Relax; we're not going to do anything mathematical at this point, but if we imagine that each side of the cube represents a different approach to the same subject, then we can picture a cube like that in Figure 7.1.

As you can see, each side of the cube contains a specific activity. The first step, of course, is to select a topic for the cube. If you have already decided on a topic for your free-choice essay, use it. Otherwise, refer to the preceding list of topics and choose one of your *C* or *B* topics. Later you might want to consider one of the *D*s as a possibility, but begin with something you have some knowledge about. Next, set yourself up to have some writing time in or out of class. It matters little

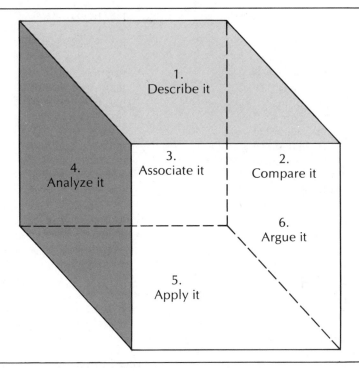

Figure 7.1 Cubing

1. *Describe it:* Look closely and tell what you see.
2. *Compare it:* What is it similar to? Different from?
3. *Associate it:* What does it remind you of? What other associations come to mind?
4. *Analyze it:* Tell how it's made; make it up if you're not sure.
5. *Apply it:* Tell what you can do with it. How can it be used?
6. *Argue for or against it:* Take a stand; give any reasons—silly or serious.

where the cubing takes place as long as you have time to take on all sides.

With your topic in mind and plenty of paper, follow the sequence suggested by the cube and outlined below, allowing yourself at least five minutes for each step of the sequence. Don't worry about editing or revising; simply write yourself out in relation to each side.

Side 1: Description   Describe your topic; look at it closely and tell what you see; give as many details as possible. Describe it from all sides—top, bottom, near, far, sideways, and so on. If your topic is not a physical object but an idea such as violence or baking, describe the physical aspects you see in relation to it. Suppose you selected spelunking; think of a particular cave and describe it. At the end of five minutes of free writing about what you *see* in connection with your topic, *stop*. Go on to side 2.

Side 2: Comparison   What is your topic similar to? What is it different from? List as many similarities and differences as you can; don't worry too much about developing any one similarity or comparison in depth; just keep listing or writing about them. Write as rapidly as you can. Stop at the end of five minutes.

Side 3: Association   Most subjects remind us of other things or of experiences we have had related to it. For five minutes list all the associations—the memories—you may have about your subject. It may happen that one particular association or memory comes to your mind and you find yourself eager to try to get down as much as possible about that association. If this happens, don't fight it; go ahead and concentrate on recording as much information as you can; such an urge may signal that your mind is beginning to supply you with a possible focus for your piece of writing. Write for five minutes and then stop.

Side 4: Analysis   What makes up your subject? Can it be broken down into small parts? Can you classify it in different ways? What are the ingredients necessary for your subject to exist? If you're not sure of all the ingredients at this point, make them up; simply let your imagination take over and be inventive. You can worry about checking the accuracy later. Write for five minutes.

Side 5: Application   What can you do with your subject? How can it be used? What are its many purposes or functions? What do you know about its uses? Which are most important? Again, if you're not entirely sure, let your imagination tell you; brainstorm and don't pass judgment on what comes out at this point. Stop at the end of five minutes.

Side 6: Argument   Argue for or against your subject; take a stand; marshal your reasons, silly or serious. What are the strengths of your topic? What are the dangers? If you run out of material on one side of the argument, switch to the other side; for the sake of later understanding, though, try to stay with one side of the argument as long as you can. Argue for five minutes.

When you've finished cubing, it's time to take a breather and see what happened. Right now you are probably looking at a collection of scribbled notes, thoughts, and inventions. As you look back through your material for each side of the cube, some items will leap out at you, others will seem even sillier than they did when you put them down.

Don't worry about this apparent inconsistency. In the preliminary stages of writing, as you know by now, you're apt to come up with some strange things. But, what do you do with all this material now? First look through your material for each side. Circle sections of your writing that seem as if they could be developed more. Then go back and look for how you might combine material from two or more sides; for example, you might not have a full topic in the side on comparison, but some details or comparisons might come in handy elsewhere. Depending on the topic you chose for cubing, some sides of the cube will yield more material than others. The association, the application, and the argument may be the richest if you're dealing with a very broad subject; on the other hand, if you were using something physical for your subject, description, comparison, and analysis may give you more.

From your survey of the different perspectives, make a preliminary decision about which one seems to hold the most promise. If you discover that none of them seems to provide a direction in which you can go, don't be discouraged. Simply use one of the prewriting strategies you encountered in previous chapters. You might want to cycle off one of the perspectives to see if you can discover a sharper focus, or you might want to do some listing. Cubing simply provides a method for exploring a topic from six different angles in the hope that something will emerge; we might call it "starting cold" on a topic. If you're already hot on the trail of a topic, you're probably well on your way to writing your first draft and won't need to spend much more time on this step of discovering your topic focus.

Audience

Once you've found something, at least of a general nature, that you believe you could develop into an essay, you'll need to take a few minutes to consider purpose and audience. Before this, you've had both supplied; now you're going to make your own decisions about them. What do you want this piece of writing to do and for whom do you want to do it?

Audience analysis can be very complex and can take a great deal of time if you're getting ready to market a new product. Advertisers, for example, spend huge sums of money to hire special research analysts who only build profiles of prospective consumers; using the material gathered in such an analysis, advertisers and product manufacturers then decide the best approach to use in marketing the product. Although you can't hire a special researcher or spend the amount of time advertisers do in deciding the best method for presenting a new product, you can ask some basic questions that may help you develop a better sense of who might be interested in reading what you have to write.

Your Relationship with the Subject

Your first concern as a writer is to make certain you understand your own connections with the subject on which you're about to write. You can do this by answering the following questions.

1. Do I have firsthand experience with the subject? If so, how fresh is that experience in my mind? Fresh enough so I can develop a thorough picture for my readers?
2. If I don't have firsthand experience with the subject, where did I get my information or how might I obtain some? How will this affect my ability to be accurate and convincing?
3. Do I like or dislike my subject? How will this affect the material I present and the way in which I present it?
4. Is the subject important or unimportant to me?
5. Is the subject only of personal interest or does it also have universal interest? Can I show how the subject relates not only to me but to others?

Your Relationship with the Audience

From your answers to the preceding questions, you'll have built some awareness of what, if any, adjustments you have to make in your knowledge and feelings about the subject. Those adjustments, of course, will be tempered by your perceptions of the connections that will link you, the subject, and the audience in your writing of this essay. The following are some additional concerns related to your audience.

1. How much can I assume my audience will know about the subject?
2. Will my audience be enthusiastic, hostile, skeptical, or apathetic about the subject?
3. Does the audience have any mistaken ideas about the subject?
4. What are the age and educational level of my audience?
5. Is the audience predominantly male, female, or mixed?

Your answers to these questions will, in large measure, determine how you will proceed with developing your topic. What do you want to do for this audience with your chosen subject: Convince them? Anger them? Entertain them? Create a new interest for them? Inform them? Make them take action? Perhaps it will be a combination of these purposes, or perhaps your purpose will not emerge entirely until you have written a draft.

Response

At this point, your ideas may still be very unformed; you may have some general sense of what you want to do but are finding it difficult to put it into words. Take some time and discuss your options with a writing group or partner; tell them some of your ideas and what you might do with them. View this talk as simply another way of exploring what you may have to say. Encourage your listeners to respond, to ask questions, and to make further suggestions. By now, you and your classmates should be comfortable with this idea of helping one another and serving as sounding boards for one another's ideas. Make notes as you talk so you'll have a record of what has been suggested, both from you and from your listeners.

The First Draft

With the responses from your partner or group fresh in your mind, take stock of where you are. Do you need more information? Do you need to do some more prewriting? Be honest with yourself. If you're not ready to write, go back and do some more talking, thinking, and prewriting. If you have some material with which you're fairly comfortable, sit down and write out a rough draft. You're familiar enough with the process to know that this initial draft is just a working out on paper of some ideas and material. Write yourself out to see what you have to say. Then review it to discover what the focus might be. Once the focus appears clear, review your answers to your audience analysis. What do you need to do to make the draft fit the audience, the subject, and the purpose? Be sure you have that fit clearly in mind before revising.

Rewriting/Revising

With the rough draft to work on and with the audience/subject fit determined, go to work on a revised draft. Cut and paste if you have to; move sections around, add and subtract material where it seems desirable. Review what you have learned about paragraph structure, about introductions and conclusions. Depending on the approach you have taken to your subject, you may find the revision suggestions in earlier chapters helpful. Build a strong draft that you feel comfortable sharing with a writing group.

Response

Decide how you would like your draft responded to; do you want to use the one-to-one system or a writing partner, or a group of readers to get several different responses? Your instructor may allow you some freedom in obtaining the response, or he or she may make suggestions about which approach seems best suited for the particular kind of writing you've developed. Whatever the choice, seek the response, consider it carefully, adjust your draft accordingly and polish, using more response sessions if you have the time and the need. Remember that this paper represents, to a large degree, an indication of how well you have absorbed earlier lessons in using the writing process to your advantage. Make the final draft a good one.

SAMPLE ESSAYS

Identity Crisis
by Carol Howard

It was a sultry summer evening several years ago when my girlfriend Sherrill and I strolled into our favorite night spot, Off 2nd. Lively music and laughter filled the dimly lit main room as we nudged our way to a circle of friends near the bar. Suddenly I felt a tap on my shoulder and turned to see a young woman's familiar smiling face. We had been friends for several years, and I had been to numerous parties at her and her husband's house. We chatted briefly, and as she was leaving, she invited me to join her and a mutual friend, Marcia, in the back room.

"Who was that?" Sherrill asked. "She seemed friendly."

"Oh, that's—" For a moment my mind was blank. I couldn't produce her name. A clear picture formed of this short, stocky girl of about twenty-seven, but she remained anonymous. I saw her medium-length, dyed-blond hair, slightly curved under, one side drooping into her face. And, of course, there was her husband—a skinny, dark-haired fellow—but I could not identify him either. The only name that came to me was Mary Lou. The girl was definitely *not* Mary Lou, but she should have been. It suddenly occurred to me how much she looked like one. Perhaps her name had a similar sound.

"She's a friend of mine who teaches at Catholic High," I told her. "She wants us to join her and another friend later on."

"Sure, I'd like to," Sherrill smiled.

"Later on" arrived in twenty minutes when Sherrill and I made our way back to the plush, contemporary sofa where Marcia and the mysterious girl were sitting. Sherrill graciously joined in the conversation although I knew she had no idea who the people were. My apprehension grew steadily as the moment of introduction became imminent. An outer me was carrying on conversation while inwardly I was ransacking my brain for a clue to her identity. Nothing surfaced but "Mary Lou."

"Won't you sit down?" Marcia said, indicating two armchairs across from them.

"Sure." Sherrill nodded. "Aren't you going to introduce us, Carol?"

Panic seized me by the throat. My heart skipped a beat, then raced madly. How can Sherrill do this to me! I silently raged. This can't be happening!

But it was. My mind desperately began to devise a strategy. Surely as I introduced Marcia, the other girl's name would follow. To tell the truth, though, I was in such a state that Marcia's name was becoming shaky, too. In a minute Sherrill's might go. . . . I had better introduce them quickly.

"Sherrill, this is Marcia—" I laughed sheepishly. "Ha . . . ha. . . . Your married name has slipped my mind. I wanted to say 'Thompson.' "

There wasn't any excuse for that. I knew her husband. We had gone to the same schools together all our lives.

"Carson," she helped me.

"And this is—" Still no name. I wanted to cry. I wanted to dive under the chair in front of me and slither out the door. How can you tell a good friend that you don't know her name without hurting her?

I didn't continue. My cough started as a nervous little irritation, but it became so interesting I decided to prolong it—to make it deeper and more convincing. I then paused for a moment as if to make sure the tickle was gone. . . . No, it was still there. . . . My choking resumed. The more I coughed, the redder my face got; the redder my face got, the more I coughed to cover it. The women stared strangely at me. They know I'm faking it, I thought, but the less convincing my act seemed, the stronger my need to convince them it was real.

Oh, heck, why not just dive into it all the way, I decided. I've already gone this far. I contorted my face and held my chest and threw myself into my act so violently that the faces were beginning to get worried. If I had continued much longer, my friends would probably have carted me off to the hospital—if not the insane asylum.

The performance drew to a close. I grimaced a few times as if to get hold of myself and then stole a glance at *the girl* to judge my effect. She seemed disappointed—as if she were still waiting. I started toward my chair pretending that the introduction was completely forgotten.

The group's focus finally shifted away from me as the conversation resumed. Sinking into my chair, I began to relax somewhat, and, of course, her name immediately flashed across my mind: Janet! Her name is Janet Hart! Her husband is Jim!

The information arrived too late, however, to salvage the introduction—or the evening. Even today the memory of that fiasco has so shaken my confidence that I face introductions with the poise of a victim before a firing squad. Outside of family members I cannot guarantee anyone recognition at that crucial moment. Former students are greeted only with a "hi" for fear I will slip. My sister's best friend has had to prompt me on her last name. Several weeks ago a friend (who knew my past history) left me cruelly dangling for five minutes until I could identify her. Perhaps my problem will remedy itself, however. My foible has proved so endearing that I sense I shall soon be free of all friends to introduce.

An Act of Contrition
by Virgil Sublett

I was having coffee at the counter of the Cadillac late one evening, watching the girls as they stopped in for a snack after working the late-night shift at the General Electric plant. As a group got out of a car and started into the restaurant, I noticed one girl in particular; we had gone to the same high school. She was two or three years behind me, but I remembered seeing her in the halls and at ball games. Although I didn't remember speaking to her, except for a few conventional hellos, I had enjoyed looking at her. Her skin was that beautiful hue often featured in the lotion ads. Even in the early spring, she had a muted bronze glow, not beautiful, but strikingly attractive. Eight years had not changed her; she was still golden through the streaked plate-glass windows. I was watching when she tripped on the concrete apron. I saw her stumble forward, reach out her arm toward the service door. I heard the glass splinter, her face paling through the glaze that webbed the glass. My own awful, helpless horror was mirrored by the startled eyes, gaping mouths, and half-raised bodies of the other customers. I waited for her to be helped up. When she didn't appear, I went outside to join the crowd around her.

She lay on her back, eyes closed, moaning softly. A white counter cloth pillowed her head from the harshness of the sidewalk cement. The blood streaming from a cut in her right upper arm pooled into an almost imperceptibly widening arc and caused a man kneeling beside her to move his foot to one side. Her Samaritan was awkward, yet somehow heroic, trying to help—but the blood still ran. So much blood from so small a wound. The pool of blood lost its color in the reflected lights, becoming translucent, like water wrung from the towel held to her arm.

I backed out of the circle. Bucky Leonard was nearby in his deputy sheriff's car, doing his official duty. Fragments of dialogue as he talked on the police radio competed with bits of conversation from the group in front of me: ". . . been more than fifteen minutes . . . no ambulance . . . on strike . . . paddy wagon . . . ambulance . . . still be a while . . . bleed to death."

She was dying. I wanted to run to her, yell at everyone to move back. Too much blood. Probably an artery under her arm, near her breast. Let people think whatever they want. Find a knife, cut through her uniform, her underwear. Bare her torso, hug her to me while I closed her wounds with my hands. I wanted to do more. I wanted to say the Act of Contrition for her. Bend close to her ear, talk louder than the jumble around us: "Oh my God, I am heartily sorry for having offended Thee. And I detest all my sins because I dread the loss of Heaven and the pains of Hell."

I didn't do either one. I ran to my car and backed it up to where the girl lay. Bucky came over to help. Many hands did what had to be done. They lowered the tailgate, put the rear seat flat, found an old blanket folded in the back, and gently eased the motionless girl onto the blanket and into the rear compartment. Bucky was already in the patrol car—lights flashing a warning, siren breathing a soft monotone. A young newspaper reporter, well dressed in a dark suit and tie, climbed in the back of my wagon to steady the girl during her ride to the hospital.

Bucky led the way. I drove behind him; a city police car fell in as a rear escort. I felt that I was seated too close to a movie version of a thrilling cops-and-robbers chase scene, light streaking and blurring onto intermittent rainbows and fog, the cacophony of whistling wind, roaring motors, and screaming sirens amplified even above the pounding of my heart. Every rise and dip of the streets exaggerated the lunging bounce of the front of the car. I could hear the soft, sticky sound of her body being swayed on the blood-soaked blanket.

The emergency room crew was ready for us. Seconds after I backed up the ramp, efficient hands took her from the wagon and placed her on a wheeled operating table. I saw the towel still pressed against her upper arm. The bright fluorescent lights dulled everything to a dusty gray: her face, her lips, her uniform, even the towel. When the door bumped shut behind them, I was alone.

I moved the car out of the way to a parking place under a light. I sat behind the wheel for a few minutes, feeling tension jerk out of my body, down my legs, through my feet that beat a spasmodic tattoo on the floorboard. I looked around for help. No one moved in the quiet parking lot. The stillness followed me to the gaping back door of the station wagon. Carefully, almost reverently, I rolled the warm, moist blanket and carried it into the hospital lobby. I took paper towels, a bucket, and some water from a janitor's closet and walked back to the wagon.

I cleaned for a long, thoughtful time. Part of a girl was being washed from the rubber matting. I watched the stains smear, the edges already drying. Was the sound from the back a final reflex as lungs strained to salvage life from collapsed arteries? Did I pray for her while I drove? My tears joined the blood and water. The damp towels absorbed them, mingled them. On hands and knees in the dark compartment, eyes closed against burning tears, I choked a barely audible whisper: "Oh my God, I am heartily sorry. . . ."

Reality

Nan Riley Flanagan

Just wait until I get my hands on him, the creative genius who plots and plans the ads for today's refrigerators. I say genius singular, not plural—there could surely be only one such combination of archfiend and fond dreamer whose work results in my complete frustration.

Understand, I have no objection to the color pictures of the *outsides* of the refrigerators: the fridge done in American Western decor, with the accompanying model dressed as a contemporary Annie Oakley, or the one with the Spanish wrought-iron influence, the model a charmingly feminine bullfighter. What really reaches out and grabs me is the picture of the box with the open door.

Look at those shelves. Invariably there are several sherbet or parfait dishes loaded with some luscious heaped-up *cordon bleu* concoction. There is also a molded salad—not just a plain old ring mold, but one of that unusual Raymond Loewy type of melon shapes, or a writhing fish, or a tiered monument. And one ham, beautifully glazed, probably with nectar and ambrosia. (Now, about that ham. It is reposing gracefully on a large platter, circled by enticing accessories. Said accessories are best with *hot* ham. What does the cook do? Cook the ham, put it in the icebox with its surrounding delights, and then before she serves it take the ham out of the box and reheat it? She'll have to wash the platter again before she can serve her meal, and I am just uncharitable enough to enjoy the thought of her hasty last-minute efforts.) The chocolate cake with white and yellow icing is quite evidently the masterpiece of some modern-day Renoir.

The fruits and vegetables are always in season—in their own season, that is, whether there are winter grapefruits and summer watermelons pictured together, or fresh raspberries and Rome Beauty apples as a color-ful duet. Celery, radishes, carrot sticks have been freshly bathed, toweled, and manicured.

Take a look at those bottles of lemon juice, soft drinks, catsup, salad dressing, fruit juice—all full. How about that stick of butter on the butter shelf? It is whole, entire.

Now for the other side of the coin. My side, and a dull side it is. Let me open my refrigerator to you. Perhaps you will shriek, as a friend of mine did once when she was helping me entertain at coffee, "*Look* at that neat-neat icebox!" I was flattered momentarily, until I realized that shelves so nearly empty could be nothing *but* neat.

The coffee can contains bacon grease—I like to fry chicken in half bacon grease and half butter. That egg yolk in the small custard cup—the egg yolk that looks, and is, slightly crusty on top—is left over from the recipe I used day before yesterday that called for one egg white. I intended to add it to several (whole) eggs to scramble for breakfast yesterday, but we decided instead on basted eggs. The three tablespoons of oatmeal were left from last Friday (the container got pushed behind the coffee can, and I just this minute noticed it).

Those three small white plastic cartons hold about a half cup of soup each. I thought I might combine them, but somehow the mixture of cream of potato, vegetarian vegetable, and Scotch broth leaves me cold. I must insist that both of those half-filled jars of preserves are really edible—one we decided we didn't care for, but how can I throw out a forty-three-cent jar of gourmet black raspberry preserves just because the seeds are so big?

The jar with the three stuffed olives in it is for a friend of ours. Occasionally she has a martini with us, but her idea of a martini is an olive surrounded by almost anything liquid, one to one, two to one, or fourteen to one. The brine in that jar is beginning to look a little doubtful, but then brine always looks doubtful—doesn't it?

Oh, the typewriter ribbon? Well, that's a spare I bought a couple of weeks ago, and it might dry out before my old ribbon needs replacing.

There are a few other small treasures—my grandmother would have called them "teeny-tonty bits." I come from a family noted for being saver-uppers of string and putter-awayers of paper bags. I might be able to do something with that bit of leftover roast. It does seem a shame to waste it, and perhaps with some artichoke hearts, mushrooms, sherry, slivered almonds, and a few other ingredients, I could whip up something delectable. I wonder if it would possibly stretch to serve two?

The imported pickled herring and the anchovy-stuffed olives are what Spouse picked up last time he went out for a loaf of bread. The two half-filled catsup bottles have me puzzled: Why two? That round mass in the corner of the bottom shelf could be a weary kernel of lettuce wrapped in a voluminous tea towel, but it's just a little ironing I didn't quite get to. (That was the day I decided to make sour-cream coffee cake and had to borrow the sour cream, the walnuts, a minimum of cinnamon, and the flour.)

The new refrigerators are beautiful, but I might as well face the fact: My family doesn't need a new refrigerator; it needs a new *me*.

Once upon a Daisy
by Martha Knight Lefebvre

The teacher and the period are both winding down while I industriously doodle in the last few empty spaces on the page. The clock clicks and a two-minute leap. Notebooks rustle, feet and books shuffle as the ɹry to cut the period a few minutes short. The teacher drones on, the ck seeming to have stopped after its last effort. A sudden buzz and ɹrackle from the p.a. system wakes the last of the dreamers and cuts the teacher short in mid-assignment.

"Is Martha Knight in this classroom?" It always amazes me how that speaker always knows where I am, kind of a "Big Brother is watching" feeling.

"Yes, she is," the teacher answers, betraying no sign of remorse.

"Would you send her to the office, please."

"Certainly."

By the time I climb two flights of stairs, my stomach returns to its original position. I pause outside the door, briefly considering flight from the country, then bravely stride through, ready to get the ordeal over. The principal's office door is shut tight, but the secretary motions me to have a seat after giving me the "I know something you don't" look. I figure she probably does, but I cross my legs and try to look as though I'm here by choice, not design. Actually, I feel like I do when I'm waiting in the dentist's office with two cavities to be filled. I can almost hear the drill and my stomach is tending to wander again, so I look around to take my mind off the situation.

"Your Career and You" in optimistic white letters blazes across the opposite wall. I find myself eye to eye with a smiling nurse taking an equally happy patient's pulse, a grinning Marine with little hair, and a college student posed dramatically in front of an ivy-covered building, carrying a load of books that would have broken a lesser man's back.

I would have been bored, but my stomach wouldn't let me forget why I was here. Tired of staring at successful young adults, my gaze wanders to the closed door again. Is there a lady or a tiger behind it? Just then the doorknob turns, but it's only another secretary who gives me a funny look as she swishes by. Now I'm beginning to wonder if I got everything on after gym class, but before I can check, she issues my sentence.

"You may go in now."

The principal doesn't even look up when I come in. He keeps on writing furiously; maybe I'm being sent up the river. His bald head glistens in the overhead light. A beached fly on its back and the pen's scratching back and forth are the only sounds. Finally the scratching stops, and he looks up, kind of fidgeting with his pen. I smile but he doesn't—a very bad sign. The clock clicks. The pen points to an empty chair. It's one of those folding metal ones that give you frostbite or a first-degree burn, depending on the weather. Today it's frostbite, but I maintain my poise after the initial shock.

He plays with the pen some more, then painstakingly adds another line to his paper. The bell rings and we both jump. I take the chair with me, and it falls with a crash. By the time the chair and I get settled again, he has disappeared from sight, presumably behind the desk. Sure enough, he emerges a few seconds later, holding up a dejected brown leather lump by one strap.

"My pocketbook!" I cry, reaching for it.

"So you admit that it's yours?" he asks me in a voice that would have done Joe Friday proud.

I nod warily, my mind frantically sorting the contents of the pocketbook, checking for incriminating evidence. I'm pretty sure I'm clean, but I've got this horrible feeling like when a cop pulls up behind you and you wonder why he's there. While I am recalling past sins, he has unzipped the bag and pulled from it a small plastic bag, neatly tied off. We both stare at it, mesmerized.

"Is this marijuana?" he asks, still in the Joe Friday voice.

"Huh?" I say, not very intelligently, but he's caught me off guard. I'm not even sure what he's got. I take another myopic look at it and, seeing what it is, have to struggle to keep from laughing in his mournful face.

"It's a party favor," I finally gasp, "a dried-flower arrangement!"

"What's it doing in your pocketbook?"

Obviously this guy has a one-track mind. Admittedly it is a little worse for the wear, but even from where I sit I can see the red and blue flowers and a small daisy, still recognizable though crunched. I decide to humor him.

"I put it there after the party," I explain patiently.

"Oh," he says, Joe Friday receding. "Well, since you are a senior and an honors student, we'll let it go."

Great, I think; since I am a senior honors student I've got permission to carry dead flowers in my pocketbook. But I say "Thanks" kind of sarcastically and grab for the pocketbook and the flowers, shaking my head slightly.

"Watch yourself in the future," he says.

"Sure," I say and back out of the office, surprising all the secretaries who had been clustered by the door. "It was a daisy," I explain kindly and run out into the hallway, swinging the pocketbook by its tired strap. I stop the first kid I see.

"Hey, Rick!" I shout. "I just got picked up for possession of a daisy."

CHAPTER 8

Workshop: Writing Effective Sentences

Although you may not be entirely conscious of the fact that you're a skillful practitioner of language skills—you are. By adolescence most people have learned just about everything worth knowing about language, vocabulary not included. They know how to put words together to form a question, state an idea, and make a sentence. They have the basic uses of language under control. It's understandable if you're just a little skeptical about such statements. After all, you're probably saying, if I'm such a skillful user of language, why is it that my writing doesn't always seem to sound, or even look, like that of published writers?

Good question—and one that has been answered in a variety of ways over the years. When we entered school, most of us didn't know how to write a sentence although we were speaking in complete sentences. The first discovery of what a sentence is probably came from reading books:

> The cat runs.
> The cat is black.
> The cat has a friend.

A teacher undoubtedly told you to read these sentences and before long you were encouraged to copy them. As a result, you came to believe sentences were short. If you didn't read a great deal as you grew up and if no one took the time to show you how short sentences could be combined to form longer and more complex sentences, your writing may still have a kind of primer quality to it.

But skilled writers have learned through practice and experimentation that sentences can be long, short, or medium; they can appear in several different forms and do many things for readers besides simply communicate information. No one, however, can write effective sentences or have effective sentence variation in writing without practice. Traditionally, people thought that everyone had to have drills on the parts of speech and rules of grammar and then do all kinds of sentence diagramming and labeling to achieve the polish and sound that experienced writers have. You might have had a healthy dose of this medicine yourself. Unfortunately, even after such a dose, most people's writing still does not reveal any consistent amount of maturity.

SENTENCE MATURITY

Let's see if we can examine the situation in a more direct way. Most of us can "hear" the difference between a smoothly written piece and one that lacks smoothness. Read the following paragraph and see what your "hearing" reaction is.

> A man lived in a farmhouse. He was old. He lived alone. The house was small. The house was on a mountain. The mountain was high. The house was on the top. He grew vegetables. He grew grain. He ate the vegetables. He ate the grain. One day he was pulling weeds. He saw something. A chicken was eating his grain. The grain was new. He caught the chicken. He put her in a pen. The pen was under his window. He planned something. He would eat the chicken for breakfast. The next morning came. It was early. A sound woke the man. He looked out the window. He saw the chicken. He saw an egg. The chicken cackled. The man thought something. He would eat the egg for breakfast. He fed the chicken a cup of his grain. The chicken talked to him. He talked to the chicken. Time passed. He thought something. He could feed the chicken more. He could feed her two cups of grain. He could feed her in the morning. He could feed her at night. Maybe she would lay two eggs every morning. He fed the chicken more grain. She got fat. She got lazy. She slept all the time. She laid no eggs. The man got angry. He blamed the chicken. He killed her. He ate her for breakfast. He had no chicken. He had no eggs. He talked to no one. No one talked to him.
>
> —Kellogg W. Hunt

Well, what's your reaction? How would you describe the smoothness of this paragraph? What seems to be the major problem? If you pinpointed the shortness and similarity of the sentences in the paragraph, as well as the repetition of words, your sentence "sense" is working well. Now that you've revealed your awareness, go one step further— show what you would do to make this paragraph a more effective piece. Rewrite the paragraph in any way you think appropriate; you may change the wording of sentences and combine and omit words, but do not change the basic facts or meaning in the passage.

When you've finished rewriting the paragraph, place your paragraph next to the original one. Look at the two paragraphs and see if you can describe the difference. What were some of the things you had to do to the original sentences to produce your version? In a short paragraph, write out a description of *how* you made improvements and what effect they have on the "sound" of your new version.

Obviously an exercise of this type does nothing more than suggest where you may be in your development as a writer of sentences. The results have nothing to do with the content of your writing, nor do they reflect the fact that different kinds of writing call for different types of sentences.

The crucial element in developing sophistication in sentence use is understanding the keys to effective sentences. It is the *connecting* devices of language that make sentences work, and the reassuring part of all this is that although there may be large numbers of words in the English language, the actual ways of connecting sentences are relatively few. Consider the following example.

> I wanted to go to the football game. My friend wanted to stay home. She said it would rain. I said it would not. I decided to go alone.

> *Although* I wanted to go to the football game, my friend wanted to stay home *because*, she said, it would rain. I said it would not *and* decided to go alone.

Both passages contain the same information but the second has been reduced to two sentences and the connections (the italicized words) have made the ideas clearer and smoother. In the first passage the reader has the sensation of reading five separate statements, all grammatically correct but not really connected. In the second, not only have the sentences been connected but the rhythm of reading has been changed. The first has a kind of staccato rhythm with short, choppy blocks of words; the combining of sentences and the use of punctuation in the second passage give a much more varied rhythm.

Here's a sample for you to try. Combine the following three statements into one economical sentence.

> The car sat in the parking lot. The car has a flat tire. The car was old.

Your solution might have come out like this: *The old car, which has a flat tire, sat in the parking lot.* The operation wasn't difficult: you looked for possible repetition (the car; the car), then you decided which details (old; flat tire) should be connected with the car; you perhaps decided that *which* would serve as a good connector. The result is a smooth, related statement of information. Of course, there are other solutions to this sentence problem. You might have produced any of the following:

> The old car, the one with the flat tire, sat in the parking lot.
> The old car, its tire flat, sat in the parking lot.
> The old car with the flat tire sat in the parking lot.
> In the parking lot sat the old car, its tire flat.

You might have found still other variations. The important point, however, is that all of these sentences are correct grammatically and all will be distinct improvements over the original three in most uses.

In this workshop, you will work with sentence structure, focusing your attention on how you can improve your sentence fluency and make your writing sound and work even better than it already does. Although there are many aspects of sentence combining, we will begin by concentrating on three: *adding, deleting,* and *embedding.* As you practice using these techniques, you will note an immediate change in the sentences that appear in your essays. The sound and flow of your writing will become much more sophisticated. As you continue to practice, you will discover that some of the patterns will become almost automatic; others will take a bit more time and may not always come out readily, but they will be there and you can tap them, using revision, when you need them.

In the following discussion, specific signals have been added to alert you to the different techniques being used, as in this example:

1. She had finished reading the note.
2. Her eyes reflected a humorous glint. (, *and*)

Here, sentence 2 is to be combined with sentence 1 by the "signal" indicated in parentheses. Hence, the combined sentence would read:

> She had finished reading the note, and her eyes reflected a humorous glint.

All you have to remember in examples like this is that the signals always appear at the end of the sentence or element that is to be combined with another and that you will move to the beginning of the material to be combined any word or mark of punctuation that is to be added.

Adding

One of the most common devices for joining ideas is to connect one idea to another, unchanged. This connecting can be done with punctuation—usually a comma or semicolon—and/or with a connecting word. Consider the following samples of adding.

1. No one has found a total cure for stagefright.
2. Being well prepared is a partial cure. (, *but*)

    No one has found a total cure for stagefright, but being well prepared is a partial cure.

1. The tornado struck the town without warning. (*when*)
2. People were caught in the middle of the street. (,)

    When the tornado struck the town without warning, people were caught in the middle of the street.

1. The noon whistle sounded.
2. The plant was already empty. (*although*)

    The noon whistle sounded although the plant was already empty.

1. The Emperor Nero chose to play his fiddle.
2. The city of Rome burned. (*while*)

    The Emperor Nero chose to play his fiddle while the city of Rome burned.

1. The news of the team's victory spread quickly.
2. The telegram arrived at midnight. (*after*)

    The news of the team's victory spread quickly after the telegram arrived at midnight.

1. Most of the room lights stayed on in the dormitories until two or three each morning.
2. Midterm exams were being given all week. (*because*)

    Most of the room lights stayed on in the dormitories until two or three each morning because midterm exams were being given all week.

Adding seems to be simple, and it is. Just because you can find a way to connect one statement with another, however, does not mean that this should be the only method you use. Too much adding can be as boring and as ineffective as too little. Overuse can produce writing that sounds like young children talking: *I had a nice day, and I went to the store, and I saw a man there, and he was a big man.* What you're looking for in using this technique are sentences that are closely related and that deal with a broader action or idea than just a simple statement of fact.

Try combining the following sentences by adding. Choose appropriate connectors.

1. The United States is a democracy.
2. Argentina is a dictatorship.

1. The politician was making her speech.
2. Her opponent waited offstage.

1. The corn crop will not be a record harvest.
2. The drought stunted the usual growth.

1. Reductions in Social Security benefits alarm older people.
2. Many of these people rely on Social Security for all their needs.

1. The new dress design was popular.
2. Few people could wear it easily.

Deleting

Frequently, instead of adding material we need to omit it. A problem that occurs in many writers' prose is repetition. During the writing of rough drafts, a writer may use the same word over and over simply because it's familiar and does not interrupt the flow of ideas at the time of writing. When the writer rereads the paper, however, these words begin to hammer away at the ear, and the effective writer knows that such repetition has to disappear. The solution is, again, a relatively simple one. Experienced writers look for ways to omit or delete parts of a sentence, particularly the repetitive words or phrases, and to combine the remaining ideas into effective sentences.

A different signal device is used in this section. Underlined words or phrases are to be saved and combined; everything else is to be deleted. The following are some examples of deleting.

1. Susan is a wonderful girl.
2. She is always smiling.
3. She is friendly.
4. She is helpful.
5. She is even-tempered. (, and)
   Susan is a wonderful girl, always smiling, friendly, helpful, and even-tempered.

1. The problem has several solutions.
2. The solutions range in difficulty. (, which)
   The problem has several solutions, which range in difficulty.

1. The people in the bus are neighbors of mine.

2. These neighbors <u>have helped me in several emergencies</u>. (who)

The people in the bus are neighbors of mine who have helped me in several emergencies.

Combine the following sentences by deleting.

1. The soup was full of floating bits of parsley.
2. The floating bits of parsley looked like mold.

1. The people watched the television program.
2. The program lasted for three hours.

1. The gown is white.
2. The gown is long.

1. In a disaster, the people most needed are doctors, firefighters, and police.
2. These people are trained for coping with a wide variety of emergency situations.

1. The president spoke at a news conference.
2. The news conference lasted one minute.

Embedding

You will often find it useful to combine two sentences into one; *embedding,* as it is called, allows us to show how two ideas are actually part of each other, not merely one idea added to another. When you decide to use embedding in your writing, you might find it helpful to think of one sentence as having an open slot in it. Most writers label this slot *something* to remind themselves of the need to fill it with a definite part of a second sentence. Here's an example:

The president knew *something.*
The economy was not in good shape. (that)
The president knew that the economy was not in good shape.

In this example, *that* moved to the front of the second sentence and the second sentence was embedded in the slot indicated by *something.*

Revision comes after *something.*
The writer has completed a first draft.
Revision comes after the writer has completed a first draft.

As in the previous example, the second sentence is embedded in the first sentence, this time using different connecting words.

The best way to recognize the need for embedding is to examine sentences to see where material occurs that might be "slotted" into another sentence, thus cutting down on the number of sentences and tightening the relationships between ideas. Embedding is particularly useful in material that deals with facts and ideas. Some variations include the use of connectors such as *what, how, when, where,* and *why:*

> Few people are anxious to reject *something.*
> They once believed. (*what*)
> Few people are anxious to reject what they once believed.
>
> No one wanted to know *something.*
> The wreck occurred. (*how, where, when,* or *why*)
> No one wanted to know how (where, when, why) the wreck occurred.

Now try embedding a few sentences. Choose appropriate connectors.

> 1. I saw *something.*
> 2. The river had risen over its banks.
>
> 1. *Something* made the teacher pleased.
> 2. Students completed all their revisions.
>
> 1. The newspaper carried *something.*
> 2. The story was about the new shopping mall.
>
> 1. The captain of the *Queen Elizabeth II* knew *something*
> 2. The troops would wreck the polished dance floor.
>
> 1. *Something* should make you avoid the display.
> 2. You are allergic to roses.

The particular sentence skills suggested so far have more or less involved adding or deleting elements of sentences. We have focused on the specific operations without looking at what they might do for the style of your writing. You will discover that by adding, deleting, or embedding, your sentences may tend to grow longer; this may lead you to believe that by merely writing longer sentences you'll be a more effective writer. The key, however, is to determine what effect you want your sentences to have on your reader and to what purpose you intend to put the material in each sentence. Short sentences are often as effective as long ones, and variety in sentence length is as important as variety in sentence type. Although you'll discover that, on the average, the sentences of effective writers are longer than those of beginning writers, the sentences tend to be more economical: they say more with fewer words.

Practice

To see if you understand the principles of adding, deleting, and embedding, use the techniques described on the previous pages to combine each cluster of sentences below. You may find it helpful to combine each cluster in several ways, experimenting to see which versions work best.

1. My classes contain some people with unusual experiences.
   These people have traveled more than I have.

2. We just received a weather bulletin.
   A severe thunderstorm is on the way.

3. I have read *something*.
   Gothic romance novels are highly popular.

4. The school has made several budget cuts.
   The budget cuts will mean fewer opportunities for extracurricular activities.

5. The season had come to an abrupt end.
   The team lost the game needed to get to the finals.

6. She asked me *something*.
   I should stay until the end of the party.

7. Some things can pollute the environment.
   Burning soft coal can pollute the environment.

8. The sun shone down on the crops below.
   It was like an overheated furnace.

9. People were caught without protection.
   The storm came rapidly.

10. The waves formed interesting patterns.
    The patterns were all over the beach.

11. The issue came to a vote.
    The chairman announced a tie.

12. The man was well dressed.
    The man was polite.
    The man was patient.

13. The people huddled against the cold.
    The sun was shining.

14. The cat had a long, narrow head.
    The head was in the shape of a spear.

15. Karate is a popular sport in America.
    It began in the Far East.

16. I hate *something*.
    I go to bed late.

ANALYZING YOUR OWN SENTENCE CONSTRUCTION

Now that you've been introduced to some principles of effective sentence construction, you can turn to your own work. Select the draft of a piece you know is going to need some revision, or work with a piece your instructor has indicated needs some attention to sentence construction. Read the piece aloud if possible or, better yet, have someone read it to you. The old saying "Familiarity breeds contempt" is appropriate here. You may be so familiar with a piece that you have ceased to hear or see some of its problems. The advantage of having other people read your work is that they usually aren't familiar enough with it to gloss over problem areas the way you might. Listen and look for repetitive wording, lack of variety in sentence openings and length, and awkwardness in the sounds of words and formation of sentences. Make notes anywhere you find such difficulties. When you've finished the reading, return to the questionable sections. If one section seems to have more notes than others, concentrate on that area first. If you happen not to spot any problems immediately, set a challenge for yourself. Select one paragraph from the piece and set out to rewrite each sentence in a different way, looking for new combinations on the basis of what we have covered so far. Then compare your new version with the old. You may discover that you like some part of the new one more than the original. Make substitutions as necessary.

One of the easiest ways to work on "sentence tuning" is to pull the questionable sentences out and look at them in isolation, as you have done in the exercises in this chapter. When you have them out by themselves, the problem often becomes quite clear—too much repetition, lack of variety in length, or perhaps incorrect or awkward connections. Experiment with several ways of solving each sentence problem. Read your solutions aloud—remember the ear is a good instrument for checking the tuning. If you have a chance, try out several versions of a sentence solution with a writing partner; see what his or her reaction is to the different versions. Remember, though, that you're the one who has to make the decision. Once you've made a choice, insert it into the original piece. Reread the section with the new version. How does it sound? If it's still not quite right, take one version out and try another one. Keep "tuning" until you're satisfied that it sounds as you want it to. Then move on to the next problem.

Test your sentence sense on the following paragraph from a student's draft about the pleasures of driving in the wilderness. Read the
paragraph to see if you can identify the trouble spots.

> I wanted to get off the main highway, so I searched for another
> road to take. I drove for a while. Then I found such a road. It was a
> beaten, old dirt road. I hoped it would lead me deep into the virgin
> woods. There I would be beyond any sign of civilization except for my
> jeep and myself.

If you decided the writer's problem with sentences seems to be in the
heart of the paragraph, you're on target. The first and last sentences of
the paragraph seem adequate at this point, so let's begin pulling out the
other four sentences to study:

> I drove for a while.
> Then I found such a road.
> It was a beaten, old dirt road.
> I hoped it would lead me deep into the virgin woods.

Isolated in white space, the sentences seem to have a little variety in
length, but the first three are very similar in form. Let's see what options
we have. We might try combining by simple addition:

> I drove for a while and then I found such a road.

Or we might decide that *and then* could be shortened, giving us this
version:

> I drove for a while *until* I found such a road.

Either choice would be fine; the writer would decide which one seems
to fit best with the others around it.

Again we have some choices with the last two sentences. We can
combine the two by addition:

> It was a beaten, old dirt road that I hoped would lead me deep into the
> virgin woods.

You've probably noticed that in the combining process, *it* was deleted in
the second part to make the sentence clearer and smoother. By this
time, though, you may have discovered still another possibility using all
four sentences:

> I drove for a while until I found a beaten, old dirt road that I hoped
> would lead me deep into the virgin woods.

Your immediate reaction to this change may be that the sentence is too
long. Perhaps so, but look at the sentences around it. In fact, let's put

the paragraph back together with the two different versions and you be the judge.

> I wanted to get off the main highway, so I searched for another road to take. I drove for a while until I found such a road. It was a beaten, old dirt road that I hoped would lead me deep into the virgin woods. There I would be beyond any sign of civilization except for my jeep and myself.

> I wanted to get off the main highway, so I searched for another road to take. I drove for a while until I found a beaten, old dirt road that I hoped would lead me deep into the virgin woods. There I would be beyond any sign of civilization except for my jeep and myself.

Although this kind of sentence tuning may appear time-consuming at first, by focusing your attention on this element of your writing you'll be developing your sentence sense. Eventually you will discover that the necessary changes will occur as you are writing and your choices of what to combine and what to leave alone will become easier. Effective writers know that some "tuning" is necessary, however, and welcome it as an opportunity to make sure that whatever they are saying comes across in the best possible way.

THE CUMULATIVE SENTENCE

The principles you've just learned are sound ones and work well in many cases. But frequently beginning writers try too hard to tighten their sentences and end up with sentences that are as ineffective as those with which they began. Consider what might happen if you took the following and applied what you have learned so far.

The man has a black hat.
The man walks slowly.
The man walks slowly into the room.
The man carries a cane.
The cane has a snake's head carved on the handle.
The cane was given to the man in Africa.
The cane was given to the man by his great-grandfather.
The man's relatives had gathered in the room.
They were gathered to honor his birthday.
His birthday marked his age of one hundred years.

If you rigorously apply the principles of adding, deleting, and embedding, you might produce the following passage:

> The man who had on the black hat and who carried a cane with a snake's head carved on the handle that had been given to him in Africa by his great-grandfather walked slowly into the room where all of the man's relatives had gathered to honor his birthday which marked his age of one hundred years.

Our initial reaction as readers is to give thanks that we do not have to read much of this type of prose. Too much of this style and readers will abandon the writer. But the revision followed the principles outlined in the previous sections of this chapter. Does that mean all your work was for nothing? Of course not. What is needed is more variation in sentence construction.

In the previous revision the writer concentrated on binding all the words together. When this is done, readers are forced to read without pause. Problems don't occur as long as the binding doesn't build too heavy a load for the reader. But many times ideas and details need to be presented in a more fluid construction so the reader gets a feel for what is happening and has time during the reading to begin to comprehend what is being said. Such attention could produce the following revision:

> Black hat on his head, carrying a cane with a snake's head carved on the handle—a present from his great-grandfather in Africa—the man walked slowly into the room where all his relatives had gathered to honor his one-hundredth birthday.

The sentence is still long, but now it gives the reader some flexibility. The addition of punctuation and the deletion of the *who, which,* and *that* connectors make for a completely different—and more pleasant—reading. It is this kind of flexibility that you want to achieve in your writing.

To understand the purpose of flexibility, you first have to understand the unit on which it is built: the sentence base. The sentence base contains the main subject and main verb along with any bound modifiers—words that can't be moved about in the sentence easily without altering the meaning. Here's an example of a sentence base:

It was a crowded store with aisles jammed with merchandise.

In this sentence, the word *crowded* is bound—it cannot go anywhere but where it is; the same can be said for *with aisles* and *jammed with merchandise.* These words and phrases are bound together. In this case, such binding does not make an inappropriate sentence, but if all your sentences followed this format you soon would encounter some problems with readers who complained about the lack of variety in your writing. Here's the same material, but this time in a different format:

> It was a crowded store, aisles jammed with merchandise.

In this version, the reading of the material changes. There's some variation in the flow of the words; the simple addition of a small amount of *free modification* has made the sentence looser and more interesting to read.

Free Modification

The principle of free modification is based on the idea that sentences have levels of meaning; that is, everything is built off the sentence base, and each detail or idea that is added to the sentence base occurs at a more specific level. People naturally qualify things as they say them. A person might say, for instance, "I just bought a super car, a Chevrolet, a Camaro, a two-door fastback with bucket seats." No one hearing this would be confused into thinking the person had bought four cars; instead, the listener is aware that each element is a more specific qualification of the previous one. Graphically we could show the relationship this way:

> I just bought a super car,
> > a Chevrolet,
> > > a Camaro,
> > > > a two-door fastback with bucket seats.

You can see that this arrangement looks like a ladder. The first part of the statement—"I just bought a super car"—is the most general level and thus at the top of the ladder; then we move down a rung because "a Chevrolet" is more specific than "super car." The next step down is "a Camaro" because that is even more specific than "a Chevrolet." Then "a two-door fastback with bucket seats" tells us more about the Camaro. Note, then, that, going down the ladder, each time the writer comments on a part or the whole of the previous element a new level occurs. You can number the levels so they become more apparent:

> 1. I just bought a super car,
> > 2. a Chevrolet,
> > > 3. a Camaro,
> > > > 4. a two-door fastback with bucket seats.

On the basis of this example, you might think that the levels all follow the sentence base, or level 1. This is not always the case. As a matter of fact, free modifiers usually can be moved around to different positions in the sentence without changing the essential meaning. For example:

> Sneezing and coughing, the hay fever addict groped blindly for his medicine.
> The hay fever addict, sneezing and coughing, groped blindly for his medicine.
> The hay fever addict groped blindly for his medicine, sneezing and coughing.

Sentences using free modification are called *cumulative;* they offer three key positions for free modifiers.

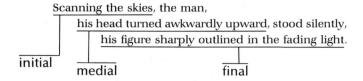

The sentence base is "the man stood silently." Free modifiers occur before, within, and after the base. Before the subject is the initial modifier, "scanning the skies"; within the sentence base, between the subject and verb, is the medial modifier, "his head turned awkwardly upward." After the main verb and its bound modifier "silently" comes the final modifier, "his figure outlined sharply in the fading light." These are the three basic positions you have to work with in a sentence when you choose to use free modification.

You may have noticed that free modifiers in the previous examples were set off with commas. Careful punctuation of free modifiers is important if they are to add to the effectiveness of the writing. Free modifiers that come at the beginning of the sentence base may or may not be set off with commas; by their very position at the front of the base, they usually are free. If they are set off, it is normally with a comma. Free modifiers that occur in the medial or middle position must always be set off by a pair of marks—commas, dashes, or parentheses. Final free modifiers also are set off, usually with a comma but occasionally with a dash, colon, or parentheses.

Several variations in the basic pattern of the cumulative sentence are possible with free modification. A sentence may begin with free modifiers, continue with the base, and then have a final free modifier.

(In the following sentences, the base is numbered 1 and modifiers are numbered 2.)

2. As the deadline for filing petitions comes closer,
1. the city council will have to decide how it intends to handle the city's sanitation problems,
    2. problems that could have been solved five years ago had the council acted promptly to obtain federal funds.

2. Forlorn and weak,
2. its legs quivering under the unaccustomed weight of the rider,
1. the newly saddled bronco, / , stood in the center of the corral,
    2/ head bowed,
    2. awaiting this new experience with fear and loathing.

In the second example, the slash mark before the phrase "head bowed" simply indicates that this modifier would be inserted in the sentence base at the other slash mark. The sentence, therefore, would read: "Forlorn and weary, its legs quivering under the unaccustomed weight of the rider, the newly saddled bronco, head bowed, stood in the center of the corral, awaiting this new experience with fear and loathing."

Free modification and the cumulative sentence, then, offer you an opportunity to loosen your writing style, to show readers more accurately the relationship between ideas, and to provide more variety in the length and type of sentences. Modern stylists have come to like the freedom the cumulative sentence provides, and you will too once you get comfortable with the necessary adjustments to punctuation and levels of meaning.

Practice

Building the cumulative sentence is not difficult. Try the following sequence:

Begin with a clear sentence base:

1. The woman walks across the room

Decide what element in the sentence base you want to tell more about and add a free modifier for that purpose:

2. her small, slippered feet making no sound on the carpet

Add another modifier:

2. her body stiff with tension

Add other modifiers, perhaps commenting on one of the previous levels:

3. the chin jutting firmly forward
3. the shoulders squared beneath the expensive dress
3. the fingers curled tightly against the palms.

The result:

The woman walks across the room, her small, slippered feet making no sound on the carpet, her body stiff with tension, the chin jutting firmly forward, the shoulders squared beneath the expensive dress, the fingers curled tightly against the palms.

Here is another sample with five possible combinations.

The paper lies on the executive's desk.
The paper is white.
The paper flutters in the breeze.
The breeze comes from the open window.
The paper awaits a signature.

Possible combinations:

1. Lying on the executive's desk, the white paper flutters in the breeze from the open window, awaiting a signature.
2. Fluttering in the breeze from the open window, the white paper lies on the executive's desk, awaiting a signature.
3. The white paper, awaiting a signature, lies on the executive's desk, fluttering in the breeze from the open window.
4. Lying on the executive's desk, the white paper that awaits a signature flutters in the breeze from the open window.
5. The white paper, fluttering in the breeze from the open window, awaits a signature while lying on the executive's desk.

Following are some sentence clusters on various subjects. Work with each cluster, using the combining techniques you have learned, to produce single sentences.

1. The conductor raised his baton.
   The baton was white.
   The baton was raised in his right hand.
   The conductor placed a finger on his lips.
   The orchestra waited.
   The orchestra looked alert.

2. Humans have been exploring.
   The exploring has gone on for years.

The exploration has been in space.
The exploration has been in the sea.
The exploration has been in the ground.
The purpose has been for knowledge.
The purpose has been for thrills and adventure.
Humans seek to test their limits.

3. Some modern artists are very inventive.
   They are inventive in how they paint.
   They use cars.
   The cars are driven through puddles of paint.
   The cars' tires pick up the paint.
   The cars' tires leave tracks.
   The tracks are colorful.
   These tracks are called "art."

4. Applying to colleges means time.
   Applying to colleges means money.
   The time is spent with forms.
   The forms must be filled out.
   The forms must be accurate.
   The forms must be neat.
   The forms must be accompanied by a fee.
   The fee usually is at least ten dollars.

Now try your hand at building cumulative sentences from the following sentence bases; remember that you have three basic positions to work with—the beginning, the middle, and the end—and that you want to work with a variety of levels.

1. The wind howled.
2. The teacher announced the assignment.
3. The mayor was late for the meeting.
4. Some insects are not mere pests.
5. The batter missed the ball.
6. The labor group announced a strike.

ANALYZING YOUR USE OF CUMULATIVE SENTENCES

Once you have grasped the importance of the cumulative sentence and the levels within a sentence, turn to your own prose. Select a passage from one of your recent essays and analyze the sentences carefully.

Remember what you have learned about adding, deleting, and embedding as well as about the cumulative sentence. Are the sentences basically alike in length and type? Do they contain different levels? Experiment with the passage. Try rewriting it using the strategies you've practiced in this workshop. Review other passages for the same purpose.

Try from now on to use your heightened sentence awareness and, particularly in revision, look for ways to make your sentences more interesting and effective.

CHAPTER 9

What Other Sources Are There?

"Now, when I was growing up. . . ." How many times do adults try to impress young people with how much life has changed? Actually, some changes are inevitable. Yet until we look at what was happening when we were born, for example, we may not fully appreciate just how much change has, or has not, occurred in our lives. Comparing the past with the present often leads to some interesting observations about our world, observations that may help us understand why things are as they are in our present situation.

All the writing you have done so far has come directly from your experiences, a familiar source by now. Writers, however, can't always depend only on their experiences to provide necessary information. Frequently they must step beyond themselves and go to other sources to discover what they need to know. You can expect more and more of that activity, starting in this chapter. But as you move from personal experience to experiences outside yourself, you'll still be able to anchor your writing in what you know best—yourself.

Using evidence drawn from sources other than your own experiences calls for some adjustments in your preparation for writing. No more brainstorming for a few minutes and then selecting the particular examples and details that will help your readers understand what you're up to. Instead, evidence from newspapers, magazines, books, and interviews will become useful resources. If you are willing to spend time looking for and analyzing various materials and then deciding what the information adds up to or how it supports the original idea that started the search, your progress will be quite rapid. Such progress is not made all at once, of course, so toss any thoughts of an all-night cram session out the window. Instead, in these next chapters you will develop some systematic approaches that you can apply not only to searches in this writing course but in your work in other areas.

ASSIGNMENT: USING OUTSIDE SOURCES

Topic and Purpose

In this writing assignment you will look at events, people, places, and things that existed at the time you were born and at events, people, places, and things that exist now. In a sense you're going to become a detective. Your job is to identify clues in the material you examine that suggest possible contrasts or comparisons between how things were when you were born and how they are now. Your purpose is to build a case to explain the significance of these contrasts and comparisons.

Audience

Your audience will be like yourself, not too well informed at the start perhaps, but rather curious to know what conclusions can be drawn from the material. Because your audience won't do the same research that you will, you must supply the details and facts you use to draw your conclusions. This will be the only way your readers will get any value from your presentation. After all, a good detective never testifies until all evidence is collected, evaluated, and presented.

Prewriting

Finding Material

The first step in obtaining evidence for your case is to go where the information is—you can start in the library. To make your task easier, select a library with a large collection of current and past issues of magazines or newspapers published about the time you were born and copies of those same publications today.

The search for this kind of material will lead you to several options. Like the good detective you are, you will have to decide which options to follow, and your decision will depend on your interests. Perhaps the easiest sources to locate are magazines such as *Time, Newsweek, U.S.*

News & World Report, Harper's, The Atlantic, the *New Yorker,* and *Esquire.* Since magazines such as *Life* and *Saturday Evening Post* have altered their publication schedules several times in the past twenty years, you may want to avoid them unless you determine first that issues are available to cover the dates you will work with in this assignment. Another source is the specialty magazine, written primarily for special audiences and special purposes; some examples of those with a national distribution include *Sports Illustrated, Road and Track, Seventeen, Popular Mechanics, Popular Science, Scientific American, Field and Stream, Ebony, Ladies' Home Journal,* and *McCall's.* As you look for these, you may discover others that cover areas or interests that never had occurred to you before.

If magazines are not readily available or prove not to be as useful as you had hoped, you may find that newspapers will work just as well as magazines in this assignment. Try to use newspapers with a national circulation such as the *New York Times, Washington Post, Wall Street Journal, San Francisco Herald,* and *Los Angeles Times;* if none of these is available, look for a newspaper that has statewide or regional distribution. Your reference librarian can help you identify which newspapers might qualify. Avoiding local papers will test your skills for dealing with unfamiliar information in a larger environment.

Don't expect all these materials to greet you at the doors of the library. On the other hand, finding the appropriate material is not really that hard. First, you'll have to determine how your library handles and stores *periodicals*—a term used to describe magazines and newspapers. Some libraries have all their newspapers on microfilm, while the magazines are bound like books and placed on shelves. If you're not familiar with the procedures for using microfilm, a librarian can show you in a few minutes how to locate and use it.

Magazines commonly are located in the periodical section of the library. Here you'll probably have to do a bit of cruising up and down the aisles, but you'll quickly discover that in almost all instances old issues of magazines are bound according to year, and the appropriate year and month appear on the spine of each bound volume. Current issues of a magazine or newspaper may be housed in one of two places: If you're seeking a magazine or newspaper published within the last month or week, it may still be on display in the general reading area of the library; earlier issues in the most recent year or years may be placed unbound on the shelves with the bound volumes. If you have trouble finding what you want, ask a librarian. Questions, after all, are part of the detective's tools.

The temptation may be overpowering to grab the nearest magazine or newspaper and start reading. You'll get better results, however, if you spend some time browsing in newspapers and magazines published on or near your birth date. Once you have a feel for the kinds of information to be found in these materials, you can narrow your search to a particular magazine or newspaper. And it's here where the selection process really begins. Suppose you were born on July 5, 1965. Look for a magazine or newspaper published on or near that date; then look for an issue of the same publication that appeared on or near your most recent birthday. If your birthday hasn't occurred yet this year, simply take the issue closest to the date or go back and use an issue from last year. You may want to select two issues in each year, one just prior to your birthday and one on or just after it. This provides a wider span of time in which events have taken place and gives you more ideas to choose from.

Focusing on the Material

If possible, put the issues from both time periods together before you try to do anything else; if you're using microfilm this may be impossible, but you should have no problems with bound materials. One word of caution—most libraries do not permit magazines or newspapers to be taken out, so you may want to find out what copying facilities are available in case you need to study your material outside library hours.

With the materials close at hand, do some skimming and page turning; as you flip through each issue, look at the covers or front pages, the advertisements and illustrations, the main features, and the general content. If you've never read the publication before, your journey through the contents may be slower than if you were working with a familiar title.

Once you've done this quick scan of the contents to get a sense of what the issue is all about, get ready for a return trip through the pages. The best preparation for the trip is to set up a work sheet on which you can record your findings. It doesn't have to be complicated but could look something like the following sample. Be sure to note on the work sheet the name of the magazine or newspaper you're working with and when it was published.

Magazine or Newspaper: _____   *Magazine or Newspaper:* _____

Date: _____   *Date:* _____

Topic 1:   *Topic 1:*

Topic 2:   *Topic 2:*

With the work sheet set up, begin your search for material with the table of contents or index. You'll probably find broad topics listed there such as Politics, Entertainment, Economy, Business, Science, Sports, Leisure, and so on. If you're using a specialty publication, special departments as well as article titles are probably listed in the table of contents; if this information is not quite as helpful, turn to the content of the magazine itself to devise appropriate general headings. This first search will establish exactly what general topics are covered in both copies so you can begin to look for areas of similarity or difference.

With the preliminary headings established and entered on your work sheet as Topic 1, Topic 2, and so on—more headings can be added as you go along—skim the material that appears under the headings in the publication. Be sure to do it in both copies; you can record parallel findings as you go. Jot down just enough information under each heading so that when you review the list you'll have a fairly clear idea of what the general focus is under each topic. At this point, of course, you're merely on a fishing trip, an essential one if you want to catch the necessary material. Your finished work sheet from this expedition should look something like the following one.

Magazine: Time

Date: February 9, 1981

1. *Cover Story:* Brooke Shields and the modern model—life and fame

2. *Nation:* Hostages welcomed home; personal accounts of imprisonment; lessons learned from Iranian crisis

3. *World:* Mideast—Islam nations unable to reach agreement on Iran/Iraq conflict; agreed to aid UN in settling Afghanistan crisis

4. *Science:* Outer-space telescope increases scientists' view of universe 350 times as much as previous instruments; no problems getting pictures back

5. *Sports:* Oakland Raiders upset Eagles; SuperBowl follow-up

6. *Advertisements:* Imported cars—Renault 18i, being sold by American Motors, "forced" partnership(?), emphasis on mileage even with Cadil-

Magazine: Time

Date: February 10, 1961

1. *Cover Story:* Speaker of House Sam Rayburn; political power moves in Congress

2. *Nation:* The economy; recession; start of Kennedy's presidency; U.S. defense capability vs. that of Russians.

3. *World:* Iraq—attitude changed toward West; Congo war.

4. *Science:* All-seeing satellite launched; "spy in the sky" function; cloaked in Air Force secrecy; problem getting pictures back to earth; chimp in space

5. *Sports:* Track-Millrose Games; skiing competition

6. *Advertisements:* Compact cars—Valiant, Dart; emphasis on suspension, quietness, classic style; image of success; V-8 Turbine; Renault—

lac; cigarette ads—wording, presence of Surgeon General's warning; Benson & Hedges—image of woman; television and stereos—video recorders; detailed specifications

40 mpg; winter car; extra-hot heater; Thunderbird; equipment—water coolers, IBM electric; computers for missiles; only one beer ad—Schlitz; several whiskey ads; cigarette ad for Philip Morris King Size Commander

Re-Viewing

After canvassing the contents of the publications, sit back and do some serious thinking about what you have found; study both sides of your work sheet to see what, if any, connections can be made. If you review the list in the sample work sheet, for instance, at least two possibilities for further study appear. You could, for starters, focus on the advertisements, but in doing so you would have to keep in mind that you probably would be unable to use just one ad from the early issue and one from the later source; ads often don't have much material in them. If you cluster similar ads together, however, then you would have a number of options to explore. You could focus on the types of ads that appear in one issue but not in the other; or you could examine the current issue to see if the same type of ad is still being carried. Cigarette ads might form the basis for comparison or contrast. Automobile advertisements could lead somewhere if you focused on changes in styles, in features, and in image for the car owner. One interesting contrast should jump out of the sample work sheet: At least one Renault ad appeared in both issues, but the ad in the older issue featured Renault by itself, stressing its winter efficiency and gas mileage; in the newer issue, Renault is paired with American Motors and nothing is said about the car's winter efficiency. You might want to study this ad and see if there were any others that you could use to show what changes have occurred in the American vision of the automobile over the last twenty years. If you find there's not enough information to support a study of specific ads, another option would be to study the ads in each issue to determine what generalizations might be made about the apparent audience the publication caters to and whether that audience has changed.

Our sample work sheet turns up another possibility under *Science*. Material here seems to be ready-made for our purposes: a spy satellite in 1961 and a space telescope in 1981. Just the words themselves suggest a possible shift in space technology from spying and military defense to scientific exploration. So it should go as you crisscross your own list from top to bottom or bottom to top, looking for any clue that will help you establish a focus for comparison or contrast. Such clues need to be followed, and that's your next step.

Narrowing the Focus and Quest

Once you've determined that at least one or two topics or areas exist about which you could develop some conclusions, return to your magazine or newspaper and study those areas carefully. Read slowly, taking notes on details, facts, examples—anything helpful for building a case. Remember that you may have only the list to work from when it's time to write because the publications can't be taken out of the library. But that doesn't mean you should go on a copying spree; just take notes, being sure to be accurate and complete.

Throughout all this, keep your basic approach of comparison and/ or contrast in mind. Try to identify specific ideas you can talk about on both sides of the comparison or contrast. If you make notes about car mileage twenty years ago, for example, remember to get information so you can talk about mileage from today's perspective as well. To put it another way, what you talk about from one time period has to be talked about from the other or you will have to explain its absence.

The following is a sample of what one student produced as a working list of ideas by looking at an issue of *Newsweek* for 1961 and then a *Newsweek* issue in 1980. The student was attracted to the topic of Cuba because in the preliminary skimming of the two issues, he noticed that Cuba was prominent in both. In returning to that topic, the student discovered that Cuba had been a problem for the United States for almost twenty years and the basic problem seemed to remain the same. Here, then, was just what any good detective would want—a ready-made case with strong clues. Going to work, the student produced the following notes.

Magazine: Newsweek, June 5, 1961

Focus: "Reason for Hope" article

Response to Bay of Pigs invasion in April 1961 (referred to in May 29, 1961, *Newsweek*).

1,214 men captured by Castro. Castro wanted to barter captives for 500 tractors; Caterpillar tractors Model D-8; worth $35,000–50,000.

Magazine: Newsweek, May 26, 1980

Focus: "Carter and the Cuban Influx" article

Result of Refugee Act of 1980 (what is that?); defined refugees as people "unable or unwilling to return to their homeland." Cubans seen as undocumented aliens seeking asylum.

Cubans numbered over 60,000 arrive in Florida.

Castro found U.S. was involved in planning stage of invasion; U.S. felt responsible for men that had been captured.

Castro thought he could ridicule U.S. by suggesting trade; U.S. took proposal seriously; thought trade would be seen as humane by rest of world.

Citizens like Walter Reuther (United Auto Workers head), Dr. Milton Eisenhower, and Eleanor Roosevelt were special Tractors for Freedom Committee members and in charge of getting private donations.

Castro saw U.S. serious so had prisoners elect 10 representatives; sent them to Miami to barter; taken to White House.

Country's reaction quite negative: "When, oh when will we stop being blackmailed by Castro?"—Sen. Homer Capeheart.

Contributions to Tractors for Freedom fund declared tax deductible; President Kennedy thought contribution was "every bit as charitable an act as a donation to CARE."

Historical notes: only other documented time men exchanged for machines or suggestion made—in WWII Nazis offered a million Jews for 10,000 trucks. Exchange of people for people has occurred many times.

Note: Tractor agreement included demand for five years of maintenance and parts.

Castro had three demands for stopping the people: U.S. give up military base in Guantánamo Bay; lift economic sanctions against Cuba; stop high-altitude intelligence flights over Cuba.

Castro saw chance to embarrass U.S. and relieve some pressure at home; encouraged migration of hundreds of social misfits and other undesirables; cleaned out prisons.

Diplomatic struggle between Castro and Pres. Carter.

Castro generated anti-American feeling in Cuba by suggesting all people leaving were traitors.

"Castro, in a way, is using people like bullets aimed at this country"— Jack Watson, White House aide.

U.S. not prepared to cope with flood; elite came; then tradesmen; then mental and criminal elements; 9,000 refugees arrived in Florida in one day; no place to house, feed, etc.

Govt. tried to stop flow: private boat owners fined if caught transporting; many boats impounded; criminal element set aside.

Negative public reaction balanced against desire of Cubans now living in America to get friends and relatives out of Cuba while the opportunity was there.

We can learn quite a bit from the student's list about the process of writing this essay. When he started the list, the student was not entirely sure of the exact material he might find, so he did not identify any specific headings ahead of time. He simply read the material and took brief but fairly specific notes on what seemed to be important information; then he turned to the other source and did the same. Of course, when the list is made first on one side, it's much easier to organize your note taking on the other side—provided, of course, the material cooperates.

Once the lists on both sides are completed, some writers find it helpful to draw lines to items that seem related, whether they are for contrast or comparison. The student's sample list, then, looked like the following when he went back through it to begin making the necessary connections. You'll see that not every item is connected to a corresponding one on the opposite side; that can be a useful discovery, suggesting either that you need more information or that perhaps there is really no need to include that material in the paper.

Magazine: Newsweek, June 5, 1961	*Magazine: Newsweek,* May 26, 1980
Focus: "Reason for Hope" article	*Focus:* "Carter and the Cuban Influx" article
Response to Bay of Pigs invasion in April 1961 (referred to in May 29, 1961, *Newsweek*)	Result of Refugee Act of 1980 (what is that?); defined refugees as people "unable or unwilling to return to their homeland." Cubans seen as undocumented aliens seeking asylum.
1,214 men captured by Castro. Castro wanted to barter captives for 500 tractors; Caterpillar tractors Model D-8; worth $35,000–50,000.	Cubans numbered over 60,000 arrive in Florida.
Castro found U.S. was involved in planning stage of invasion; U.S. felt responsible for men that had been captured.	Castro had three demands for stopping the people: U.S. give up military base in Guantánamo Bay; lift economic sanctions against Cuba; stop high-altitude intelligence flights over Cuba.
Castro thought he could ridicule U.S. by suggesting trade; U.S. took proposal seriously; thought trade would be seen as humane by rest of world.	Castro saw chance to embarrass U.S. and relieve some pressure at home; encouraged migration of hundreds of social misfits and other undesirables; cleaned out prisons.
Citizens like Walter Reuther (United Auto Workers head), Dr. Milton Eisenhower, and Eleanor Roosevelt were special Tractors for Freedom Committee members and in charge of getting private donations.	Diplomatic struggle between Castro and Pres. Carter.
Castro saw U.S. serious so had prisoners elect 10 representatives; sent them to Miami to barter; taken to White House.	Castro generated anti-American feeling in Cuba by suggesting all people leaving were traitors.

Country's reaction quite negative: "When, oh when will we stop being blackmailed by Castro?"—Sen. Homer Capeheart.

Contributions to Tractors for Freedom fund declared tax deductible; President Kennedy thought contribution was "every bit as charitable an act as a donation to CARE."

Historical notes: only other documented time men exchanged for machines or suggestion made—in WWII Nazis offered a million Jews for 10,000 trucks. Exchange of people for people has occurred many times.

Note: tractor agreement included demand for five years of maintenance and parts.

"Castro, in a way, is using people like bullets aimed at this country"—Jack Watson, White House aide.

U.S. not prepared to cope with flood; elite came; then tradesmen; then mental and criminal elements; 9,000 refugees arrived in Florida in one day; no place to house, feed, etc.

Govt. tried to stop flow: private boat owners fined if caught transporting; many boats impounded; criminal element set aside.

Negative public reaction balanced against desire of Cubans now living in America to get friends and relatives out of Cuba while the opportunity was there.

After identifying connections, try matching items in a more systematic way to determine what conclusions you might draw. What general statements do the connections seem to support? Pull your material out and make a brief outline of the apparent similarities and/or differences. If the student were to do that with his sample list, the result might look something like this:

1. Both incidents were caused by some action of the U.S.
   1961—invasion of Cuba
   1980—passage of Refugee Act
2. Both incidents involved exchange of people for benefit of Cuba.
   1961—gained tractors
   1980—asked for military base, removal of economic sanctions, and stopping of intelligence flights; got as a bare minimum relief of population overcrowding and removal of many undesirables
3. Both incidents caused negative reactions in U.S.
   1961—Senator Capeheart's comment
   1980—White House aide's statement
4. U.S. responded to both incidents on "humanitarian" grounds.
   1961—get men out of jail
   1980—could not turn people away who were seeking refuge in America, "the land of the free"

Conclusion: Both incidents demonstrate that in twenty years the U.S. has been unable to find an effective way of keeping Castro and Cuba from putting us on the defensive and embarrassing us in the eyes of the world.

Organizing

Having arrived at a conclusion and having examined the material to see how it supports the conclusion, you next have to determine the most effective way to present the information. Actually, organizing this essay should not be too difficult, since the options are limited by the nature of the material. You have past and present, both of which have to be covered. The primary question is, then, which method you use. Do you use the familiar whole-to-whole method—put all aspects dealing with the past together and then present all the aspects of the present, or start with the present and then go to the past? Or do you follow the part-to-part approach, a model for which is seen quite clearly in the student's listing of the basic similarities? With the part-to-part approach, each general connection in the material that supports the similarities or differences in the subject becomes the focus for one section; the amount of material you have available will help you determine whether to carry out the part-to-part approach in separate paragraphs or within paragraphs. If this approach is used, you also must decide how to arrange the topics in such a way that they lead the reader from the least significant connection to the most important one. (Review the descriptions of these options in Chapter 6.)

Response

At this point it's time to have a talk with someone not familiar with the material. Find a partner or a group and fill them in on what you have discovered; stress what the main point of your discovery is and see if they believe you. If you're still a bit shaky about how accurate your conclusion may be, say so and let them draw you out. Invite the challenge, don't back away. Finding out now whether you have a real point to make can save you many hours of frustration later. Perhaps your partner or group can spot some clues you missed or can suggest a way to make the information clearer. Try not to dominate the discussion; your partners need help as well. Supply as much help as you can so everyone feels the dialogue has been worth the time.

The First Draft

Once you've made the necessary decisions about organization, your next step is to complete a rough draft so you can see what you have and how convincing it is. You'll probably make a discovery about this draft that will surprise you. Up to now you've been relying on your memory for information in your writing; now you've got notes. Since notes are just fragments of information, you have to weave them together in your own words to form a whole picture. That means thoughts and interpretations come into the process, and they have to be added to the notes to help the information stick together. If you ignore this aspect, you'll have a draft that looks like a reject from Western Union. No need to get concerned at this point—you haven't started your draft yet. But to get an idea of what can emerge from all this exploration, take time to read closely the student essays at the end of this chapter and note how the writers integrate the factual material into their own writing style and add their own observations.

After you've read the essays, begin your own draft. Keep in mind at all times the case or point you want to make and observe the following guidelines:

1. The main idea must be sharply focused throughout the essay.
2. Any information presented in the essay must be clearly related to the main idea.
3. Keep a consistent pattern of comparison/contrast throughout the essay.
4. Make the specific sources and dates for information clear to readers.
5. If you use quotations, names, and dates, be sure they are accurate.

Go ahead now and take the plunge; write yourself out, remembering this is your first draft and that there is time for changes if necessary, once you've got the words on paper.

Re-Viewing

After the first draft, which may be a little muddled because you are writing with material not directly from your own experience, take a few minutes to see what you have. Put yourself in the place of readers who haven't done the search for information that you have. Review the guidelines in the previous section. If you're satisfied that you have followed those guidelines, move on to the next consideration—your opening and closing.

Introduction and Conclusion

In writing a paper of this sort, you may find that the introduction and conclusion are rather difficult to write. Your key concern in your introduction is to set your readers up and let them have some sense of the significance to be found in the material. Remember, everyone does not automatically get excited or interested about reading history; you need an approach to convince readers that by looking at the past with you they will understand the present better. Your choice of openings varies. Starting off with part of a dramatic incident, as in the essay on integration at the end of this chapter, or using an unusual statistic may catch readers' attention; even a variation in style may be enough to attract attention. In the essay about Cuba the reader immediately receives the key elements in the Cuban situation. Introductions, or leads, call for experimentation; try several different ways and test them on various readers if possible. Refer to the workshop in Chapter 4 for more advice on writing introductions.

The same attention should go into a conclusion. Many writers choose to bring out the full impact of their comparison or contrast in the conclusion. Like the preacher who wants to end on a strong note so the congregation will go away with the final words ringing in their ears, you want to push home the significance of what you have written. You do not have to do this in a way that insults anybody, however; your readers, after all, are pretty intelligent people and presumably are the wiser for having read what you've offered. Still, they'll appreciate a summing up, a key paragraph or two that tries to bring your whole point into sharp focus. Again, note how the writers of the essays at the end of this chapter leave their readers with both a question and a suggestion that something needs to be done. Don't just mimic that kind of ending, but see if you can come up with some variation of it.

Response

Once you're satisfied that the introduction and conclusion work effectively and that other details of your usual revising have been attended to, you'll need an audience test. Before releasing the text of your essay, however, try writing a self-evaluation of what you have accomplished. Later, after you have received some audience response to your draft, you'll have a chance to compare your reactions with those of your readers.

1. Write in a clear sentence the key idea that you attempted to prove or show.
2. Identify what you consider the strongest part of the essay and explain why; give several specific examples in this part that are particularly effective.
3. Identify what you consider the weakest part of the essay and explain why.
4. Identify the pattern of organization and explain why you used it.

With your responses to these aspects of your writing recorded, form a group of four people plus yourself. Follow the response procedure that you have used earlier in the course: Exchange your draft with someone in your group. Read the draft carefully and respond to it on the basis of the following questions:

1. What is the main idea or conclusion developed in the essay? Where does this main idea become the clearest for the reader and is this the most effective place for it to appear?
2. Study the organization of the paper carefully; identify places where the writer has signaled the reader well about the relationship of ideas, facts, or incidents; if there are places where the organization seems less effective, point those out.
3. How clearly and how often does the writer cite evidence drawn from the reading of outside sources? How do you as a reader know the information is from such sources?
4. How effectively does the writer handle the shift from past to present or from present to past? Identify places where this effectiveness is evident. If there are places where the shift does not work, indicate those and make suggestions for improvement.
5. Examine the opening and closing of the essay. What are the strong and weak points of each?
6. What single major improvement would you recommend the writer make in this draft and why?

If you and your group members address these areas carefully and provide comprehensive answers, you probably won't read four papers in the time you have, but each person in the group should receive a minimum of two responses.

The Final Draft

After you have received the critiques from your group, compare the responses with the assessment you made before sharing your draft; how much agreement is there about the key points? Where does any disagreement center? You may, of course, choose not to follow all of the suggestions made by your classmates, but give each idea some thought before accepting or rejecting it. Remember, a reader's questions about what he or she sees on the page should alert you to what you are communicating and how well you are doing it. After considering these responses, you may discover the need for some further revising of small sections of your draft—perhaps a tightening and clarifying of your introduction or conclusion; perhaps the addition of some facts. Address these issues first and be sure you have them under control. Then move to your final editing.

Just as you have with other drafts, spend some time fine-tuning your prose in this draft. Have you spelled all names correctly from your sources? Have you got the dates right? It's easy to make a slip when working from notes, so always triple-check. What about a title for the essay? Remember that titles can help attract readers while also focusing their attention on the main point of your discussion.

This essay will become an important step across that gap between total reliance on personal experience and relating personal experience and information drawn from outside sources. Make this first step a strong one so you'll have a solid foundation to build upon in the next few assignments.

SAMPLE ESSAYS

Big Problem, Small Cuba

The year is 1959, the country is Cuba, and the man is Fidel Castro. Add these ingredients together and the result is one big headache for the United States. In 1959, Fidel Castro led a band of guerrillas from the mountain region of Oriente into positions of power in the Cuban government. Shortly after taking control of the country, Castro began a campaign to blame many of Cuba's problems on the United States. By the end of 1960, Castro had seized over one billion dollars' worth of American investments in return for what he termed American interference. Finally, on January 3, 1961, the United States broke diplomatic relations with Castro's government. Most people probably thought at the time that this would solve the Cuban problem.

Castro, however, continued to be a headache. The May 29, 1961, issue of *Newsweek* reveals in an article titled "Reason for Hope" that a small band of anti-Castro guerrillas tried to invade Castro's country and overthrow the government. The revolutionaries were unsuccessful and instead found themselves held as political prisoners. After questioning the prisoners, Castro's forces discovered that the United States had been involved in the organizational phase of the whole operation. With this information, Castro quickly moved to embarrass the United States once again.

This time Castro proposed a trade, one that would put America in a bad position. From the 1,214 prisoners who had been captured during the Bay of Pigs invasion, as it was called, ten prisoners were selected and returned to the United States where they were to barter with U.S. authorities for the lives of the 1,204 prisoners still being held in Cuban jails. The price for freedom was five hundred Caterpillar tractors, Model D-8, each of which was worth $35,000 to $50,000. In addition, Castro demanded a guarantee from the United States that it would supply parts and maintenance for five years. Such a demand might seem to be the first of its kind, but actually in World War II the Nazis offered a million Jews in return for 10,000 trucks. Castro needed machinery badly to replace worn-out equipment; besides, Castro must have been delighted to present the United States with an equation that made machines as valuable as human lives.

As might be expected, there was mixed reaction from the citizens of the United States. On the one hand, Senator Homer Capeheart expressed the feeling of many Americans when he said during a debate, "When, oh when will we stop being blackmailed by Castro?" President Kennedy, however, indicated that he felt a contribution to the Tractors for Freedom fund, as it was called, was "every bit as charitable an act as a donation to CARE." The government itself refused to get involved directly in raising the necessary money for the tractors; this was handled by a special committee headed by citizens such as Walter Reuther, head of the United Auto Workers, Dr. Milton Eisenhower, and Eleanor Roosevelt. Although the Tractors for Freedom idea was not terribly popular in the country, the money was raised and the U.S. State Department agreed to the trade on "humanitarian" grounds.

Twenty years have passed since that 1961 Bay of Pigs invasion, but Castro continues, as Jack Watson, White House aide, puts it, to use "people as bullets aimed at this country." Things have not gone well for Castro's Cuba in these twenty years, in spite of all his efforts. Crops have not been good; world trade has not been as rewarding as expected due to economic sanctions imposed by the U.S., and Castro continues to have difficulties developing and maintaining the resources of his country while meeting the needs of his people. Apparently, unknown to the U.S., Castro decided to use the Americans once again to ease some of his problems.

Newsweek once again provided evidence of this use. The May 26, 1980, issue carries an article titled "Carter and the Cuban Influx," which offers yet another account of Castro's using human bodies to humiliate the U.S. Shortly after Congress passed the Refugee Act of 1980, Castro began to allow selected Cubans to emigrate to the U.S. Slowly a trickle of elite Cubans began flowing into Florida ports; then a second wave of Cuban immigrants flooded the Florida beaches; in one day 9,000 refugees arrived. The second wave was followed by one of hardened criminals and mental patients that Castro had flushed out of the dark corners of cells. Before the U.S. could realize the size of the immigration, the numbers of Cuban refugees had risen to over 60,000 and the American government once again had to rush to meet this new embarrassment.

Just as with the Tractors for Freedom movement, dealing with the Cuban refugees caused strong public reaction. Part of the problem stemmed from the wording of the Refugee Act itself, which defined refugees as people "unable to or unwilling to return to their homeland." Most of the Cubans arriving in the U.S. were viewed as undocumented aliens seeking asylum. Florida was caught in the middle of the problem because much of Florida's population around Miami is of Cuban descent and many of the refugees were members of their families who had taken this opportunity to get out of Cuba and join their relatives in the U.S.

The government attempted to stop the flow of refugees by fining any private boat owners who were caught transporting Cubans and by impounding as many boats as possible. Recognized criminals from Cuba were placed in a special camp to await deportation back to Cuba. Castro, of course, was quite willing to stop the refugee flood if the U.S. would give him what he wanted. This time no tractors were involved; instead he wanted the U.S. to give up its military base in Guantánamo Bay, lift economic sanctions against Cuba, and stop high-altitude intelligence-gathering flights over his country. The diplomatic struggle between President Carter and Fidel Castro continued, with the U.S. actually on the losing side.

The U.S. had to accept the refugees, or so it thought, to maintain its image of a humanitarian society in the eyes of the world. Castro, on the other hand, had little to lose and much to gain. Although he might not get all he asked for, in the process he reduced the overcrowding in his country, relieved the population in the jails and mental hospitals, and rid his country of "undesirable elements." He even convinced many Cubans who stayed behind that those who left were traitors and therefore the country was better off without them.

The Cuban situation should have been resolved more than twenty years ago. The inevitable confrontation repeatedly has been postponed and Cuba remains a large black spot on the map of America's foreign policy as a result. One might think that the U.S. would have learned from the repeated lessons taught by Castro's Cuba, but the Iranian hostage crisis of 1980 suggests that we haven't. While we fumble for answers, other countries have been watching Castro and getting free lessons on how to make a big nation look rather foolish. Dare we hope that before another twenty years passes we will have learned our lesson?

The Fight for Integration

On the first day of school in September 1957, the streets surrounding Central High were lined with hundreds of armed Arkansas Guardsmen. Their objective was to keep nine Negro children from entering the Little Rock school. This was the scene described in the September 16, 1957, Newsweek. The Guardsmen were there at the request of Arkansas Governor Orval Faubus, who was acting in open defiance of a federal court ruling of 1954 that called for an end to segregation in schools.

In a few days, Governor Faubus had left President Eisenhower with no choice but to federalize the Arkansas Guard, creating a new crisis. Where did federal authority end and where did states' rights begin? The nation was divided and there was talk of forming a third political party, the "Dixiecrats," who would take a segregation stand. Some criticized Governor Faubus's action; A. B. (Happy) Chandler of Kentucky pointed out that Kentucky was eighty percent integrated and said, "We're not allowing anyone to use force to stop anyone from going to school." Others felt President Eisenhower was acting as a dictator by using federal troops to force integration.

The South's tightly knit society was being torn apart. The people of the South opposed integration for deep-seated reasons. They felt the southern Negro, at this time, was simply inferior, that integration would upset their traditional way of life and lower their children's morals, and that it would lead to intermarriages.

Though it was now clear that the Supreme Court decision would stand and integration would proceed, there were still seven states in which no steps had been taken toward desegregation. The people of these southern states were ready to completely abolish their public school system if desegregation was forced upon them. Only in Kentucky and Maryland, where integration had a strong foothold, did people appear to be resigned to the idea of mixed races in classes together. Some still did not like the idea, but the general consensus seemed to be that it was working out better than had been expected.

Twenty-three years later, the September 15, 1980, *Newsweek* had a much happier story to tell of the first day of school at Cleveland High in St. Louis. The entire Cleveland High football team was in full uniform, standing in front of the school to welcome six hundred black students who were integrating the once almost all-white school. Across town, at Soldan High, which went from ninety-nine percent black to only thirty-nine percent black in 1979, students and neighborhood residents handed new white students ribbons that read: "Let's make it work."

The difference here is that these children are not only attending racially mixed schools, they are being bused into alien neighborhoods as courts try to cure decades of intentional, illegal segregation. Almost one-third of the blacks in large northern states still attend all-black schools. In many of these states, the cities are virtually all black and the suburbs are all white. Since the Supreme Court ruling on busing does not include areas of the states outside of the cities, busing cannot guarantee complete integration, and many city school systems will continue to be dominated by minority students. Cities such as Houston, Boston, and Milwaukee, however, are trying out "magnet schools," offering special music and academic programs to attract white children to city schools.

In schools where segregation has proved to be intentional, the federal government has appointed integration czars, or desegregation administrators. One such administrator, Donald Waldrip of Cincinnati, says, "I think people are tired of fighting and want solutions." Evidently some people don't want solutions very badly; Waldrip is protected by a twenty-four-hour armed guard.

Many resentful parents feel the money spent on gasoline to bus children miles out of their own neighborhoods would be better spent on books. Some just pull their children out of the public schools. Private schools were in a decline ten years ago, but according to *Newsweek* private school enrollment has increased sixty percent since busing began.

Overall, the case of school desegregation in 1980 is light-years away from 1957 and the story of Little Rock. According to recent statistics, the South is now better integrated than anywhere else in the country. Integration has shown itself to be harmless at worst, and often beneficial. The general conclusion is that black children have made an educational gain from integration and white children have not suffered.

Although federal laws have brought about the acceptance of integration in schools, it is still largely a resentful acceptance. Many people still believe that blacks have no business in white schools. This is not a matter of sense, morals, or reasoning as much as it is an attitude. Perhaps with desegregation working for them, the next generation will see past their parents' prejudices. But perhaps fifteen-year-old Elizabeth Eckford, a black child trying to enter a Little Rock school, said it best, "The best things in life are never easy."

CHAPTER 10

How Do You Analyze and Respond?

With few exceptions, your writing so far has come from familiar sources—your personal experiences and observations. But you're undoubtedly aware that much writing, especially in college, focuses on responses to someone else's ideas. Hence, being able to read, analyze, and respond effectively are valuable skills. For that reason, in this chapter you will develop procedures for analyzing something you read and for responding to it in writing.

At this point the thought of book reports may flash across your mind. But we will move beyond the mere summary of plot, character, and theme to emphasize two aspects: your personal response to readings and your analysis of writers' purposes and techniques. You might be wondering why all of this is so important. Reading without involvement is like watching rain running down the outside of a window—you see the words, or drops, but you're not in touch with them. The only way reading will stay with you and have some effect on your thinking is if you react to it actively. By responding actively, you begin to understand what the words mean, what you believe and disbelieve, what's really important to you and what is not. Sometimes, in fact, you may find yourself caught up in your reading, fascinated by what is unfolding in front of you, not able to wait for what may appear on the next page.

Involvement with reading doesn't always come easily. Frequently you have to work at this involvement before the message begins to have any impact. As you begin to read an assignment, for example, you may have little idea of what lies ahead; here and there as you proceed, a glimmer of an idea or response may surface, but it may be quickly forgotten as you turn the page. Other concerns may interfere, like the desire for a cup of coffee or a walk outside with a favorite person. If you make no conscious effort to sort out what you read and how it relates to you, ideas from reading quickly fade away. Later you have only faint memories of the reading and can usually only characterize it as somewhat interesting or dull.

What this boils down to, then, is the necessity for understanding that reading is not a passive process—it's a reactive one. You may claim boredom when reading, but true boredom comes only when you are reading something you already know too well; fake boredom comes when you're simply too lazy to figure out the new meanings of ideas and facts you may not have encountered before. The mind often backs away from new and unusual challenges. The solution for real boredom is to find something more advanced that will challenge you; the cure for fake boredom is to become fully and personally involved with what you are reading. That's where reading and writing can come together to work for your advantage.

REACTING TO WHAT YOU READ

To begin sorting out your initial reactions to reading, you need to talk or write. The difficulty is finding someone who is not quick to condemn your first ideas and gropings for understanding about what you're reading. At first you might doubt that you have anything to say or that it might be correct or appropriate. Sometimes a friend will hear you out, or someone who is studying the same material may want to test his or her ideas too. But this kind of response is not always available every time you read, so it's necessary to look for some other way to capture these reactions.

Marginal Annotation

Because even your best friends leave you alone now and then, a useful practice while you're reading is to write down your thoughts, reactions, observations, and questions as they occur—right next to the sections that touch off the responses. At first you may have some difficulty doing this, since most people have been cautioned repeatedly not to write in books. If the book is yours—not the library's or a friend's—there should be no reason for holding back. Once you've overcome this barrier, you should find that, with little difficulty, you'll begin to talk back to the writer. Actually this practice is only one step beyond what many students already do—highlight certain passages with colors or underlining. The only difficulty with the color coding and underlining is that all you've done is mark a passage, not respond to it or interpret it; when you return later to that passage, you probably will have to read it again because you have no idea why you thought it was significant. Written comments called *marginal annotations* relieve you of that problem; by glancing at the annotations, you'll know what you liked, what you didn't, or why you thought something was important or ridiculous.

When you start to read, you may have several different purposes in mind. You may want to read strictly for the information and how you respond to it, for example. This will mean that some of your comments in the margins will be designed to help you understand the meaning of the text and others will indicate your own impressions, associations, and evaluations. Another reason for reading can be to understand authors' purposes and techniques—how writers achieve what they do. In all cases, there's no particular rule to follow; some readers like to put certain types of comments in one margin, other types of comments in another margin and still other comments in the third or fourth margin; some pages will be covered with your responses, others may have little. For the most part, no one will see these annotations except you. Think of them as being another form of prewriting—you're exploring the territory to see what may be there. In that sense, no comment is too foolish or too serious. Go ahead and express your feelings. If you want to disagree with the writer—do so! If you want to use question marks and exclamation points—why not? Any type of phrase, mark, or sign that conveys your response—and that you will understand later—is appropriate. Here are some possible types of comments you might use:

> *Marks of approval or disapproval:* !!!, ???, **, Yes, No, Insane, How true, Exactly, Rubbish
>
> *Disagreement:* That's not so because. . . . I've never heard of. . . . If that's so, how do you account for. . . ?
>
> *Exceptions:* May work except for. . . .
>
> *Extensions:* This would apply to . . . as well.
>
> *Personal connections:* Reminds me of Uncle Luke. I did that the other day.
>
> *Other connections:* Prof. talked about this in class last week. Read an essay on this in . . . check to see if it agrees.

Once you're accustomed to thinking out loud on paper through marginal annotation, you'll wonder why you never did it before. You'll also discover quickly an approach that seems most comfortable for you but that may vary somewhat depending upon the kind of material and the purpose of your reading. In the following sample of marginal annotation, notice the questions and the personal flavor of the responses.

I like this word—describes situation perfectly

The rapid and startling changes rocking our society today force the classroom teacher to face the fact that her words are not necessarily wisdom, and that, in fact, even if they are wisdom at the moment they are uttered, they may be obsolete the next moment. The student has every right to mistrust the generalizations delivered in the classroom unless she or he had the opportunity to test their correctness against the real world. This means that the student must have an opportunity to become what William Boyer calls "a causal agent in historical change." Only by attempting to make change in the social and physical environment around him can the student test the accuracy and relevance of what the school proclaims as knowledge.

true – we can't seem to keep up

do you call this "real learning" then?

pompous quote

who's he?

how will teachers & principals react to this idea?

It is the task of the teacher to help give students the tools and attitudes that will help them and us survive in the midst of a historical transformation. There is a need, too, for positive images of the future. People need to feel they can cope, and the place to start that feeling is in the schools.

right – but what are the tools and attitudes?

everyone seems to use this word – does it mean merely survive?

—Priscilla P. Griffith, "Teaching the Twenty-First Century in a Twentieth Century High School"

This kind of personal response is the first step toward making reading more useful to you as a reader and as a writer. Before you begin to look at other aspects of a piece of writing, you must understand what the material is about. But there comes a time when you must react not only to the content of a piece of writing but also to the author's purpose and technique.

Identifying the Purpose

Everything you read has some purpose that helped create the words on the paper. As you have discovered, the more control and understanding a writer has of the purpose of a piece of writing, the more fully developed will be the design of that purpose in the writing. The reader, of course, has to determine this design and the purpose that led to it. With an awareness of this, the reader can then determine to what extent the writer was or was not successful.

Purposes vary. A fiction writer may simply want to entertain; a reporter may want to present the facts about a situation; a letter writer may want to offer his or her side of the story for our sympathy and understanding. Most writing is not highly manipulative. Instead, the writers let us know what they expect of us and, as readers, we can then comply or not as we wish. If we were to put together a catalogue of purposes for writing, it would be rather extensive, but here are a few of the most frequently used.

Research
To present the results of experiments, recent information, and new findings
To offer new interpretations, ideas
To gather together all that is currently known on a subject to see how it fits together and to reach some new conclusions
To show how one field of study relates to another.

Sharing with a Wide Audience
To satisfy curiosity
To offer practical information for everyday application
To introduce a new area of knowledge
To offer instruction about the latest material, skills, or techniques

Conducting Business and Government
To report information needed for making decisions
To argue for certain positions or regulations
To sell, advertise
To form laws, regulations, and guidelines

Supporting a Community of Shared Beliefs
To state one's beliefs; take a stand
To encourage and reflect the beliefs of a certain group
To share developments of common concern
To gain acceptance of one's beliefs in a wider community
To recruit active support

Promoting Public Action
To raise questions
To criticize the actions of others
To persuade to act
To inform about issues of concern

Providing Entertainment
To offer amusement
To arouse emotions and sympathies
To stimulate imagination and fantasy

Naturally, when you start to read something, there's little chance that the author will be right there to tell you what he or she intended to do in the piece. Instead, you have to rely on certain clues and information in the writing. The signals are not usually hard to find.

Direct statements. Some authors simply tell at the beginning of a piece what their intentions are. Titles, for instance, often provide useful clues: "How to . . . ," "The Case for (or Against) . . . ," "A Report on. . . ." In rather formal books—and in many textbooks—the writers will indicate in their introductions what their purpose is.

Indirect clues. Even if the writer chooses not to tell directly what the purpose of a piece is, you can examine some indirect clues and come up with useful information. When was the work published, by whom, and where? Answers to these questions will give you a sense of the particular conditions in existence at the time the article or book was written, and the name of the publisher will give you a clue about the audience for which the piece was originally written. An article that appeared in a general-circulation magazine, for example, probably was designed for the nonspecialist. You can even determine to some extent the relative level of education of the audience: magazines like *Harper's*, *The Atlantic*, and *Saturday Review*, although general-circulation magazines have an audience predominantly of college graduates, many with advanced degrees; *Time, Newsweek,* and *Reader's Digest* may have some of those people in their audience, but they also have many people with a high school education. This does not mean that a piece that appears in one magazine is necessarily better or worse than that in another; the source of publication simply provides us with some sense of the way an author might have viewed the audience and of his or her particular purpose in writing for that group.

In the same way, knowledge about the author may be helpful, although not always entirely reliable. A certain writer may be associated primarily with a certain type of writing—but writers can switch, of course, and write on many things and in many ways. Still, if a writer is known to be a supporter of some cause, any writing on that subject probably reflects that support. Articles and books by famous people more often than not are devoted to some kind of image building, such as a Mr. Universe writing about a certain kind of diet or body-building program. Scholars may attempt to build a case for a particular interpretation of their work. So some awareness of the background of the author can help, but you should not rely on it exclusively as an indicator of purpose.

ANALYSIS/RESPONSE: A SAMPLE

All of the techniques mentioned so far are ways to accumulate a better understanding of what you read and to produce something to say about your reading. But the single best way to determine a writer's purpose is careful reading and analysis of what appears in the article or book. Because a writer's purpose reveals itself in the way words are combined, the writer's technique appears in every word and sentence, as well as in every paragraph. To understand the technique and purpose of a writer, therefore, you have to bring together everything you know about reading and writing. As a result of the work you have done in this course, you should have a good understanding of how a writer constructs an effective piece of writing, but in this assignment you will need to draw on not only that information but also everything else you may have learned previously about reading and your own writing.

Because you're bringing together a number of skills for this assignment, some preliminary practice won't hurt. The following essay, "Surveyor in the Woods," is well suited to this assignment. Use the following procedure as a warm-up for your own reading.

Step 1: Read through the entire essay at least once, disregarding the questions in the margin.

Step 2: Reread the essay, slowly this time, focusing your attention on the writer's technique. Use the marginal questions as a guide and, wherever possible, jot down your answers in the margins. (This practice will be useful later in your own annotations.)

Step 3: Discuss your responses and perceptions with your classmates, referring to your notes.

Your class discussion will help you identify areas where your skills in analysis worked well and other areas where you need to be more alert in your reading. Go back to those questions and sections of the essay that seemed to give you the most difficulty; analyze what happened and see if you can work out a way that will make it easier in the future to deal with such problems.

Surveyor in the Woods
by Kenneth Andler

1   I want to tell you about a woodsman, what he was like, what his work was, and what it meant. His name was Alfred D. Teare

1 What does the writer promise to deliver in this essay? As a reader how do you like this

and he came originally from Nova Scotia, but all the time I knew him his home was in Berlin, New Hampshire. Probably the best surveyor of old lines in New England, he was—in his way—a genius.

2 I saw him for the first time when I was a boy of twelve; he was visiting my stepfather, a lawyer, who was then engaged in litigation involving boundary lines. Mr. Teare, a wonderful storyteller, held our family entranced with his tales of the woods. He conjured up a marvelous land of mountains, rivers, and lakes, peopled it with lumberjacks, rivermen, timber cruisers, Maine guides, and plenty of bears and moose for good measure. Just the expression "the Maine woods," as he used it, tingled along my spine. He visited our house several times after that and always brought my stepfather a bundle of pipe-lighters, little sticks about a foot long, taken from the roots of an old-growth pine windfall, for use with an open fire. They smelled good; they had the woods in them as a sea shell has the roar of the sea.

3 The summer I was fourteen, in 1918, I had a chance to work as a chainer for Mr. Teare, who then was running lines near Reading and Plymouth, Vermont; and I spent several seasons with him thereafter.

4 At the time he was nearing sixty years of age. Over average height in spite of a pronounced stoop to his shoulders and quite heavily set, he appeared to be coming at you aggressively with his head lowered like a buffalo. Although his back was quite bent he had powerful arms and shoulders, and somehow he seemed stronger that way than if he had been erect, particularly when he carried an enormous pack by means of a tumpline.

5 He had a forceful, weatherbeaten, almost leathery face; a dewlap like a bulldog's; a bald pate bounded by a horseshoe of black hair turning gray; blue eyes, and short, strong, even teeth with spaces between them. One of the curious little tricks he delighted in, when occasion required, was biting a fish

kind of introduction? How does the writer make you aware of the most important point to be made in the essay?

2 What does the writer accomplish in this paragraph? From the way the writer explains "pipe-lighters," what do you think is his understanding of the audience for this essay?

3 Of what value to the reader is the information in this paragraph?

4, 5 What does the writer attempt to accomplish in these paragraphs? How successful is he? Why is the detail about the mosquito included?

line in two with hardly more than one snap. His hands, remarkably square with large blunt fingers, were tough and work-hardened with skin like brown leather. A mosquito never could drill through this hide of his, and often, when one tried, Mr. Teare would watch it with a tolerant amusement until it staggered off bewildered.

6   He took a peculiar pride in his eyesight; but he must have been farsighted like many outdoor men, for he had a sturdy pair of glasses which hung from a fish line about his neck and nestled snugly under his shirt in the abundant hair on his chest. To use them, he always hauled them up through his open shirt, and taking them by one end with his blunt fingers, perched them on his nose. He had the characteristic habit of always sitting on his left foot, his left leg bent under him, his right leg out straight. He was nimble enough to do this as long as he lived and it provided him a cushion of sorts on ground no matter how cold or wet. When he made his survey notes he would seat himself thus, affix his glasses with a kind of clumsy ease and write laboriously in a red-covered notebook with a hard smudgeless drawing pencil which seemed lost in his great, rough paw.

6 How is this paragraph an example of "showing, not telling," readers?

7   Summer or winter he always wore heavy woolen socks, and in summer, ankle-height moccasins, half-soled and hobnailed (really the best footgear imaginable), trousers of heavy khaki, a faded blue denim work shirt, and a slouch hat. He never would wear corduroy as he said corduroy gets wet two weeks before a rain.

7, 8 Why are the details about clothing and language included? How effective is the paragraph hook connecting these two paragraphs? Why does the writer use the parentheses in paragraph 7?

8   Of Scottish descent and old-fashioned in manner, he used rare and almost obsolete expressions seldom if ever heard nowadays. He used "gran'sir" for "grandfather," spoke of building up a good fire "against the night," and was the only person I ever heard use the archaic "an" for "if." One favorite expression he coined himself, I believe: of an honest man he would say, "He's as square as ninety degrees."

9   Of course, he reeked with ordinary woods lore. He pointed out to me what a widow-maker was: the dead top of a tree which would come crashing down when an axeman started to cut at the base. A fool-killer, equally dangerous, was a live tree bent over by a fallen one so that when an unwary chopper drove an axe into it the tremendous tension, suddenly released, sent the tree splitting and charging up to catch him under the chin. A smudge of brakes warded off mosquitoes, of course, but it was news to me that only a bright fire would stop midges or "no-see-ums," for they'd fly right into it. Nothing in the world could stop an onslaught of black flies while we were at work on the line, although the best protection was a smudge pot and smearing our faces and hands with tobacco juice. Mr. Teare advised these things for our sakes; insects didn't irritate him. When we got soaked from a sudden shower, as we often did, and came tramping back to camp through water-laden brush, Mr. Teare said we wouldn't catch cold if we let our clothes dry on us. We always took his advice and slogged around camp like saturated dishrags while we built up a fire, but we never did catch cold from our wettings.

9 Why does the writer say "Of course, he reeked . . ."? What has the writer assumed about his audience? Is he correct? What other assumptions about audience has the author made in this paragraph? Were they safe to make in your case? How would you describe the kind of information Teare possesses?

10   He was ingenious to a degree and a wizard with an axe. When a tree became lodged, he employed what he called a "Samson Pole" to make it fall in a different direction. This was a strong pole which he held upright, in a notch of which another strong pole fitted, running as a cross bar to a notch in the recalcitrant tree, and with this device he could exert a tremendous leverage. If an axe handle got cracked he fixed it by binding a fish line tightly about it in a manner few could duplicate. He always had in camp an awl with waxed ends with which he could sew up his moccasins, and if he was far enough back in the woods and the need arose, he would tap them, sometimes using bark for leather.

10 How is this paragraph related to the previous one? What technique does Andler use here that he has used in previous paragraphs?

11   He was full of lore and ideas of his own concerning the curative properties of herbs. For bronchial trouble he advised the sticky gum which exudes from cherry trees. Balsam blisters were also good. If he had a bad enough cough he mixed up a mysterious concoction which someone called "spruce gum and blue vitriol," and he downed it with a bear-like roar of distaste. When I cut my fingers deeply near the knuckles with an axe he rushed to my side where I was leaning against a tree, faint from loss of blood in July heat, and mopping up the gash with a handkerchief, he told me to wiggle my fingers. They wiggled; he could see the cords move, and he acted relieved. Then he took his plug of tobacco, chewed up a piece to a soft cud and placed it in the gash. He bound up my fingers with a splint and a handkerchief to keep in the tobacco. No infection set in thanks to the nicotine, and although some stitches would have been a good idea, none were taken. The cut healed perfectly, though I shall always bear the scar.

11 Why does Andler use the word *lore* in the opening sentence? Where else in the essay have you heard this word? Is there any connection? What does the account about the axe incident do for us as readers besides show us Teare as a man of action?

12   His medicinal theories carried more weight with me when I learned that many years before, when a doctor had given him six months to live because of his weakened and, I gathered, consumptive condition, he had struck out for the woods where he slept on the ground and gulped a prodigious number of raw eggs every day. He came out of it all right and throughout the rest of his years was as rugged as an old gnarled oak.

12 Why do you suppose Andler waits until this point to present this information about Teare? Why does Andler use the comparison "rugged as an old gnarled oak"? How effective is it? What is your response to Alfred Teare and to Andler's presentation of him up to this point?

II

13   He was not by any means simply a backwoodsman. He had traveled extensively throughout the United States; his work brought him into contact with the executives of large companies; but most of his life he spent in the woods. They were really home to him although he had a conventional home, a remarkable wife, and five grownup children.

13 What connection is made between Part I and Part II? Why is it done this way? How does this second part of the essay relate to the purpose of the essay announced in the introduction? Why is the information about travel and home life presented here? Is this effective?

14   While I worked with him we usually camped out in a lean-to tent, open on one side, and before this side we built with huge flat rocks a fireplace in which on chilly nights we kept a fire of four foot wood. Sometimes we threw into the fire great pieces of punk, a fungus black on the outside, reddish within, which grows in nubs on old birch trees, and then we'd have coals for the morning. We made our bed on the ground from the tips of fir branches, set upright very close together and then pushed backward at an angle.

15   At the opening of the tent we had a bench made from saplings, or from a board if we had one, which Mr. Teare called the "deacon seat." Sometimes where a tent would be a nuisance and we weren't going to stay long we built a bark lean-to, and often we reveled luxuriously in deserted and almost ruined farmhouses.

16   Although the company furnished us a cook one summer in Vermont when we had two timber cruisers with us, almost all the time I was with him, Mr. Teare did the cooking. He was very good at it, too. When we got in from work he would don a white apron (at least it had been white originally), mix up a batch of biscuits on a table of saplings covered with birch bark, put them in his little tin baker which faced the open fire, fry some meat, turn out a rice pudding to which we helpers contributed raspberries or blueberries in season, brew tea, and in no time produce an excellent meal. He delighted in baking beans in the ground, fried excellent doughnuts and a somewhat similar product which he called "doughgods."

17   We always carried our lunch for the noon meal together with a nest of metal cups and a tin tea pail. Invariably we would stop by a spring or brook and build a fire. Mr. Teare would sit on his left foot, hunched forward and intent, holding the pail over the fire on a long pole, and he never paid the slightest attention if the smoke engulfed him. When the water boiled, he would swing the

14, 15 What seems to be the focus of these paragraphs? How can you tell?

16 Why does the reader need to know about Teare's cooking skills?

17,18 What does the word *invariably* in paragraph 17 suggest about Teare? What words in paragraph 18 remind us of *invariably*? Why does Andler use this technique? How did you feel reading the first sentence of paragraph 18? What is unusual about its construc-

pail out for one of us to toss in a handful of good black tea, and then he'd swing it back over the fire for a momentary re-boiling in the interest of strength and power. Our pail had seen so much service that merely boiling water in it produced stronger tea than most people would care to drink.

18   After lunch Mr. Teare would get out his long-bladed jackknife, pare off some shavings from his strong plug tobacco, and with the knife still held, blade upright, between thumb and forefinger of his right hand (lest more paring be necessary) he'd work the tobacco with a semicircular motion, between the palms of his hands—grist between millstones—then fill and light his pipe. He never, never used a match for this purpose if a fire was going, principally, I think, because he regarded matches in the woods as precious. He always took a brand from the fire, blew on it prodigiously to bring it to a bright coal, and lighted up with that. Often he would have only embers to choose from and these too he used, holding one somehow in his tough paw. He would press the ignited tobacco down with an impervious thumb and then, when the smoke rolled out, he would settle back to spellbind us with some yarn. The whole business of the noon meal was a never-varied rite.

19   He worked summer and winter on every passably workable day. In the winter, if camping out, he used a square tent with a stove in it. He wore ordinary snowshoes for fairly level country but bearpaws for rough and hilly terrain. As our lunch always froze we toasted our sandwiches over the fire. When Mr. Teare knocked the icy clods from his snowshoes, stood them up in the snow, and hunched over to start a fire with birch bark and dry sticks, he seemed as integral a part of winter in the woods as the snow upon the ground.

20   Sometimes he would stay at farmhouses instead of camping out. During the last forty years of his life, he worked mostly for such

tion? Why might it be constructed this way?

19 What key element about Teare already emphasized earlier appears in this paragraph? Why does Andler repeat it here?

20 Why is this information offered?

large corporations as the International Paper Company, the Mt. Tom Sulphite & Pulp Company, the Draper Corporation, the Brown Company and others. He traveled extensively through the back country of northern New England and stayed at literally hundreds of isolated farmhouses, using them either to work from directly or as bases from which he could pack his "wangan" into the woods for a camp. Lonely farm families whose homes he had previously visited looked forward eagerly to his coming, for he brought to their routine existence an inexhaustible store of adventure tales and to their drab lives a fresh and lively color.

III

21   The problem of surveying in the timberland of northern New England is one of the most difficult and fascinating things in the world. It's difficult because it consists largely of relocating the old lines of original lots and ranges run by pioneers with crude compasses as much as one hundred and seventy-five years ago. The early surveyors blazed or spotted the trees along these lines, and for corners set posts, marked trees, or piled up stones. They also blazed trees about the corners for "witnesses." Succeeding surveyors have respotted the lines infrequently, perhaps not oftener than once in twenty years, and in many instances the original lines have not been renewed at all.

21 How does the opening sentence of this paragraph relate to the essay's introduction? Are the Roman numerals helpful or distracting to you as a reader?

22   When a tree is spotted with an axe the wood grows over the blaze in a few years and leaves nothing on the bark but a scar which only an experienced woodsman can recognize. A novice either notices no spot at all or thinks that every scar he sees is a spot whether it's a hedgehog mark, a windgall, or just a natural blemish.

22–24 What is the purpose of this information? What feeling do you think the writer wants you to have about paragraph 23? How do you know? What connection does the feeling have to the purpose of the essay?

23   The original lots, laid out by the proprietors of each township, classified by number in ranges and divisions, usually contained about one hundred acres each and were described quite accurately and specifically by

the early surveyors, who gave points of compass and definite distances in the title deeds;
but as these lots were either split up or amal-
gamated with other lots, people grew very
careless when conveying real estate, and fell
into the habit of bounding land by the names
of the adjoining owners, as in the classic example Mr. Teare used to quote from a Vermont deed: "Bounded on the North by
Brother Jim, on the West by Brother Bill, on
the South by Sister Sal, and on the East by
Mother."

24   With the migration of farmers to the
West, or to the cities, immense areas of rural
farm land reverted to the wilderness. Even
many New Englanders do not realize how far
this went and how extensively the forests
have crept in over once-tilled fields. We have
seen sites of villages silent in the woods,
crumbling cellar holes through which great
trees are growing, once proud highways
which are now only dim trails, and even a
graveyard in Vermont from which three crops
of pulp wood have been cut. Gone are the
people who owned these farms, their most
lasting works faded like old ink, their names
nothing but an echo in the land records.

25   Consequently, in these abandoned dis-
tricts, now merely a wilderness, a reference
in an old deed such as "bounded on the
North by land of Abijah Davis," which may
have been perfectly plain to the contracting
parties in 1860, means very little now. A surveyor must trace the title deeds in the regis-
try, draw tentative diagrams and fit them together like a jigsaw puzzle, and somehow or
other get the chain of title back to the older
deeds where references to compass courses
and distances provide something definite to
work on. By this research one may discover
that Abijah Davis owned Lot Number 2 in the
3rd Range and 1st Division and that the line
in question was originally "North 85° East 88
Rods and 17 Links."

26   To his task Mr. Teare brought very peculiar educational equipment. He never went
beyond the seventh grade in school as he had

26 Why is the information
about Teare's educational
background provided?

to leave and go to work, but in his early years he had followed the sea and had become skipper of a three-masted schooner, and thus he had learned navigation.

27   As a surveyor he brought this navigation inland. It was really dead reckoning on land. A college-trained engineer would have thought his methods rule of thumb, but where such an engineer would have seen only woods, Mr. Teare could read them like an open book. For instance, he would go up to some old spruce on which, once he'd pointed it out, you could see a small scar, then taking an axe he'd swing with great true blows; and as large flying chips began to litter the ground he would lay open the white flesh of the tree in a larger and larger gash. After a while he would begin to strike more slowly and carefully, now and then peering into the opening, until finally he had disclosed an old blaze, black and flat with the original axe-marks in it.

27 How is the connection made between paragraphs 26 and 27? How effective is it?

28   Then he would fish up his glasses from his shirt and holding them to his eyes would count the annual rings of growth. More than once I have seen him cut out spots made more than a hundred years before, and he once found spots on the old Masonian curved line, run in 1751 by Joseph Blanchard—the first line surveyed in New Hampshire. Mr. Teare had a spiritual affinity with the pioneer surveyors. He saw at a glance what they'd done, what they meant by their marks. He would sometimes look at a spot which definitely had been made with an axe, glance around and growl: "Not a line, just a trapper's trail."

28 Why is the detail about the glasses brought up? Is this the first time this detail is used?

29   He could follow not only the original spotted lines but the "lines of occupancy" as well, such as the trail of an old brush fence, all obvious remnants of which had disappeared at least twenty-five years before. This he would do by noting the crooked growth of trees here and there along its course, or a stretch of hazel bushes (which are likely to grow up along the remains of a brush fence),

29 How does the material in this paragraph support Andler's original purpose?

or piles of moss-covered stones in which fence posts had once been set. Whenever Mr. Teare, scattering the leaf mould near one of these stone heaps, uncovered a split ash rail, he would pick it up and fondle it lovingly. "They never rot," he would say with a solid approval of the wood itself and of the pioneer farmer who had taken pains to use it.

30   For equipment he used an open-sight compass with about a five-inch needle. There was no telescope on it but sight vanes instead with slits in them, and this compass rested not on a tripod, which would be too awkward in the woods, but rather on a single staff called a "Jacob staff." That was the kind of compass George Washington and Abraham Lincoln used when they were land surveyors, but Mr. Teare's was considerably more accurate. He referred affectionately to his compass as "Mary Jane" and almost always called it an "instrument" instead of a "compass."

30, 31 Why is the reader offered this information? How helpful is it?

31   When I first went with him he used a Gunter's chain, two rods in length, but in later years a steel tape of the same length. The Gunter's chain is an actual chain with real links and it can be folded up instead of rolled. It is very durable; it can be used to help a man go down over steep ledges, and will perform a hundred and one odd jobs that it would be sacrilege to force on a tape, which couldn't do them anyhow. He never wanted a chain or tape longer than two rods because the ground he had to work on was so hilly and rough. Somehow or other the Gunter's chain seemed to fit him better than a tape.

32   This type of surveying, difficult and requiring an analytical mind as well as woodcraft, is a fascinating pursuit—a sort of treasure hunt for old lines and corners. The problem was posed more than a century ago by men who marked those lines and corners in the wilderness and left cryptic directions on how to find them. In deserted areas it is a search through a forest-buried civilization as

32 Is Andler speaking for himself or for Teare in this paragraph?

dead as the bottom layer of an Egyptian city. The fascination of it for Mr. Teare never left him.

33   I can see him now hunched over his compass while the needle settles on the proper course, then standing behind it and shouting directions to his axemen, while the two chainers bring up the rear. He is full of anticipation at what he may find at a given distance where he thinks a corner ought to be. He assiduously examines the trees alongside the line to see if he is following the old spotting, and now and then breaks into some rollicking song. His joy in living radiates around him.

33 How is this paragraph different from previous ones?

34   Mr. Teare's genius, true to the proverb, consisted largely in his capacity for taking infinite pains. He would always make sure of a starting point that could not be questioned. Once he ran twenty-four miles of trail line to locate one corner. Furthermore, he would never let an obstacle or a series of them block him. If a swamp were deep and cold he crossed it nevertheless. If towering cliffs barred his way he scaled them, if blown down trees strewed his path he slashed his way through, if a swollen river cut across a line he felled a tree for a bridge and kept on going. He was absolutely indomitable and he followed an old line as a hound follows a fox.

34 How is this paragraph connected to the introduction to the essay?

35   He hated to see the woods cut by the companies for which he was working, even though he well knew that timber like other crops must be harvested. Often people asked him what he considered the most beautiful thing he had seen and he always gave them the same reply—sunset over the Adirondacks and Lake Champlain, from Mt. Mansfield. He worked most of a lifetime in the woods of northern New England and in spite of hardships and privation he never lost his love for these wild and wooded hills, for the silence of the deep forest in winter, the splendor of the mountains in the winey tang of autumn days.

35 What contradiction is pointed out about Teare's work? Why does Andler do this?

36   The infinite variety of his daily scenes of activity pleased him. One day he might stand

36 Why is this information included?

among tall spruces high up on some mountain, sighting, far below, an isolated farmhouse on which he could take a "triangulation shot"; another day he might be following a hardwood ridge of beech and maple, or working in the bear-wallow sort of land that often lies atop a mountain, or following the stone walls of abandoned fields. Often he made a traverse survey of the great roaring brooks which come tumbling out of mountain ponds and cut their resounding way down deep ravines; he loved to drive a canoe across a lake or down a river through white water.

37   Often he would pause at the summit of some hill. Then with his Jacob staff, he would point out to us the mountains and hills as they rolled away into blue distance, calling them by name and referring to certain jobs he had done on each. He knew them all as a father knows his children.

IV

38   The thing that staggers me when I get to thinking about Mr. Teare is the stupendous amount of work he accomplished in his long career. He surveyed thousands upon thousands of acres in Maine, New Hampshire, and Vermont. And he did not work merely for a monthly pay check; a craftsman, he labored so that his work would endure.

39   Many if not most surveyors in timberlands leave few marks or monuments. Some of them figure that they'll soon be hired to resurvey the land if the lines become easily lost. Most make a half-hearted attempt to mark their lines and corners, but their work is like snow upon the desert, for the resurgent life in New England woods is almost tropical, as anyone knows who has tried to keep brush out of a field.

40   Mr. Teare, on the other hand, when he was sure a line was finally right—and if he was sure it was right, it *was*—would have the axemen blaze almost every tree along the whole line. One that stood exactly on line he'd spot on both sides, while a tree that

37 Why does the writer use the comparison in the last line?

38 How is this paragraph related to the essay's introduction?

39–43 What is the purpose of these paragraphs?

stood off a little way to one side or the other he'd blaze with "quarter spots," that is, blazes which were quartered on the bole, not centered, and these faced toward the line.

41   He made his blazes deep enough to take out a shaving of the wood, and they were large man-sized spots, not boy's work. Some foresters and engineers complained that every tree would die but Mr. Teare knew better and he was right. He knew one great primary truth: you can't mark a line in New England's fast-growing woods a bit too plain.

42   Iron rods are impractical to carry in the woods and also a menace to the compass, so for a corner he set a large wooden post, fashioned from a suitable tree nearby, hewn flat on three sides or four as circumstances demanded, sharpened at the bottom and topped at an angle for a "roof." He never pounded it into the ground as that would soften the top and let the rain in, but instead forced it in with its own weight. Around it he piled rocks. He stripped the bark off so it would last longer and with a timber scribe— a fascinating little instrument with which he could carve letters almost as fast as one can print on paper—he marked the names of the adjoining owners, the date, and his mark which was two parallel lines with a circle between them. He always said with a twinkle in his eye when he finished a corner and straightened up from piling stones, "There, that'll stand till Gabriel calls all good surveyors home."

43   About the corner he blazed witness trees in a circle facing the post and inscribed on them the date and his mark. These words, figures, and symbols, being only in the bark, never grow over. One could stand at a corner and, looking back into the woods, see the line stretching straight and true and well brushed out, its blazes shining new and startlingly clear. Few things give one quite the sense of accomplishment that this does—to go forth to a tract of land as nebulous in location as the scene of a fantasy, to find the old

lines and corners, and to leave them well marked and definite.

44   These lines of Mr. Teare's, reaching for hundreds of miles in the aggregate through the deep woods of northern New England, live on today as I can testify, for while working as a land surveyor myself and later while abstracting titles, I have followed many of them. One of the companies had Mr. Teare respot its lines at seven-year intervals and, of course, these are exceptionally plain. But I have followed easily, and without a compass, lines which he had established thirty-five years before and which had never been touched since. The wooden corner posts needed renewing, yes, but that was easily accomplished. One can follow his lines even through the areas devastated by the hurricane of September, 1938, where the blazed trees, no longer upright, lie in a tangled snarl upon the ground.

44, 45 What quality of Teare is emphasized?

45   In scores, even hundreds of towns in northern New England, his lines form a reliable basic network from which almost any survey of land in their general neighborhood would be started today. The local people, farmers, timber operators, and investors would no more think of questioning his lines than they would the law of gravitation. More than once when I have told some timber buyer that several lines of a proposed tract had been run by Mr. Teare I have seen his face light up—he knew that *those* boundaries would be distinct, at any rate. Quite often I have heard one of Mr. Teare's old friends use the expression, "Why it's as plain as one of Teare's lines."

46   Whenever I happen to come upon one of his corners now that he is gone and, in the solemn hush of the forest, see the post in its cairn standing there, the trees about it alive with dates of those years when we worked together, and with his mark and perhaps the initials of the old crew members, I feel an ineffable sadness not only because he is gone but because everything in those woods seems

46 What feeling comes through in this paragraph? How does the author sound? Is it the same as or different from previous paragraphs?

to inquire for him—and he would be enjoying himself so much if he were there.

47   But he did his work well and it survives
him. No more can a mortal really ask. His
lines are impressed into the living forest, his
corners stand in wooded solitudes silently
eloquent of his skill, and his witness trees
bear witness not only to them but to him.
Wherever he worked he brought order out of
confusion and established a lasting thing.

47 How effective is this last
paragraph? What is empha-
sized most?

ASSIGNMENT: WRITING AN ANALYSIS/RESPONSE ESSAY

The only way to understand technique and purpose is by analyzing
individual pieces of writing. You've been doing this partially in your
responses to your own and your classmates' drafts throughout the
assignments in this course. Now you are going to approach a piece of
writing with the specific assignment of thoroughly analyzing technique
and purpose.

Purpose

Your own purpose in this assignment will be twofold:

1. To show how the writer has put together the piece of writing and to
   comment on the effectiveness or ineffectiveness of the technique.
2. To express the impact the essay had on you as a reader: how the
   subject matter may or may not relate to your own life and to the
   lives of others.

To do this, you will select an essay—one in this chapter, one from
another chapter in the text, one of your own selection, or one desig-
nated by your instructor—and develop an analysis/response essay.

Audience

You will need to make some decisions about an audience for your
analysis/response. Will your audience have had access to the piece of
writing you select to analyze? If so, then you will be writing to relatively
well informed readers. If you assume the majority of your audience has

not seen the piece you will analyze, then you'll have to keep that in mind and provide the necessary information so they will understand what you are referring to in your analysis.

Prewriting

Locate an essay that you have some interest in reading. Two sample essays, "Surveying the Wilderness" by Donald Hall and "Shoot-out at the Red Horse Barn" by John O'Dell, appear at the end of this chapter for possible use in the assignment. You may want to select one of the essays that appear elsewhere in the text or, with your instructor's permission, you may want to work with a reading assignment from another course.

First Reading

If possible, before reading your selected essay, number the paragraphs for later reference. Refer to the sample marginal annotation on page 189 and, if you wish, reread the section on annotation in which it appears before starting to read. Then read the essay you have chosen and record your reactions to the content. Make your comments as direct as you can and as extensive as possible; these comments are simply working notes, nothing more.

When you finish this first annotation, look over your comments and group them into categories. Some simply may be questions you have about the material—list those together. Other comments may have to do with personal associations—you remembered something in your own life or in other readings that agrees or disagrees with what the author says—list those items together, remembering to indicate by paragraph number where in the essay they occurred.

Second Reading

The second reading—or perhaps it will be the third or fourth since you may want to read the essay several times to feel fully familiar with its content and style—should be devoted to observing the writer's technique and purpose. You may have already recorded some preliminary notations on these items in your previous reading; if so, simply add to them. Following are some guidelines to assist you in looking for various aspects of the writer's technique and purpose. You don't have to address each question, but make annotations about as many as you can so you'll have plenty of information to draw on in your own essay. Refer also to the marginal questions in "Surveyor in the Woods."

GUIDELINES FOR ANALYSIS ANNOTATION

Whole Structure

1. What keeps the writing together as a whole?
2. How does the writer lead you from one paragraph to the next, from one section to the next?
3. How does progress through the text occur: by topics, by time, by comparison, by actions, by building up of details, by steps, by breaking the topic into parts? What is the best evidence of this in the piece?

Content Selection

1. What parts of the subject does the writer devote the most time to? The least? Why?
2. What statements does the writer make that are based on the assumption that everyone knows they're true (that is, no proof is offered)?
3. What topics that might be included are ignored by the writer? Why?

Selection of Evidence

1. What types of information are used to support main statements: statistics, examples, anecdotes, original observations, scientific evidence, appeals to emotion, quotations, definitions, common sense?
2. In what ways are individual topics developed? In what ways are arguments given, anecdotes told?
3. Does the expansion of statements prove the statements? Help the reader understand? Keep the reader interested? Suggest implications?

Use of References

1. How much does the writer rely on other sources? Frequent mention of books, articles? Indirect references to the work of others?
2. What methods are used to refer to other works: name, summary, direct quotation?
3. What kinds of material does the writer cite: newspapers, magazines, books, articles, documents?

Level of Accuracy

1. Is the subject oversimplified or overcomplex?
2. Does the writer bring out all the important distinctions or points?
3. Does the writer provide many supporting details or only state broad principles or observations?

Style Characteristics

1. Are the sentences matched to the content and purpose of the essay? Do they show variety of length and type? Describe actions, physical qualities, relate actual events, discuss abstractions?
2. Does the writer's choice of words reveal an awareness of audience?

Writer and Reader Relationship

1. Does the writer address the reader as an expert talking to another expert? As an expert talking to a general reader?
2. Does the writer make certain that ample signals are available to allow the reader to follow the discussion?
3. Does the writer make a definite attempt to interest the reader through humor, drama, unusual examples?

After noting the various techniques the writer uses in the selection, think about the overall purpose the writer might have had in mind. Look at your annotations—do they all seem to be pointing toward a central purpose? See if you can formulate a statement in your mind—perhaps even write it out—about the overall purpose of the author.

The First Draft

You're ready to begin thinking about a preliminary draft of your essay when you have a clear understanding of the material with which you've been working. When the author's purpose is in your mind, you need to think about your own purpose. What do you want to show in your analysis/response essay? Return to the original purpose given for this assignment.

You may discover that the material you have selected is too comprehensive for you to discuss every aspect of the writer's technique. In that case, you can isolate what you consider some of the key examples of the writer's efforts and concentrate on them. They might be the writer's descriptive powers, the ability to make complex subjects accessible, or the ability to re-create action for the reader.

Once you've made the decision about the major focus your essay will have, it's time to assemble the material from your marginal annotations that relates to your focus. You may even reread the piece of writing one last time to check for the following:

1. How well does my major focus fit with the evidence I have?
2. How can I organize my observations and evidence to match the original design of the writing with which I'm working?

3. Have I missed any pieces of evidence from the original that might help me at this point?

Although it may seem as though you're taking an extraordinary amount of time to prepare for the writing of this assignment, the careful preparation can save you considerable frustration during the writing. Because you're relying on someone else's thoughts and techniques as the content for your own writing, you must know that other material very well. Otherwise your own writing will be disorganized and little more than a summary of your reading.

The main purpose of your essay is to present a major insight into the overall design and content of a selected piece of writing. Because this task is so specific, you must be wary of sliding off into other areas, such as merely repeating what the piece said. If that begins to happen during the drafting, stop, reconsider your purpose, and then continue. Of course, at times it will be necessary for you to summarize or even quote small parts of the original as evidence for what you claim happens in the piece, but that should be done only as support for your own points. The same can be said for your personal response—relate it to the overall design of the original.

Organizing

As with your other essays, you have some options in how you present your material. One option is to present your findings and reactions according to specific topics. You might use some of the headings from the guidelines on pages 206–207. If you do this, you can relate each aspect of the writer's technique to the overall design of his or her essay; in other words, you can determine whether each aspect contributes to the effective or ineffective development of the writer's purpose. Simply isolating each part of the writer's technique is not enough; the reader needs to be reminded of how one part fits with another. For this reason, you must pay particular attention to your transitions in this approach. You'll want to plan the most logical progression of topics; that progression will depend, again, largely on what point you want to make about the writer's efforts.

A second option is to cover all the techniques in one section at a time. We might call this a chronological approach, because you will proceed from paragraph to paragraph or section to section just as the original is organized. This approach works well if the original selection goes through several distinct stages. Using such an approach, you can show how the writer does or does not build from one stage to the next.

The danger that lurks behind this approach is that you easily can slip into merely summarizing what the original selection says: "The first point the writer makes . . ." followed by "The second point the writer makes. . . ." The way to avoid this is to show how one argument or point affects or shapes another; in this way you focus on the purpose of the author's technique and stay away from a simple retelling of the author's content.

Another concern in organizing is the introduction and conclusion. Although you have discovered by now the wisdom of not laboring forever over the perfect introduction in a first draft, you also know that some focus in the introduction, even at this early stage, helps. To launch into the essay strongly, concentrate on acknowledging your audience, the source of your material—including some reference to title and author—and then the major purpose and techniques of the selection. From that point, you can go on to build your assessment of the degree of success the writer had and your personal response to the piece. In your review of the draft later, you can make further refinements in light of what you know about introductions.

In the conclusion of your essay you will need to do more than simply repeat your major points. You may discover, for example, that in the concluding paragraphs (note the plural—*paragraphs*—here) you may want to bring yourself and your readers together by providing your personal reactions to the selection. After having shown your readers all the evidence you've accumulated, you should be able to build a connection between your evidence, yourself, and your readers. What is the significance of what happened in the selection? How does it relate to you and your readers? If you have some moral, ethical, or emotional reactions to the selection, this is where you can bring them up and examine them. By now you know that there is no single approach to a conclusion; in this first draft, give it a good try but realize that you can return to it and tinker with the arrangement and the content until it meets your approval and that of your readers.

At this point, you should be ready to write a draft. Rough it out, putting in material as you go but not lingering on any one section too long; if you can't find just the right example, leave a space or make a note to yourself and go on. In this writing, if you have done all the suggested rereading of the original and the required thinking about the point you want to make, you should find a startling flow of information coming from your head to the paper. Details you may not have known you absorbed will suddenly spring to print. Enjoy this feeling of power and go with it as long as you can.

Before reviewing your first draft, take time to read the essay on "Surveyor in the Woods" that was written in response to this assignment. As you read, keep in mind the following questions and determine how well the writer deals with each one. These are questions you can ask yourself later about your own draft.

1. Does the introduction clearly establish for readers the focus of the essay and how it may be of interest to them?
2. How does the writer reveal an understanding of audience?
3. Has the writer clearly identified a point or series of points about the material being analyzed?
4. Does the writer relate the content of his essay to those points?
5. Does the writer provide enough examples to support the analysis?
6. How does the writer avoid merely summarizing the material being analyzed?
7. Does the essay have a strong closing that puts the writer's analysis and response clearly into focus and demonstrates the impact of the material on the writer?

A Matter of Purpose: Kenneth Andler's "Surveyor in the Woods"

Many of us may have read about wilderness living, about carving an existence out of virgin land, but few of us probably have had the opportunity to know someone whose life was devoted to bringing order to the wilderness. Kenneth Andler in an essay entitled "Surveyor in the Woods" makes it possible for us to meet such a person. This surveyor of the woods, Alfred D. Teare, was not exactly the most ordinary of men. His toughness, his expertise in matters of wilderness life, and the complicated skills, knowledge, and natural instincts he used in his chosen work of surveying the New England woods gave him a peculiar genius. But Andler shares his memories of Alfred D. Teare not only for these qualities but also to suggest that here is an individual who represents a level of dedication rarely seen. Alfred D. Teare's motivation in life is not to accumulate great wealth or even fame; instead, an inner pride and a personal set of standards far above the ordinary demand that even work in the wilderness, where most people will never see the results, must be done at all times to the best of his ability. It's that drive and how Andler presents it to the reader that makes "Surveyor in the Woods" an unforgettable essay.

Andler takes a cue in his own writing from the man he portrays. The essay is precisely constructed, divided into four parts, each section bringing the reader a different aspect of Alfred Teare. The first two deal with the characteristics of the man himself; his physical appearance, his background and unusual habits and abilities; the last two relate his skills in surveying and the significance of his achievement.

It takes little time for us to build a mental picture of Alfred Teare. Andler sketches details so vividly that in no time we can see the toughened old man ". . . quite heavily set . . . with powerful arms and shoulders . . . sitting on his left foot, his left leg bent under him, his right leg out straight." His was "a forceful, weatherbeaten, almost leathery face. . . . His hands, remarkably square with blunt fingers, were tough and work-hardened." These signs of a man used to hard work and to living outside are echoed in Andler's description of Teare's dress: heavy woolen socks, uniquely hobnailed ankle-high moccasins, khaki trousers, a denim work shirt—all topped off with a comfortable slouch hat.

Teare was a practical man. Nothing was wasted and the best cure was a natural one: concoctions of tree gums for bronchial troubles; chewed tobacco spread on open wounds to prevent infection. Along with his medicinal skills, Teare also was an expert cook, serving up biscuits, rice pudding embellished with an area's in-season fruits, and even producing doughnuts from his campfire kitchen.

One might suspect from such description that Alfred Teare is simply another New England backwoodsman; this suspicion lasts only until Andler begins to discuss Teare's skill as a surveyor. A surveyor fills a need in our world, providing the accuracy for our mapping of our environment. Surveying this environment is not easy. New growth of trees covers old boundary blazes, and vague title deeds—"Bounded on the North by Brother Jim, on the West by Brother Bill . . . "—hinder the process greatly. But Andler describes Teare as having an almost uncanny knack for untangling the puzzles of the past; he seemed to sense rather than see the small scars upon old tree trunks and knew instinctively when the mark was "not a line, just a trapper's trail." Teare's ability was strengthened by his fascination and his satisfaction in his work. He was a detective tracing title deeds, drawing tentative diagrams, and fitting together unlikely clues like parts of a jigsaw puzzle. He was an archeologist searching "through a forest-buried civilization as dead as the bottomless layer of an Egyptian city"—and he loved every minute of the work.

As I read Andler's account, I began to feel real affection and pride for this man who always "appeared to be coming at you aggressively with his head lowered like a buffalo." He never allowed swamps, cliffs, swollen rivers, or fallen trees to draw him from his trail. Once his goal of discovering the boundaries of a piece of land was achieved, he took enormous care in the marking of his lines. His blazes cut deep and clear into the surface of the tree trunks, his corners were painstakingly marked with carefully lettered posts and surrounded by a circle of "witness" trees, each bearing the date and Teare's own mark. In fact, Teare was so well known for the accuracy of his work that a friend once coined the phrase "as plain as one of Teare's lines" and timber buyers never bothered to resurvey a timber lot if they knew Alfred Teare had done the surveying.

It might seem from my analysis thus far that this essay is only a character sketch. Such is not the case. The reader gains valuable knowledge not only about the woods but also about surveying. In fact, Andler's account of surveying is a skillful mini-essay in itself. From it, any reader should gain a new appreciation for the significance of boundaries in our lives and the degree of difficulty in keeping those boundaries true.

I have praised the essay for its effective description and organization. For the most part the essay does work well. I had little difficulty following the development of thought and I enjoyed the detailed descriptions of Teare in his environment. The four-part organization was clearly indicated and proved to have only one weakness when, in the opening paragraph of Part II, Andler made reference to Teare's travels outside the woods and to his wife and children. Both subjects, although perhaps of some interest to readers, seemed out of focus for the principal purpose of the essay— Teare's achievements in the woods. Undoubtedly Andler wanted to let readers know that Teare was not a hermit, but the effort was undeveloped. Other minor slips in technique occur when Andler fails to define a word such as "tumpline" and offers an incomplete explanation of how a Gunter's chain is used. These slips are noticeable only because he is so painstaking in explaining and defining everything else.

On the whole, this is an essay that ought to cause readers to stop and think. Reading about Teare's pride in his work and the great satisfaction he derived from his efforts makes me wonder how many Alfred Teares may be left in today's world. Perhaps there were not many back in 1947 when Andler wrote this essay for *Harper's* magazine. Quite possibly, he wanted his readers to perceive this and think about the quality of their own contributions to the environment around them. All of us probably would like to be remembered after we're gone—I know I would. And I can't think of a better epitaph than the one Andler provides for Alfred D. Teare:

> But he did his work well and it survives him. No more can a mortal really ask. . . . Wherever he worked he brought order out of confusion and established a lasting thing.

Re-Viewing

As you wrote your first draft, you might have discovered gaps in your knowledge. Those gaps will come into focus now as you review the draft. As you reread and think about what you've said, note also any statements that have no real evidence to support them. Put a check mark next to those sections and, when you finish reading your draft, return to the original selection to locate evidence that might shore up those parts of your essay.

One particular area of concern in this kind of essay is that you do not recopy words from the original without giving appropriate credit; merely changing a word or two in an original passage is not enough to make the material yours. Be careful not to distort what the original author said. When in doubt, use a direct quotation from the original. In some cases, however, you may decide that you do not want to quote an entire passage from the original. Instead, you can use ellipsis marks to indicate the omitted part of the quotation. If you were to select a sentence from this paragraph to quote, but wanted to trim it for length, you might come up with something like this: "One particular area of concern . . . is that you do not recopy words . . . without giving appropriate credit."

The revision uses ellipsis marks (the three dots) to indicate to the reader that material has been omitted. As long as the omission does not change the basic meaning of the statement, the use is permissible. Selective quoting in an essay helps readers gain a sense of what the original was like; such evidence becomes particularly important in cases where readers of your essay may not be familiar with the material you're discussing. The sample response to this assignment contains good examples of how to handle selective quoting.

When you're certain that the content of your essay is satisfactory, study your draft using the questions on page 210. See if you can answer each question with confidence, even going so far as to locate the exact places in the essay where the evidence supports your answers. In addition to the items already mentioned, you should be concerned with the usual aspects of your writing: paragraphing, transitions, sentence structure, and word choice. Take pains to get all the elements working together smoothly. Then you're ready to seek an audience.

Response

The response you receive to your revised draft should be quite helpful. By now, you and your classmates are skilled at offering each other constructive feedback about writing. In this assignment, the comments should be most helpful because in the responding you can do what you have just done in writing your essay; that is, as you read and respond to one another's drafts, you can apply marginal annotation, offering both personal response and analytical comments. You can use the following questions in preparing your response:

1. How effective is the introduction in establishing a clear focus for the essay?
2. What assumptions about readers' prior knowledge are revealed? Are those assumptions appropriate?
3. What are the points the writer promises to make about the reading? Does the writer deliver on those promises satisfactorily?
4. How effectively and consistently does the writer offer both personal and analytical responses? Point out specific strong and/or weak examples.
5. Does the writer provide enough evidence to support the analysis? Point out examples where there is strong evidence and places where more evidence could be used.
6. How effective is the conclusion?
7. What recommendations can you make for strengthening the piece?

When you receive the responses to your draft, study the comments carefully and make any adjustments that seem necessary; if questions arise about the comments, try to get some clarification from your readers before making changes. Then put your essay in final form, polish it carefully, and proofread slowly. When you are satisfied it meets your highest standards, submit it to your instructor.

SAMPLE ESSAYS FOR ANALYSIS/RESPONSE

Surveying the Wilderness
by Donald Hall

One day last August I went surveying with Heman Chase, who has been measuring land in Vermont and New Hampshire most of the time since 1928. In order to start first thing in the morning, I stayed overnight in the house that Heman and Edith built in 1936, in the town of East Alstead, New Hampshire, where Heman has spent most of his many-sided life. Being a surveyor is only Heman's vocation; by avocation he writes books, runs a watermill, invents useful devices, philosophizes, writes poems, and uncovers local history.

But surveying was the morning's task. After breakfast we descended to the under-house garage where Heman keeps the truck he uses for surveying. His Bronco is twelve years old, with eighty-seven thousand miles on it—and a lot besides miles. Heman has equipped it as ingeniously as the British Secret Service outfits a sports car for James Bond. A clock, an altimeter, and a pencil sharpener screw to the dashboard. At the front of the hood he has fixed an antique bell from Manchester, Vermont, bartered from a dealer for whom Heman felled an elm. On the front bumpers Heman has a telescoping device for pushing cars without doing damage to the pusher or pushed. As he shows me how it works, Heman remembers a story: in 1928 his Model T got stuck in a snowstorm at Craig's Four Corners; he slogged uphill to Ike Craig's farmhouse, and Ike hitched up his oxen to a logging chain to pull him out. When Heman tried to pay him, Ike waved him off. "Pass it on," said Ike Craig—and Heman has been passing it on ever since.

Surveying equipment fills the Bronco's truck bed. It will be a warm day, and Heman wears a tank top, heavy trousers against the brush, and old sneakers for his work in the woods. Today Heman says that he will use compasses, to save the client time and money. Machines that measure more precisely are expensive and time consuming. "We are always being pushed to be more technological." Heman has found a favorite subject. "A compass survey is accurate within one in three hundred fifty or so, adequate where we're going. People who spend their time in an easy chair in an office now say we ought to get it one in five thousand." Heman snorts, and seems to change the subject by referring to old-fashioned telephone operations: "Back when Mrs. Buzzle was Central, I tried to call Mr. Marsh the minister, and Mrs. Buzzle said, 'You'd better wait five minutes, he just walked past the window.' "

Heman looks over to see if I get the point. "Maybe all this homogeneity," he says, "leaves us free to read poetry and do inward things. . . ." He is being ironical. It is not that Heman dislikes machines. In fact, he has invented many useful devices. As we get ready to back out of the garage, I observe a Chase invention: as Heman pushes lightly against the garage door, it lifts up easily, its weight balanced by an egg-shaped stone fixed to the end of a twelve-foot wooden spoke. When the door is open, its granite counterweight poises in air like a dinosaur's egg over a cave mouth.

As we drive to Alstead Center, Heman discusses the *appropriate technology* of surveying, in his crisp, deliberate voice. He parks on a wooded road by the parcel of land we will survey for possible subdividing and selling. Heman opens drawers and panels in the Bronco's back end—as compartmentalized as a Swiss Army Knife—and removes some tools of the trade: a compass on a tripod, a hundred-foot spool of metal surveyor's tape, a red-and-white striped pole for sighting through the compass, a machete, and bug spray.

Now Hallie Whitcomb arrives, Heman's coworker, a slim woman in her late twenties, strong, friendly, giving off the sense both of farm girl and intellectual. On his stationery Heman lists Hallie as his assistant. When he first told me about her, he spoke of Hallie as if she were a miracle: six years back, a total stranger, she dropped over, *out of the blue,* to visit Heman and Edith. She had grown up on a farm in Springfield, Vermont—where she still lives—and had studied geologic mapping at Earlham College in Indiana; she thought she would like to try surveying for a while. After the visit, Edith told Heman: *"Give her a chance."* Heman gave her a chance. "I call her a partner now," he says. "She just about as often tells *me* what to do as I tell *her* what to do." About one social matter Heman feels especially grateful: "I'm glad that I lived into an age—or *to* an age—such that it's not considered improper for her to work with me."

Heman has already explained the morning's task: we will follow the old backline through eight hundred feet of forest, and set a new corner for the putative subdivision. Heman leads the way. We set off for the starting point. We head into the woods; the woods take us over—up precipitous banks slippery with pine needles, down steep sides to streams layered with flat round stones as black as slate. We clutch at saplings, we dig our fists into cliff faces of needles. Our leader in his tank top wields his machete rapidly, cuts off sharp dead hemlock boughs with a quick, powerful wrist stroke—intrepid, single-minded, and overheated.

A great hemlock tree marks the corner from which we begin to measure. Heman nails on the trunk a metal plate that bears his name, the initials of the owner, and the date. From this tree we set out, Heman leading with his barber pole in one hand and his brush-cutting machete in the other, slashing blazes on trees on either side of his path, progressing at north fifty-four degrees west. Hallie takes up the rear with compass and tripod. When Heman has traveled eighty or ninety feet ahead and is still visible, he stops for Hallie to check the line. She sights Heman's barber pole in the open sights of the compass and tells him to move a foot to the right, or six inches to the left. With his own hand-held compass Heman counterchecks the reading; if his compass differs, he moves to split the difference. The tape counts the distance traveled, and Hallie keeps track.

Sometimes I forge ahead with Heman, sometimes stay behind with Hallie. As I scramble up and down, following our bearing down gullies and up hills, I lose the lens cap of my camera; then I manage to lose my reading glasses from my shirt pocket. This loss annoys me, because I was foolish to bring my reading glasses into the woods. Heman, of course, stops what he is doing and crawls around on his hands and knees searching for my glasses. "What color are they?" asks Heman, and I tell him that the rims are gold. "Well," he says drily, "if I find any silver ones, I won't pick them up." I think of how, in fifty years, someone surveying these woods again— or digging in a suburban garden; or starved and scrabbling for a root to eat—will discover a pair of old-fashioned glasses buried deep in leaf mold.

Finally I persuade Heman to return to the attack, and I talk with Hallie as he marches forward, carrying his skinny pole before him like a relay racer with a six-foot baton. At the family farm in Springfield, Hallie keeps a big garden, she tells me; and surveying is a good job for her; she works no more than half time, three or four days a week, nine months a year; she wants only as much money as she needs. She loves surveying, loves Heman, approves of using the compass. "He keeps the client in mind," says Hallie. "Land values are rising, though . . . We may have to be more precise."

As we talk, we keep moving. Ninety feet and eighty-seven and ninety-four. We are two hundred seventy-one feet toward our eight-hundred-foot goal, where we will make a corner and head for the road. Heman draws a line through trackless wood, which was probably pasture once. This land was never cultivated: too many stones—granite and quartz—and no feel underfoot of ridges that a plow made. Its pasture days are a long way back: maybe fifty years, maybe a hundred. Old trees have given up the ghost and they lie across our path with trunks two feet thick. Sharp branches scrape our skin. Although Heman hacks a gap, it is a Heman-sized gap, for a body smaller and more supple than mine.

Everywhere the prolix morbidity of the natural world has toppled old trees to the ground and started new ones up. No atom of space is unoccupied, by infant or by corpse, by needle or moss or tiny purple flower. Young trees stretch out in a row, pushed over by one gust; old trees root deep to endure. One hardy birch grips its roots into earth around a ball of quartz, the way a six-fingered pitcher might grasp a baseball. Everywhere among roots and in mosses there are holes for snake, mink, rabbit, skunk, and the bigger holes of woodchuck. We find the droppings of deer and fox, yet nowhere do we see an animal; insects and the birds that eat them fly around us, but nothing larger shows its face.

Through it all—hacking, indomitable—Heman Chase draws a map maker's line, making a human mark on the vital, moribund, unstoppable energy and decay of the natural world. He draws a line through the wilderness, order imposed on chaos, the way a railroad draws a line through valley and forest, over stream and past meadow. I remember something Heman told me earlier, about a day when he and Hallie, setting a line, came to "one of those wonderful stone culverts the railroad built in the 1850s." Deep in the woods, in by-passed rural New Hampshire, they found the stone culvert supporting abandoned railroad track, and marveled at its beauty and its construction: "Cut granite stones about three feet by a foot and a half, laid up without mortar in an arch to support a deep fill, a hundred feet through." Marveling, they ate a lunch together in the woods—Heman a sandwich, Hallie "some vegetable concoction." In summary, Heman told me, "We go around and find out what history was."

When Heman draws a map maker's approximate line through the moral wilderness, he does it by anecdote and by reference to his secular saints. Last night after dinner—under trees near his house, over Warren's Pond—he spoke about some of his professors at the University of Wisconsin. (He likes to say that his father thought Harvard the only place, his stepfather thought MIT the only place—and his mother packed him off to Wisconsin.) Professor Louis Kahlenberg was a moral example, an outstanding scientist who was forced to teach freshman chemistry—to the benefit of the freshmen—because he refused to work on chemical warfare during World War I. Of course a teacher can provide a counterexample: another engineering professor, to whom Heman mentioned that he would take a philosophy course, observed: "All right, but it won't get you ahead."

For Heman the greatest ethical model is Henry George, American economist, author of *Progress and Poverty*, who proposed a single tax on land. In Heman's first book, *American Ideals*, he connected George's ideas with the society envisioned by this nation's founders. With land the ultimate source of wealth and power, George saw the concentration of land ownership as the greatest source of inequality and inequity in the world. If a land tax were our only source of revenue, then no one could aggregate masses of land and everyone could share in it—a democracy of small landowners. "George was the man who, more than any other, understood how the earth would have to be *shared.*"

But Henry George's ideas do not find general acceptance among economists. One time Heman picked up a hitchhiking college student who majored in economics at Middlebury College in Vermont. Naturally enough, Heman asked his guest what he had learned in his classes about Henry George. The senior graduating in economics had never heard the name.

Back home, after simmering down, Heman wrote a letter to the chairman of economics at Middlebury, offering his services as an unpaid lecturer on Henry George. After a long delay he was invited to address a class and he enjoyed his visit to Middlebury, which ended in a lengthy discussion with students who adjourned to the house of a history professor. Heman realized that he had lost the class's economics teacher. He had emphasized that under George's scheme there would be no income tax at all, and the professor, looking incredulous, asked, "Not even for Ted Williams?" Now Heman's interests are wide-ranging but not universal: he had no idea who Ted Williams was. From the tone of the question, Williams was obviously an important figure. In the recesses of his mind Heman suddenly recollected that Ted Williams belonged to the sporting world. Figuring that his ignorance would undermine his advocacy, he merely affirmed: "Not even for Ted Williams." The professor of economics allowed that he could not countenance any tax scheme that refused to tax an income of a *hundred thousand dollars.*

Supper done, we walked back to the house carrying trays. Heman always walks tilted slightly forward, as if he were trudging uphill. Or he leans like the tower at Pisa, as tough as Pisan stone, with abrupt angular energy. He speaks little of age. Sometimes he remembers that he is old—as if with surprise. Back in the house he told a story about a lawsuit in 1940, when he had been hired to map a crossroads where a young man and an old one had collided in their automobiles. The young man sued and lost, but that was not the point. When the young man testified he was asked his age, and he replied brightly, as if he were proclaiming virtue, "Twenty-seven!" When the old man took the stand he was asked the same question. As Heman mimics his answer, the old man pronounced his years with a mixture of tones: bemusement, bewilderment, recognition that it did not matter, amazement that he should have lived so long. He said, in a lingering tone, "Seventy-seven." As Heman spoke, he was seventy-seven.

Before bed, we visited Chase's Mill, where hundreds of children and adults have learned the old ways of water power. One of Heman's books, *Short History of Mill Hollow,* tells the story of the various water-powered mills that used Mill Brook or Warren Brook, flowing out of Warren's Pond. It is a remarkable book, combining archeological detective work with a spirited defense of water power.

Chase's Mill is a large building topped by a great loft with a fireplace, site of community gatherings. Outside, set into the ground, is an enormous grindstone from an earlier mill. On the ground floor above the mill's workings is the shop, with water-powered lumber planer, large table saw, and jointer, together with electric-powered drill presses, band saw, table saw, wood lathe, machinist's lathe, and emery wheels. Here Heman and Edith have held shop classes for local children, teaching them to work in wood and metal.

As we entered the shop in August, I noticed a large woodstove backed against a wall, out of the way. Heman showed how the cast-iron body pivots on skids into the room's center for the winter cold, its stovepipe artfully jointed to pivot in agreement. The shop is equipped to manufacture whatever ingenuity requires. Here Heman has implemented inventions: tripods for surveying, his own screw for splitting cordwood; he has made Windsor foot stools and dump-cart bodies, trestle tables, cradles, and coffins for his mother and stepfather.

Heman stepped excitedly over the busy floor, pointing out, ex-plaining, and I realized that he is one of nature's professors—a doer who enjoys professing what he does. Although I am ignorant of mechanics and machines, Heman's enthusiasm pulled me in; I found myself watching intently as Heman cut a zigzag piece of brass, polished, trimmed. . . .

Then we descended to the floor beneath, and moved inward toward the source of the old mill's power. The walls were rough stone, primitive, and I heard water dripping. Plunging in front of us, a nineteen-inch iron penstock channeled water to a turbine two stories down. At the moment the mill was quiet: alert, suspended, waiting. Lower down, at mid-level, we walked in a maze of pulleys, belts and shafts now silent as the works of a huge abandoned clock.

Then Heman pulled a lever: *crash,* and a hurtle of water deafened us inside these deep narrow chambers, as a liquid column smashed into the turbine, urging it into spinning life. All over the mill wheels whirled, cogs spun, gears groaned—interlocking—and long belts turned their quarter turns. An immense intricacy of mechanical power—the power of the clockmaker-engineer—loosed by Heman's hand on a lever, resurged; we lived inside a clock of power, shaking, whirling with the power of twenty tumultuous horses straining to pull smoothly and steadily—a system, a church, a cave, the thunderous center of the earth. And as Heman saw its effect, he grinned like a boy.

We descended toward the tumult of water. Heman recounted, shouting, a sequence of sluices—an old wooden one, an iron one that he rescued from an abandoned mill, this new one only seven years old. Then he pointed to another pipe, a second smaller sluice as if the big one had dropped a foal, which connected to a tiny version of the big turbine. Over the small sluice was a hand lever that Heman asked me to pull. When I did, water spun into the small turbine, from which a wire moved upward to a little machine on a level above. The little machine was a car's generator, and over it Heman had hung an electric light. As the small turbine spun it generated electricity; slowly, flickering at first, a light bulb illuminated the deep hollow of Chase's Mill.

Heman offered congratulations: "You just lit a light by hydro-electric power!"

Now in the woods, surveying, we have come eight hundred feet, and it is time to make a corner. First we gather rocks, mostly lumps of granite from football size to the size of a basketball. To pry out medium stones Heman wedges his machete under them. For larger rocks he takes a stick of hemlock, sharpens the end, uses another stone as a fulcrum, and lifts the rock out to roll toward the pile. In twenty minutes we have collected a small quarry. Then Heman wedges a stout hemlock stake in the middle of the rockpile, big stones at the bottom showing their moss, smaller stones wedged closer in. Taking another metal patch from his pocket he pokes his initials into it and the date of this day and this year when we set out this line and made this corner.

Then we all stand back to look at it—a cairn of stones embodying purpose, a stick with metal tag announcing a deed—and I feel for a moment as if I had taken part in a ritual, partly because this artifact resembles a grave. Out of the silence Heman's voice declares this sign a sacrament, and Hallie adds:

"Nobody makes a corner like Heman Chase!"

Shoot-out at the Red-Horse Barn
by John O'Dell

As far as Forrest Youngblood and I knew, the barn had always been there, leaning precariously against a large sweet-gum tree in the pasture between my house and the railroad tracks. Its weathered siding sagged in protest against the elements and time, and the pitifully small clusters of hand-split shingles remaining on its skeletal roof pointed brittle fingers at the Oklahoma sky. On the gable above the loft door a faded, red-painted prancing horse was vaguely perceptible.

One of the barn's massive doors was weather-welded shut; the other still swayed on rusty hinges. When the southwest wind of summer swept over the Grand River bluff and caught the door just right, we kids in Fort Gibson would swear that folks could hear the screeching hinges all the way over in Muskogee, 12 miles away.

During the school year, Frosty (for Forrest) and I had the barn to ourselves: it was our fortress, castle, pirate ship; our Last Chance Saloon— or whatever our ten-year-old imaginations desired. But when summer recess kicked off the rubber-gun season, we were hard put to defend it against takeover by a gang of owl-hooters who called themselves "The Red River Renegades."

The Renegades were nicknamed Sticker, Kong, Whetstone and Killer. Killer was their undisputed leader, and we were semi-afraid of him. Killer wasn't any bigger than Frosty (who was lots bigger than me), but he had a tough reputation. Without even flinching, he could crack open scaly-bark nuts with his back teeth, or pop all the knuckles on his right hand three times in a row before they stopped making any noise.

In our eyes, the Renegades were "rich kids." They lived in the big stone houses on the hill. And Killer, as if to flaunt his wealth, sported a cream-colored Hopalong Cassidy hat (that I would have died for), and wore low on his hips a brace of the most beautiful rubber guns you've ever seen—made of bowdarc wood, hand carved and handsomely checkered.

"Oklahoma" rubber guns, whether fancy or plain, were usually homemade. A crude pistol shape was sawed from scrap lumber, with a barrel about 12 inches long. A spring-type clothespin was wrapped tightly to the rear of the grip (jaws up) with half-inch-wide rubber bands cut from old inner tubes. Similar rubber bands were used for ammunition. The gun was loaded by anchoring a band in the clothespin jaws, then stretching and looping it over the front of the barrel. The band shot forward from the gun when you squeezed the lower part of the clothespin. Maximum range was about 12 feet. The striking force was like the slap of a cow's tail. Cost? One cent (if your mother wouldn't give you a clothespin).

The first big shoot-out in the summer of 1934 began with a formal challenge on the second Friday of school vacation. Frosty and I were playing in the barn when Killer and Whetstone entered. The short, fat Whetstone tried to look mean while he sucked on a candy cigarette. The tall, slim Killer, hat pulled low on his forehead, *did* look mean. He patted the checkered grips of his guns and said, "We aim to take over the Red Horse come daybreak." Frosty pigeon-toed over to look Killer square in the face. He squinted his coal-black eyes and said calmly, "We'll be a-waitin'!"

After supper at Frosty's house, we hastened to plan our strategy. Frosty said he didn't like the odds of four against two, and maybe we should hire a couple of mercenaries. Actually, those weren't his words verbatim. What he said was: "Let's see if we can bribe Waldo." Waldo was 12 years old, and sometimes helped his father at the lumber mill. And he had real muscles.

With only two hours of recruiting time remaining before dark, I hung sidesaddle on the bar of Frosty's ancient bike while he pumped us up the rutted road to Waldo's house. But Waldo, it turned out, had to help his dad at the mill all day Saturday.

We hurried off to Pete Fullbright's, and had better luck. We hired on Pete and two others: Eskimo, Pete's cousin, who spent his ten-cents-a-week allowance on Eskimo Pies; and Bluegill Turner, the only kid I've ever known brave enough to bait his own hook with live catalpa worms. Our mercenaries cost us dearly: 20 unchipped marbles, two Big Little Books, and a cross-our-heart promise of one Eskimo Pie each at my father's drugstore.

Later, in Mr. Youngblood's tool shed, we prepared ammunition. Frosty cut bands from the old inner tubes, while I knotted them into figure-eight-shaped double-zingers.

We were worried, knowing that Killer would cheat, as always. Especially on Rule 1. The three rules for rubber guns, "Oklahoma style," were as follows:

1. When a fighter receives a torso or head shot, he is "dead-and-out" on the spot. After a few moans, he is to lie still and not utter a word, either of warning or encouragement.

2. A hand/arm or foot/leg hit constitutes a "wingling," and the fighter may continue the battle. But he is on scout's honor not to use the wounded limb for walking, running, loading or shooting.

3. No one may be granted a time out. The only exception to this rule is a parent-command of: "If you don't come home this instant, I'll skin you alive!"

While we worked, Frosty came up with a diabolical scheme that would prove when Killer *really* was dead-and-out. He dipped a double-zinger into a can of creosote, then wrapped it in a piece of oilcloth to preserve its tar-like potency. "This one's got Killer's name on it," he said. Delicious shivers started up my backbone, and played there right till bedtime. Born gunslinger that I was, I slept like a log.

Day broke quietly over the Red-Horse Barn. But not for long. Suddenly the serenity of Muskogee County was rent with war whoops, and the screams of the wounded and near-dead pierced the air.

On the opening skirmish, the battle went decidedly against us. Eskimo was quickly dead-and-out and I was winged in the kneecap. But I managed to barricade myself behind the poker table (an oak barrel with two staves missing), and soon was holding my own.

The tide turned in our favor when Frosty nailed both Whetstone and Sticker with his fantastic "act-like-you're-running-away, then-fall-to-the-ground, roll-over-three-times, and let-'em-have-it-right-in-the-belly" shot.

I got off two remarkably fast shots at Killer when he came tearing through the front doors and out the back. But my guns had warped some, or Killer was cheating again, because he yelled, "Yah! You just creased me!" and kept on going.

Good old Pete took care of Kong with his "act-like-you're-loadin'-when-it's-already-loaded" trick; then he took two fatal hits in the back from above—bushwacked by Killer, who had sneaked up the sweet-gum tree and down into the loft.

Taking a steady uphill bead on the coward, I was squeezing off my shot when his scorching double-zinger caught me square between the eyes. While they watered, I saw a blurry Bluegill bite the dust. I counted bodies. It was now one on one: Killer vs. Frosty.

A graveyard silence fell over the barn. Killer moved slowly down the ladder, approached the front door, reloaded his guns. Cautiously, he peeked outside, then whirled around as Frosty jumped catlike from the loft to land a foot or two from my corpse. His hands were smeared with creosote. He was loaded for bear!

The antagonists inched toward each other. "This barn ain't big enough for both of us," Killer snarled. Then, moving faster than the eye could follow, his carved guns came up and belched a pair of double-zingers at Frosty.

But Frosty wasn't there. At the last second he rolled to his left and fired from his famous prone position. Killer's hat spun off and fell at his feet. He looked at it, unbelieving. A black smudge of creosote desecrated the crown—proof of a fatal hit.

"You're dead-and-out, Killer," Frosty said softly. "And this here Red-Horse Barn still belongs to us."

All that was 42 years ago. The barn is gone now, of course, and the pasture where it stood is a modern subdivision. I went back recently, just to have a look.

In the manicured front yard of one house some children played on a gym set underneath an old sweet-gum tree. Could this be our tree? Do sweet gums live so long? As I watched the kids at play I felt a little sad for them. They would probably never experience the thrill of hearing an old barn door squeal on rusty hinges—a sound so loud that folks could hear it all the way over in Muskogee.

CHAPTER 11

What's Out There?

When students hear the word *research,* they think of the library; traditionally that's been where most people go to find answers to questions or problems—and rightly so. Yet relying only on the library restricts the person seeking information from discovering some of the richest, most interesting, and most informative resources that exist—other people. Up to now, your writing assignments in this course have followed the traditional classroom approach. Much of your academic writing will be of this type. But occasionally you will find yourself in situations where the ordinary kinds of information won't do the job for you. This may be particularly true once you leave the classroom and enter the world of work.

So what you're about to embark upon is a writing experience designed to help you operate outside the classroom as a writer and also to help you pull together a variety of skills and approaches that you've used in past assignments. You've done a character sketch in which you learned the importance of detail, dialogue, action, and dominant impression—you'll need all of those things. You've completed several assignments that asked you to bring together material of different types and viewpoints to illustrate or make a particular point, most noticeably in the comparison/contrast assignments. You've finished an assignment in process analysis where you learned the importance of sequence and explanation. And you've learned to analyze a piece of writing to determine its strong and weak points. Here, then, is an opportunity to demonstrate your skill in using all of these aspects of writing in one piece.

ASSIGNMENT: WRITING AN INTERVIEW ESSAY

"What makes you think you'd like to work for us?"

"How do you get to Monkey's Elbow from here?"

"Have you always put the plastic down first and then covered it with sand?"

"What's so special about your work that you can't leave it at the office?"

If you were to consider how many times each day you ask or answer questions, both simple and complex, about what you're doing or what others are doing, you'd probably be amazed at how much of your interaction with people results from questions. You'd probably also be amazed to discover how much of your knowledge and skill in various areas comes from your ability to ask and answer questions effectively. But what does this have to do with writing? Simple. The effective writer knows that one of the most useful resources in developing a subject is people and that to get information from people, one has to talk to them.

Purpose

This assignment will involve you with people outside the classroom. You will visit some place of business or other enterprise and talk with the people there. Watch what goes on: how do people act while carrying out their work; what do they say? Using the information you collect from this visit, you are to develop a piece of writing in which you convey as much information as possible about the enterprise and about the people involved to demonstrate a main idea that emerges from your visit.

Audience

Consider that your audience is people like yourself, curious but not necessarily well informed about the subject, who will be interested in your perceptions.

Prewriting

Since it's highly unlikely that you've had a great deal of practice with this kind of writing, let's take a few moments to consider the nature of the experience. First, no one is expecting you to go to Hollywood and interview a movie star, nor are you expected to hit the road with a rock band and "saturate" yourself in the environment. As a matter of fact, you'll need to work within a relatively small area within a specified time limit and with the knowledge that most, if not all, of your information will have to be gathered during one visit. Right now you may be living on a college campus miles from your home. Your first thought may be: I don't know anybody to interview or I don't know my way around so how will I be able to find a subject? Actually, both conditions may turn out to be in your favor. Sources of information exist all around you. But if you have to discover your subject, you may have fewer preconceptions about it and that may encourage you to ask more questions and be more observant, which means that you as well as your readers will gain valuable information and understanding.

Before rushing into the street and hailing the first person who passes or barging into someone's place of business to ask questions, take some time to approach this assignment in an organized way. By now you should understand the importance of the prewriting stage—a time to examine your options, think about what you might like to accomplish, and organize your approach to the writing.

Begin by assessing the various activities and places that might yield some interesting and informative material. For the most part, you're interested in the workplace and how people relate to their work. This restriction will help you in making a preliminary list of subjects. The following list might help you get started; add to it as other possibilities occur to you.

doctor's office	juvenile detention center
emergency room	riverboat
humane shelter	post office
landfill or dump	real estate business
mine	road or building construction
restaurant	plumbing or electrical business
federal, state, or local park	sewage disposal plant
campus security	car dealership/garage
car wash	farm
pawnshop	train, bus, or air terminal
bank	trucking firm

resort	fire station
refinery	secondhand store
prison	hairdresser's shop
bakery	dentist's office
newspaper office	theater
drugstore	print shop
factory	tannery
art studio	courthouse
bookstore	funeral parlor
photography studio	auction barn
bar	

You'll notice that the items on the list are all names of places where different kinds of work occur. But remember that within each place a number of different kinds of work can be performed and that people may have different responsibilities. An inventory of just one place might yield many rich areas for exploration. Consider a courthouse, for instance; in that one place of business, how many different types of people might be found? Here's a start:

clerks	secretaries
lawyers	custodians
judges	criminals
bail bondsmen	regular customers
newspaper reporters	

After you've spotted a few potential topics in the previous list or produced some of your own, take a moment to rank them according to the following criteria.

Interest

1. How interested am I in the activity represented by the person or place?
   Unless you're interested in the subject and have some genuine curiosity about what goes on or how the person feels about the work, there's little point pursuing the topic. Since success with this assignment will depend largely on your curiosity and involvement,

choosing a subject about which you have little enthusiasm will probably result in a less than satisfactory piece of writing.

2. What potential does there seem to be in the topic for developing audience interest?

You should be able to gauge the interest level fairly well by your ability to ask questions about the topic. Chances are good that if you're curious about the subject, your readers will be too and will read the results of your observations with interest.

Accessibility

1. What arrangements will have to be made for a visit?

Although you may be able to think of exactly the person you would like to interview and observe, that person (or place) may be too far away or unavailable at this time. Be realistic, remembering your time and travel restrictions. Select a topic that can be managed within your limitations.

2. Will one visit be sufficient to obtain the necessary information?

Of all the questions you need to answer, this one may be the most difficult, since you probably aren't sure how much information you'll need; on the other hand, the larger the topic, the more likely it is that you will have to restrict what you do with it. It's one thing to interview one person at a certain time, it's another to try to interview ten people at the same place and come away with a clear sense of what to write about.

Complexity

1. How technical is this subject likely to be and what background knowledge do I already have to draw upon?

Let's say you decide to interview a petrochemical engineer or a physicist. How much knowledge do you have of those jobs that you could use as a basis for carrying on a conversation? Some work and workers are more familiar and understandable than others; this doesn't mean that you should avoid complex workplaces or people with very sophisticated training, but you need to have some knowledge if you're to succeed in obtaining useful information.

2. How many aspects of the work will I need to explore?

You can only offer a limited view of what is involved in a particular line of work. If you were talking to a doctor in a hospital, for example, it wouldn't be necessary to deal with every part of his or her work; you could focus on one or two aspects that seem relevant to your own interests and those of your readers.

Questioning Dialogue

Once you've made some tentative choices of topics, the next step is to think about what you might like to know as a result of your visit. The material for this piece of writing will not be laid out for you, waiting for you to pick it up as you enter the front door. Take one of your top choices and engage in some questioning dialogue with a partner. This technique is similar to the prewriting device of dialoguing, which you encountered in Chapter 5. One question should trigger another so that as you proceed you begin to build a series of questions about the subject that you might like to have answered.

Work for five minutes with your partner to see how many different questions the two of you can generate about the topic; then switch to your partner's topic and do the same thing. Listen carefully during both sessions; you may discover a question from your partner's list that you want to add to your own. Such a session might go like this:

Topic: Female hairdresser who cuts men's hair

Voice 1: Okay, she cuts men's hair—what do I want to know?

Voice 2: Well, how did she get started cutting men's hair?

Voice 1: Yes, and that could lead to what kind of training she had.

Voice 2: And whether hairdressers have to take more training and if they're licensed?

Voice 1: Yeah, and what about the money she makes—although some people don't like to talk about that.

Voice 2: You're right, but we can put it down for now—remember, we're just trying to come up with possible questions.

Voice 1: Oh, yeah, I forgot. Let's see, I know something I'd really like to know—do men gossip as much as women do when they have their hair cut?

Voice 2: Dynamite—yeah, that would be really interesting; oh, and what does she say—does she gossip with them or keep her mouth shut?

Voice 1: How about different cuts—which ones she finds easiest? Hardest?

Voice 2: How does she feel being on her feet all day and putting her hands in all those different kinds of hair—yech, I don't think I could stand it.

Voice 1: Yeah, how about the guy with the bad case of dandruff—do you say anything to him or just sterilize all your tools when you're through?

Refining the Questions

Asking good questions that will elicit good information is not a chance thing; it takes some thought and preparation. You're probably familiar with the standardized question format found in public surveys, in which a number of people are asked the same questions and their responses are counted to show the percentage of responses that agreed or disagreed with each question. In that context, the wording of the question becomes especially important; if the wording varies even just a small bit from person to person, the validity of the final statistics can be suspect because of possible variations in interpretation. Fortunately, you won't have to worry about standardizing your questions; the questions you use can be quite different from those your classmates ask. By now, with the help of your partner, you've generated quite a few possible questions. They probably are not in any particular order, so the first step is to review the questions and decide if there are some groupings you can make. Although you can't anticipate all the questions you may ask, you probably can go through your early list and sort out questions that relate to the following three areas:

The Activity/Job Itself: What it is; how it operates; the different stages or steps, particular problems, tools or materials involved; degree of difficulty and danger.

The People Involved: Who they are; what they are like; the feelings they have about their work; training they need; ambitions in terms of their work; how they act during their workday.

The Environment: Where the activity takes place; special characteristics of the workplace; sights, sounds, smells, feelings associated with the workplace.

After you have your questions clustered in some fashion to suggest the areas you are most interested in, the next step is to examine the wording of your questions carefully. Interviews fail more often because of weak phrasing of questions than for any other reason. If you follow some basic guidelines in developing your questions, you should find that your subject will answer fully and easily.

1. Ask questions that invite the person responding to expand beyond a simple yes or no.
   Questions that can be answered in only one word mean that the

questioner has to follow up with another question almost immediately; if this happens too many times, the person being interviewed feels as though he or she is being grilled and soon will hesitate to respond even to the one-answer questions. The person may just end the interview. Consider the following:

Weak question: Did you receive training for this job?
Stronger question: How did you prepare yourself for this work?

Weak question: Do you like your work?
Stronger question: How do you feel about doing this kind of work?

2. Ask questions that allow the person being interviewed to indicate his or her own views, not yours.

Sometimes we may go into an interview looking for support for some preconceived ideas; as a result, we may, consciously or unconsciously, phrase our questions so as to force the person answering to support our position.

Weak question: The _____ has always struck me as being a big waste of money; don't you agree?
Stronger question: How do you feel about the amount of money being spent on this project?

3. Ask questions that seek factual information.

In this assignment, you are particularly interested in how a person feels about his or her work, but you also need basic information about the work itself. Design questions that encourage the responder to provide that information.

Weak question: I guess you've got a pretty complicated job here, huh?
Stronger question: How many steps are there in this process?

4. Design questions to obtain insights about the person or people involved in the work.

Factual information alone can be useful, but you can make it more interesting to the average reader if you also know something about the people behind the job. Each worker has a unique personality and different ways of looking at a subject. Seek out those insights.

Weak question: Are you pretty happy with your job?
Stronger question: What gives you the most satisfaction from this job?

With these guidelines in mind, construct ten to fifteen questions that you would feel comfortable using during an interview on the subject you've chosen. Try to balance your questions, in terms of both the type and the areas you explore. At this point you are developing a basic pool of questions that you can draw on to get your interview going and that you can return to if necessary during the interview.

Response

With your list of questions written out, take a few minutes and go over them with a partner, preferably the one who worked with you on the original question session. Get your partner's response to the phrasing of the questions, using the previous guidelines, and also to the balance of the questions. Do the same with your partner's questions.

Getting Ready for the Visit

Depending on the topic you have selected, you may or may not have to make arrangements ahead of time for your visit to a workplace. Certainly if you are visiting a person during working hours, it is common courtesy to determine by telephone or in person the most convenient time for your visit. If you are interested in doing your observing and interviewing in a more indirect way and want to see what you can gather just by being on the scene, you can dispense with advance arrangements. Realize, however, that off-the-cuff interviews can leave you empty-handed; people may question your motives if you get too curious and may simply not talk to you.

Assuming that you've decided on a time to visit and have made the necessary arrangements, what should you do next prior to the visit? First, review the purpose of your assignment. Tempting as it may be initially in this piece of writing just to report what you see or hear, the assignment asks for a bit more. You should be looking for some focal point in your interview/visit. When you write up the results of your observations, you will need to make some key point or points to the reader; otherwise you'll have nothing but a conglomeration of facts, details, and impressions. Your point may be as simple and direct as underscoring the importance of the operation or the person or people involved with it; or you may want to demonstrate the uniqueness you discovered during the visit—a uniqueness of environment, of dedication from people; or you may want to offer an explanation that brings new understanding to a subject often misunderstood or ignored by many people.

A second consideration is the actual skills you will need during the interview/visit. One of these skills is *observation*. A keen eye for detail, as you have already discovered, is crucial for the successful writer. You should note exactly where you are and what's happening during the visit, and your "sensory recorder" should be going full blast throughout the visit. Soak up all the concrete detail that you can and be an active reporter of what you see, hear, feel, and taste.

You'll have to realize, of course, that the place you visit will determine in large measure the kind of information you receive. For example, if you visit a real estate office, most of what you'll see will consist of desks, filing cabinets, and some display pictures of houses and property. As a result, most of your recording of information will probably center on conversations that you have with the real estate salespeople. That in itself is not inappropriate but it means that you will use different kinds of sensory details; your emphasis will be primarily on the people, what they say, and how they say it—unless you approach the visit with a bit of ingenuity. A visit to a realtor, for example, might include some time spent traveling to different real estate listings, watching and listening as the agent works with a customer, and so on. Originality and thoughtfulness toward your approach may pay large dividends in obtaining insights and information that might not otherwise appear.

Note Taking

One of the principal problems for interviewers is keeping track of all the information they accumulate during a visit. Trusting your memory is hazardous unless you have had good training in instant recall. But writers often encounter mixed reactions when they try to take notes during an interview; sometimes people get quite nervous when they see someone writing down everything they say and they may even ask to see what is being written. As a result, interviewers may rely heavily on their memories and then right after an interview sit down to record as much as they can of the visit. A reasonable compromise is to begin writing down casually an occasional statement, particularly those with facts and figures, as a person speaks, and mention that you want to be certain to get the material down accurately so you don't lose it. Frequently a conversation can be summarized in a few brief notes, but a good quotation can often add color and interest to a piece, so you should be alert for such opportunities and get the words down. Misquoting people is a cardinal sin in interviewing so be accurate, even asking for a repeat if you have any doubt; otherwise, an incomplete or inaccurate quotation will have to be discarded.

Although you may think most frequently about getting down what a person says, you should not forget that people are not the only sources of useful information. You should note carefully details of environment and process, even in abbreviated form, as concretely as possible: colors, shapes, sizes, speeds, brands, locations, textures, smells, sounds. Get as much as possible because these items will give you necessary background detail for convincing your readers that you have been where you say you've been.

The process of note taking is somewhat similar to taking class notes, but you may want to practice by going to a place such as a cafeteria and recording all you can in a five- or ten-minute span; soak up the details, the snatches of conversation, and try to get down as much as possible. Such practice should make you accustomed to concentration and should help you develop a fast form of shorthand that makes sense to you, if to no one else.

The temptation to use a tape recorder may be strong. The idea of simply sitting back and having everything recorded on tape is attractive, but it has some drawbacks. First, although many people are not afraid of tape recorders, some are and will "freeze" the minute they see a microphone. If you use a recorder, the best type is one with a built-in microphone. Such a recorder can be set on a table or chair and left running during an interview, and usually the person being interviewed will forget its presence after a time, as long as there is no apparent sound and no microphone constantly in view. A second problem with tape recorders is that they can malfunction. The operator forgets to push the right buttons or set the volume adequately; or, even worse, the tape runs out in the middle of an important comment and you discover that all your cassettes are in the car. A third problem is transcription. Tape has to be transcribed, in most cases, onto paper, and that is a laborious task. It usually has to be done before any real writing can begin so you must count on extra hours in preparing your material if you use a tape recorder. Some people compromise, using the recorder but also taking notes; then, in preparing for their writing, they listen to the tape to refresh their memories and add to their already existing notes. Whichever method you choose, the pen and paper will figure prominently throughout.

During the Interview

Conversations and observations may take place in many different settings, and you will need to adjust to each accordingly, tailoring your behavior and your observation and questioning to fit changing situations. A few guidelines may be helpful in making the visit successful.

1. Remain casual in your approach but remember your purpose for the visit. Everyone's time is valuable so don't waste it, but don't rush either. Try as much as you can to let individuals speak on their own without constant prodding; don't panic if one of your questions

doesn't get an immediate answer. People need time to think about how they might want to phrase an answer; your thoughtfulness in giving your interviewee time may pay off in a more complete and revealing answer than if you jump in with another question.

2. Listen closely to what people say, and when you believe more information might be helpful or a clarification seems necessary, ask a follow-up question or a "probe" to carry the response deeper. Remember that the person responding to your question doesn't always know what you understand or don't understand unless you indicate it. *Sample:* "I think I understand how the operation works but I'm still not sure why it will be more effective. Could you explain it another way?"

3. Remain alert at all times to catch not only what people say but how they say it. Recording the answer as well as brief notes about the method in which the answer was given may tell you more about the individual and his or her feelings than an extended conversation will.

4. Keep track of the passage of time; it may give you a way of organizing your material later. Note the stages in your visit and where you are physically during each stage. If you are moving around a factory, for example, your observations on that movement may be useful later in providing hints about the relative importance of various parts of your visit.

5. Make notes about your own reactions as well as the reactions of those around you. Although you will be concentrating primarily on what others are doing, keep track of things that surprise you, interest you, or cause some other reaction. Your responses may be helpful later in trying to determine an overall focus for your writing.

You're almost ready for your interview now. The interview—and its success—are in your hands; you have the full responsibility for making the visit worthwhile. If you follow the guidelines outlined in this chapter, you should have few problems; in fact, you're probably going to discover that you enjoy your visit and may even want to repeat it at a later date. Before you go, take some time to read the following interview with one of the most practiced interviewers in the United States. Studs Terkel has produced several books, among them *Hard Times* (1970), a collection of interviews with people who lived through the Great Depression in the 1930s; *Division Street: America* (1966), a collection of interviews with people living in Chicago; *Working* (1974), a collection of interviews in which different kinds of workers from all over the country talk about their work; and *American Dreams* (1980), a series of interviews with Americans, famous and not famous, who talk about their ambitions and what America means to them.

Note as you read this interview how Terkel stresses the importance of letting people talk and how important it is to let them feel you are sincerely interested in hearing what they have to say. The key to Terkel's phenomenal success as an interviewer of so many different types of people is that he is a good listener. Note also how he suggests that the good interviewer is flexible and never becomes locked to a particular viewpoint. Remaining alert and flexible, the good interviewer pursues the leads that the subject provides and suggests some that the person may not have thought about before. Keep his advice in mind as you get ready for your visit.

An Interview with Studs Terkel
by Gail Steinberg

Writing! (W!): How much editing do you have to do after the interview is completed?

Terkel: I do a lot of editing. I may start with a hundred pages of transcript, and then I go through it and cut out all the repetition. After that I start looking at it, and there are certain phrases, certain revelations, that just jump out at me. When I'm through, I may have cut those initial one hundred pages down to eight. And that's the gold. Being an interviewer is like being a prospector. He finds the place. I find the person. And then he digs. And then we talk. And then he filters out the ore. And then I edit. Finally, what's left is the gold.

W!: You compare yourself to a prospector, and I know you also compare yourself to a carpenter. You've said that you consider your preparation for an interview to be the tools of your trade, just as the carpenter has his hammer and saw.

Terkel: I call myself a craftsman. A lot of the writers I interview for my radio show say that I'm the only interviewer who reads their books, and they think it's great. I think it's sad. After all, that kind of preparation should be par for the course. Do you compliment a carpenter who comes to the house with his tool chest? It's expected. Well, interviewing is my trade, and I have to be well equipped and well prepared. I'm a carpenter who carries his tool chest.

W!: You do that kind of preparation for your author interviews. Do you do the same kind of preparation for the people you interview for your books?

Terkel: Since the heroes and heroines of my books don't write books, there's no preparation as far as their lives are concerned. They tell me about their lives, so I don't go in with prepared questions. I listen to what they have to say, and I go where my curiosity and their stories lead me.

W!: One of the things that stands out most in the interviews that fill your books is that you seem to bring out the best in your subjects.

Terkel: Yes, you see, to me it's the potentialities in people. It's easy to do what *is*. It's what *can be* that fascinates me. A man I know says he looks at a person through two different eyes. One eye tells him what that person is and the other eye tells him what that person can be. In my interviews I'm saying that the possibilities of people are as yet untapped. I look for that other aspect of them.

W!: You make it sound so easy. It's not.

Terkel: Well, after a while there's a rhythm. I listen, and I have to cut through and figure out what it is that each person is saying. I talk and listen, and I remember certain phrases that just ring. A man once shared with me his memories of waiting in a line of one thousand guys vying for two job openings. He told me, "The men were fighting with each other like a pack of Alaskan dogs." See, that's a phrase that jumps at you. Or there's Peggy Terry, an Appalachian woman who has been in several of my books. She told me about her memory of the Depression. "What can I tell you about the Depression," she said, "except that I was hungry?" Except that I was hungry. You see? People speak a kind of poetry at times. And I pull out that poetry. That's what it amounts to.

W!: If you could offer advice to student interviewers, what would it be?

Terkel: Listen to people. Make the interview in the form of a conversation. I guess, too, that I would also encourage curiosity. And I'd advise them to try to determine what counts and what doesn't. That's a lot of advice, but I guess that what it amounts to is that an interviewer has to determine, does the conversation reveal something, or is it just chatter?

W!: Are the people you talk to usually pleased with the finished interview?

Terkel: You know, the people I interview are always pleased with the part of them that makes it into print. People are so accustomed to being humiliated as part of their regular routine, but I won't do that to them. With my interviews I fight humiliation in my way.

W!: In your books and on your radio program, you elevate the interview to an art form. What makes a good interview, and how do
you select your interview subjects?

Terkel: My emphasis in all of my books is on those people who are not
famous. I do include some celebrated people in *American
Dreams*—Joan Crawford, for instance—because they figure in a
certain moment in the book. But generally speaking, it is the
uncelebrated people, those whose lives never have been
chronicled, that interest me.

W!: Do you, then, have a theory or a philosophy about the art of
interviewing?

Terkel: My theory, if it is a theory, is that here are people who never
are in the history books. Histories deal with kings and presidents
and powerful people, hardly with the anonymous people, who in
a sense make the world go around through the years. Who, for
example, built the pyramids? It wasn't the pharaohs. They didn't
lift a finger. Anonymous slaves built the pyramids. What were
their lives like? I always say, suppose I had a tape recorder at the
foot of Calvary on Good Friday—or, I should say, Bad Friday.
Well, what were the people thinking about down below? Who
were they, these witnesses to such an event? We read that when
the Spanish Armada sank, Philip, the King of Spain, wept. Were
there no other tears?

W!: When you search out these "ordinary people," as you call them,
how can you tell who is going to be a good interview subject?

Terkel: Ah, I don't know. I feel my way through. There are certain
kinds of people—ordinary, so called—who are able to articulate
something their neighbor can't. And ultimately I find them.

W!: How?

Terkel: Oh, no rule. I hear about someone or know about someone.
While I was working on *Division Street: America,* for instance,
someone listening to my radio show called me up and bawled me
out about something I'd said. He told me I sounded just like his
mother. So I said, "Who's your mother? Where does she live?"
And as a result, very accidentally, I found this marvelous woman
to interview.

W!: When you interview people, you get to the heart of their characters—of their souls. How do you manage to do that? Is there a
secret?

Terkel: The secret is there is no secret. I am a good listener. People
know I'm interested in them in the first place. But there is no rule.
Sometimes in hearing people talk, I find that one thing leads to

another. There might be a laugh that comes at a strange moment, say, when a person is recounting a moment of bitterness or humiliation. Why is he laughing? A good interviewer probes that. You know, there is a joke about the kinds of superficial interviews we have so much of today on television and radio. The interviewer has his notes in front of him, and the person being interviewed says, "My mother and father died in a terrible crash." And the interviewer says, "Oh, that's nice." And then he goes on. You see, he wasn't listening.

W!: Then that's one of the tricks—listening.

Terkel: That's right. And when in doubt, call on childhood, a memory of childhood, and that always opens the dam gates. When I interviewed Cesar Chavez for *Hard Times,* he recalled from his childhood seeing his father, a Mexican, go into this restaurant, and the waitress, talking to a customer, didn't even turn around. She just said, "We don't serve Mexicans." And that seven-year-old Cesar remembered this episode all these years. The memory stayed with him, but the waitress didn't even know what she had done or what kind of impact she had made. But, as I've said, there's no rule. And there's no rule about the question I ask first. When I edit, I can shift the order in which a person gave a response. I'm not altering what that person said. That order was arbitrary to begin with. I want to get at the truth of what that person said. What I always try to do in an interview piece is highlight the truth.

Resources

Before you go on your visit, you also might want to read the following essays, or you might prefer to wait until your interviewing is done. In either case, it will help you considerably if you take some time to examine the following essays before writing your own. Each provides a different approach to the interview essay. Study the essays carefully and answer the questions that follow each one. As you read, think about how the different approaches and techniques you see in these essays might be of use to you in the development of your own essay.

SAMPLE INTERVIEW ESSAYS

Life of a Saleswoman

by Tina Poveromo

8:30 A.M.

The commuter traffic along the Brooklyn-Queens Expressway is bumper-to-bumper. Carol Dixon throws her '76 Buick Apollo into low gear and checks her gold Seiko watch. The 25-year-old Xerox sales trainee is going to be late for work.

Ordinarily she's at the Brooklyn office by 9 A.M. sipping coffee and making phone calls. But today the traffic is unusually heavy; we are crawling at 30 miles per hour, still 45 minutes from Brooklyn. She fumbles through her leather briefcase and pulls out a cigarette.

"I think a lot of women have misconceptions about sales," she says. "I know *I* did—in fact, I'd never even considered the field. I had an M.B.A. *I* wasn't going to sell."

Her M.B.A. is from Pace University. Her undergraduate degree from New York University is in journalism. For the next few months she will make her living stumping the streets of downtown and industrial Brooklyn, pounding on the door of every business that looks remotely in need of a photocopier. Her starting salary is $16,000. When she becomes a full-fledged geographic sales representative and is assigned a permanent territory, she could earn as much as $50,000 a year—or more. The average income for the 70-person Xerox sales staff last year was $28,000.

"I would be less than honest to say that sales is for everyone," she says. "It's not. If you need constant emotional reassurance, forget it, because you're going to hear 'no' more times than you've ever heard it before in your life. If you have a low self-image, you'll never survive in sales.

"But if you're an ambitious, self-motivated person, sales is an extremely lucrative field. The money is there for the taking if you're willing to put in the work."

From her rust-colored, tailored skirt suit to the tips of her sensible shoes, Carol Dixon is dressed for success. Her brown hair curls softly around her shoulders and is clipped neatly away from her face. Makeup and jewelry are minimal: lip gloss, blush, and mascara, the Seiko and two tiny gold earrings. Her long fingernails are flawlessly glossed. By any standards Carol Dixon is an attractive, well-groomed woman, with sparkling brown eyes and a milewide Pepsodent smile.

"Being a woman hasn't hindered me at all in my job." She is emphatic on this point. "Sure, you develop a rapport with the clients, and some of them do ask you out. But it's nothing a woman can't handle. When someone makes a comment, you either ignore it or you say something to make them realize you're calling on them not as a woman but as a professional. It's all related to your self-image and your sense of respect for yourself.

"And all this business that men are going to buy from you because you're a woman," she adds, "is crap."

Dixon parks the Buick in her usual space in a lot near Xerox's Brooklyn office. We grab some coffee and the morning paper and head to the office, where she'll start with some "telephonics"—picking up the telephone book and cold-calling potential customers.

"Hello, may I speak with Mr. Cohen, please? Mr. Cohen, this is Carol Dixon from Xerox Corporation?" She is new at this; her introduction ends in a question. "I called to tell you that Xerox is offering a trade-in on old machines. We're buying back all brands of copiers for up to $2,000. Have you thought any more about a new machine? I see. Well, keep us in mind when you do. You have my card, don't you? Mr. Cohen, thanks very much for your time."

For 30 minutes Dixon makes phone calls. The dialogue varies only slightly. No one in Brooklyn needs a Xerox. But she is not discouraged; this is a typical morning.

"You can't be at all sensitive in this job, and you can't take the rejection personally. You have to understand that 'no' is meant at the business level," she says. Coffee and phone calls finished, we're ready to hit the street.

10:00 A.M.

Downtown Brooklyn is a compressed, dirty, and crumbling area. Theoretically, Dixon will knock on every business door in the borough. Most of her visits are cold-calls. More often than not the only clue to what lurks behind an office door is the name of the business. Nine times out of 10 Dixon walks in unannounced in the midst of the business day.

"Don't ever get the idea that they roll out the carpet and take the phone off the hook when you make a sales call," she warns. "Most of the time people are scurrying in and out of the office, and you're standing there trying to get a word in. Sometimes you never make it past the secretary."

The first building we try is a modern, professional high-rise. "I've been wanting to cold-call this building for a while now," she says. She smooths her skirt and takes a breath. "Come on. Let's take it from the top."

Before we knock on the first door, she takes a minute to collect herself, making sure her business cards are in reach. "When I first started canvassing, I handed a customer someone else's card," she says. "I had to take it back and say, 'Wait a minute—that's not me.' Ever since then I double-check."

Canvassing with Carol Dixon is a bit like campaigning for office. She shakes hands and distributes business cards. Most calls are brief, cordial, and direct. She is persistent but not overbearing. She likes to get the last word in and won't leave until the customer has her card. But she knows when enough is enough.

"Hello, I'm Carol Dixon from Xerox? Is the person in charge of purchasing available?" We are in a law office, talking to the bleached-blonde, bespectacled secretary.

"I'm sorry, there's no one else here."

"Who is the purchasing agent? Is it Mr. McCarthy?"

"Yes, but I can tell you right now he's not interested. We're very satisfied with our machine." In the sales game, the secretary is functioning as the "screen." The first step in the game plan is to break past the screen and go directly for the decision-maker.

"When will Mr. McCarthy be in, please?"

"I'm not sure. Try after lunch. But I really don't think he's interested."

"One thing you might be interested in is Xerox's new trade-in policy. We're buying back used machines for up to $2,000."

"Yes, well, I'll let Mr. McCarthy know."

"What is the phone number here?"

The secretary loses her ground. Dixon gets the phone number. The secretary gets a card.

"Thanks very much for your time."

We canvass for an hour, riding elevators, climbing stairs, knocking on doors, and distributing cards. Most of the people we see are male lawyers who are not interested in Xerox machines. But Dixon remains undaunted. After each stop she records the name, address, and phone number in a yellow notebook called the Daily Success Planner. Comments are scrawled in the margin—"call back," "send literature," "not interested."

"The easiest thing in the world is to give up and say, 'I quit!' When you sell for a while," she says, "you find out quickly how much inner strength you really have."

At 11:30 we head back to the office, where Dixon has scheduled a demonstration with a lawyer she canvassed the previous week. We are on time. The lawyer is late. She worries. "I hope he shows," she says. She checks and rechecks the copier to make sure all systems are go. "I think the hardest thing to take is when an appointment stands you up. That shows a total disregard for my time."

At 12:15 the lawyer arrives.

It takes nine months to train a Xerox sales rep. Trainees must memorize the prices and learn the mechanics of all Xerox copiers, as well as those of the competitors. New reps take intensive classes in Manhattan and Leesburg, Virginia, then spend seven months in the field. Carol Dixon has learned her lines.

"You look like a man who knows where he's headed," she begins. "I think you believe, like me, that to make money you have to spend money. This is not just a machine—it's an office system. With this machine you can send out mass mailings on your own letterhead. You can make transparencies for court. You can even do mailing labels. Think of how much time your secretary will save."

At first she is stiff, as though she's reading her lines from a TelePrompTer. But the demo comes off without a hitch. Also without a sale.

"I want this machine," says the lawyer. "But right now it's a question of money. You see, I work with my father, and he can't see what a machine like this will do for our image. Right now he thinks only in dollar signs."

After a morning of casting out lines, Carol Dixon finally has a bite. She reels him in. She offers low interest rates and monthly installment plans. She stresses the trade-in and reiterates the guarantees. She even offers to visit his office and speak to his father herself.

"I'll get back in touch with you," he says. "Perhaps in a couple of months. . . ."

"Fine. You do have my card, don't you?" They continue discussing as she escorts him to the door.

"I thought that demo went well," she says after he leaves. "He'll buy. He just doesn't have the money right now. But one day he'll get so fed up with his old copier he'll want to throw it out the window. Then he'll pick up my card and he'll call," she says.

Then, almost as a postscript:

"You know this morning when I said being a woman makes no difference? It just did. That lawyer told me not to come to his office. He said his father wouldn't do business with a woman who sells machines."

We eat lunch—corn muffins and Tabs—at the Brooklyn office. Dixon wants to make a few calls. When we arrive, several salesmen are clustered in a tiny office. Briefcases and phone books are open. Suit jackets are thrown casually over the backs of chairs and across metal desks. The Xerox Brooklyn sales force is collectively taking five.

Dixon banters back and forth with the men for a minute, then heads back to the solitude of the conference room. "It's times like this when I wish I had a woman to talk to," she says. "The guys are great and we get along, but I don't always feel comfortable." She picks at her corn muffin, breaking it into little pieces and popping them into her mouth.

At 1 P.M. Dixon is starting to fade. Her hair is pulled back in a ponytail. Her voice is more subdued. The down side of sales comes up.

"I guess I'm a paradox," she says, "because I'm really a very private person. I treasure the time by myself.

"It's not easy constantly being on. I was supposed to go to a party last night and couldn't face it. I couldn't converse with anyone. All day long I'm constantly asking and answering questions and talking to people.

"Yesterday was the worst day of my career," Dixon continues. "I lost a sale. The guy had the pen in his hand and backed out at the last minute. I went back to my car and my first impulse was to cry. It was one of those days when you say, 'Oh, my God, what am I doing with my life? What's my purpose? Why am I in sales? I can't handle any more rejection.'"

Her voice trails off, and for a moment Carol Dixon is silent. "Not to change the subject," she quips, "but that was a pretty good corn muffin."

Earlier in the day Dixon had remarked that the one characteristic all salespeople must have is the ability to bounce back quickly. After lunch she generally makes more phone calls. This time she has a lead. A manufacturing firm in Brooklyn's industrial section has called the Woodbury, Long Island, office for information. She runs a comb through her hair, splashes water on her face, and checks the map for directions. We drive into an area of narrow cobblestone streets, dirty gray smokestacks, and old crumbling warehouses. "In this section of Brooklyn you don't want anyone to know you're lost," she says. To our mutual relief the directions are accurate.

The office is at the top of a long staircase inside a dingy, brown, brick building. The color scheme is metallic gray; there are gray metal desks, gray metal filing cabinets, and gray floors. Cigar smoke hangs in the air. An old man sits behind a battered wooden desk, a guest register spread out on the desktop. We sign in.

Dixon asks for the purchasing agent, who to her delight is a woman. They discuss copiers with the ease and authority of two housewives bantering about food prices. They talk over prices, guarantees, supplies, and service contracts. The desktop is strewn with Xerox charts, tables, and pamphlets. Thirty minutes into the call, Mr. Warner, owner and president of the firm, struts into the lobby. Dixon is introduced.

"How do you do," says Warner. "Do you know Sol Linowitz?"

She thinks for a moment. "The name is familiar."

Warner gives her a worldly, I-caught-you grin. "You *should* know. He's a past president of Xerox and is presently our ambassador to the Middle East." The message is clear.

Carol blushes but recovers. "If you have a minute, could I speak with you?" she asks him.

"I'm sorry, I'm busy. Deal with my alter ego here." Warner disappears behind a door.

A few minutes later a younger, thinner version of Warner enters the lobby. Where Warner was smug, his clone is inexcusably rude. "Excuse me, honey, but I must tell you that Xerox prices are way out of line," he says. "The bottom line is the cost per copy, and your machines just can't compete." Having put in his unsolicited two cents' worth, he leaves.

The two women are silent. "Well, I guess that cuts our visit short," says the purchasing agent. "I will keep this material and look it over. Thank you very much for your time."

On a typical day Carol Dixon would get back on the street and canvass. On this day she's had enough. She heads back to the car without pausing to record the call in the Daily Success Planner.

At 4 P.M. she is visibly tired. What's more, she's lost. A gray-haired man in a jogging suit points us toward the Brooklyn-Queens Expressway, which of course is bumper-to-bumper.

"Well, today wasn't exactly a stunning success," she says, lighting a cigarette. "Sometimes I get so frustrated by my inexperience. If I had more practice at this, I wouldn't be so intimidated by certain objections customers have. I'd be much more aggressive."

After eight hours of what seems like constant rejection, why does she like her job, I ask.

"I'm a very ambitious person," she says. "If you're self-motivated, there's nothing like this job because you're going to get out of it whatever you put into it. Every day, every situation, every call is different. You're constantly challenging yourself. And if you do well, you can live well."

We pull into the parking lot of the Woodbury office just as most of the employees are pulling out. Carol Dixon shakes my hand and gives me a business card. She makes a quick time check. "Five-thirty. I still have time to make some phone calls," she says and reaches for the Daily Success Planner.

Questions

1. How does the writer maintain a clear sense of order in this piece?
2. Why does the writer note details like the following:
   the expressway traffic
   '76 Buick Apollo
   gold Seiko watch
   leather briefcase
   physical appearance of Carol Dixon
   corn muffin
3. Identify at least three questions the writer must have had to ask

Carol Dixon in order to obtain some of the information in this article.

4. What facts about Carol Dixon's job interest you? Why?
5. What special techniques of selling are explained? Why are these important to the article?
6. What key point or points does the writer want to make?

Elmer Ruiz
from Working, *by Studs Terkel*

Not anybody can be a gravedigger. You can dig a hole any way they come. A gravedigger, you have to make a neat job. I had a fella once, he wanted to see a grave. He was a fella that digged sewers. He was impressed when he seen me diggin' this grave—how square and how perfect it was. A human body is goin' into this grave. That's why you need skill when you're gonna dig a grave.

He has dug graves for eight years, as the assistant to the foreman. "I been living on the grounds for almost twelve years." During the first four years "I used to cut grass and other things. I never had a dream to have this kind of job. I used to drive a trailer from Texas to Chicago." He is married and has five children, ranging in age from two to sixteen. It is a bitter cold Sunday morning.

The gravedigger today, they have to be somebody to operate a machine. You just use a shovel to push the dirt loose. Otherwise you don't use 'em. We're tryin' a new machine, a ground hog. This machine is supposed to go through heavy frost. It do very good job so far. When the weather is mild, like fifteen degrees above zero, you can do it very easy.

But when the weather is below zero, believe me, you just really workin' hard. I have to use a mask. Your skin hurts so much when it's cold—like you put a hot flame near your face. I'm talkin' about two, three hours standin' outside. You have to wear a mask, otherwise you can't stand it at all.

Last year we had a frost up to thirty-five inches deep, from the ground down. That was difficult to have a funeral. The frost and cement, it's almost the same thing. I believe cement would break easier than frost. Cement is real solid, but when you hit 'em they just crack. The frost, you just hit 'em and they won't give up that easy. Last year we had to use an air hammer when we had thirty-five inches frost.

The most graves I dig is about six, seven a day. This is in the summer. In the winter it's a little difficult. In the winter you have four funerals, that's a pretty busy day.

I been workin' kinda hard with this snow. We use charcoal heaters, it's the same charcoal you use to make barbeque ribs or hot dogs. I go and mark where the grave is gonna be tomorrow and put a layer of charcoal the same size of a box. And this fifteen inches of frost will be completely melt by tomorrow morning. I start early, about seven o'clock in the morning, and I have the park cleaned before the funeral. We have two funerals for tomorrow, eleven and one o'clock. That's my life.

In the old days it was supposed to be four men. Two on each end with a rope, keep lowerin' little by little. I imagine that was kinda hard, because I imagine some fellas must weigh, two hundred pounds, and I can feel that weight. We had a burial about five years ago, a fella that weighed four hundred pounds. He didn't fit on the lowerin' device. We had a big machine tractor that we coulda used, but that woulda looked kinda bad, because lowerin' a casket with a tractor is like lowerin' anything. You have to respect . . . We did it by hand. There were about a half a dozen men.

The grave will be covered in less than two minutes, complete. We just open the hoppers with the right amount of earth. We just press it and then we lay out a layer of black earth. Then we put the sod that belongs there. After a couple of weeks you wouldn't know it's a grave there. It's complete flat. Very rarely you see a grave that is sunk.

To dig a grave would take from an hour and a half to an hour and forty-five minutes. Only two fellas do it. The operator of the ground hog or back hoe and the other fella, with the trailer, where we put the earth.

When the boss is gone I have to take care of everything myself. That includes givin' orders to the fellas and layin' graves and so on. They make it hard for me when the fellas won't show. Like this new fella we have. He's just great but he's not very dependable. He miss a lot. This fella, he's about twenty-four years old. I'm the only one that really knows how to operate that machine.

I usually tell 'em I'm a caretaker. I don't think the name sound as bad. I have to look at the park, so after the day's over that everything's closed, that nobody do damage to the park. Some occasions some people just come and steal and loot and do bad things in the park, destroy some things. I believe it would be some young fellas. A man with responsibility, he wouldn't do things like that. Finally we had to put up some gates and close 'em at sundown. Before, we didn't, no. We have a fence of roses. Always in cars you can come after sundown.

When you tell people you work in a cemetry, do they change the subject?

Some, they want to know. Especially Spanish people who come from Mexico. They ask me if it is true that when we bury somebody we dig 'em out in four, five years and replace 'em with another one. I tell 'em no. When these people is buried, he's buried here for life.

It's like a trade. It's the same as a mechanic or a doctor. You have to present your job correct, it's like an operation. If you don't know where to make the cut, you're not gonna have a success. The same thing here. You have to have a little skill. I'm not talkin' about college or anything like that. Myself, I didn't have no grade school, but you have to know what you're doin'. You have some fellas been up for many years and still don't know whether they're comin' or goin'. I feel proud when everything became smooth and when Mr. Back congratulate us. Four years ago, when the foreman had a heart attack, I took over. That was a real tough year for myself. I had to dig the graves and I had to show the fellas what to do.

A gravedigger is a very important person. You must have hear about the strike we had in New York about two years ago. There were twenty thousand bodies layin' and nobody could bury 'em. The cost of funerals they raised and they didn't want to raise the price of the workers. The way they're livin', everything wanna go up, and I don't know what's gonna happen.

Can you imagine if I wouldn't show up tomorrow morning and this other fella—he usually comes late—and sometimes he don't show. We have a funeral for eleven o'clock. Imagine what happens? The funeral arrive and where you gonna bury it?

We put water, the aspirins, in case somebody pass out. They have those capsules that you break and put up by their nose—smelling salts. And we put heaters for inside the tents so the place be a little warm.

There are some funerals, they really affect you. Some young kid. We buried lots of young. You have emotions, you turn in, believe me, you turn. I had a burial about two years ago of teen-agers, a young boy and a young girl. This was a real sad funeral because there was nobody but young teen-agers. I'm so used to going to funerals every day—of course, it bothers me—but I don't feel as bad as when I bury a young child. You really turn.

I usually will wear myself some black sunglasses. I never go to a funeral without sunglasses. It's a good idea because your eyes is the first thing that shows when you have a big emotion. Always these black sunglasses.

This grief that I see every day, I'm really used to somebody's crying every day. But there is some that are real bad, when you just have to take it. Some people just don't want to give up. You have to understand that when somebody pass away, there's nothing you can do and you have to take it. If you don't want to take it, you're just gonna make your life worse, become sick. People seems to take it more easier these days. They miss the person, but not as much.

There's some funerals that people, they show they're not sad. This is different kinds of people. I believe they are happy to see this person—not in a way of singing—because this person is out of his sufferin' in this world. This person is gone and at rest for the rest of his life. I have this questions lots of times: "How can I take it?" They ask if I'm calm when I bury people. If you stop and think, a funeral is one of the natural things in the world.

I enjoy it very much, especially in summer. I don't think any job inside a factory or an office is so nice. You have the air all day and it's just beautiful. The smell of the grass when it's cut, it's just fantastic. Winter goes so fast sometimes you just don't feel it.

When I finish my work here, I just don't remember my work. I like music so much that I have lots more time listenin' to music or playin'. That's where I spend my time. I don't drink, I don't smoke. I play Spanish bass and guitar. I play accordion. I would like to be a musician. I was born and raised in Texas and I never had a good school. I learned music myself from here and there. After I close the gate I play. I don't think it would be nice to play music when the funeral's goin' by. But after everything . . .

I believe we are not a rich people, but I think we're livin' fair. We're not sufferin'. Like I know lotsa people are havin' a rough time to live on this world because of crises of the world. My wife, sometimes she's tired of stayin' in here. I try to take her out as much as possible. Not to parties or clubs, but to go to stores and sometimes to go to drive-ins and so on.

She's used to funerals, too. I go to eat at noon and she asks me, "How many funerals you got today? How many you buried today?" "Oh, we buried two." "How many more you got?" "Another." Some other people, you go to your office, they say, "How many letters you write today?" Mine says, "How many funerals you had today?" (Laughs.)

My children are used to everything. They start playin' ball right against the house. They're not authorized to go across the road because it's the burial in there. Whenever a funeral gonna be across from the house, the kids are not permitted to play. One thing a kid love, like every kid, is dogs. In a way, a dog in here would be the best thing to take care of the place, especially a German Shepherd. But they don't want dogs in here. It's not nice to see a dog around a funeral. Or cats or things like that. So they don't have no pet, no.

I believe I'm gonna have to stay here probably until I die. It's not gonna be too bad for me because I been livin' twelve years already in the cemetery. I'm still gonna be livin' in the cemetery. (Laughs.) So that's gonna be all right with me whenever I go. I think I may be buried here it look like.

Questions

1. What makes this interview different from the previous one?
2. What indications are there that the interview has been edited?
3. What central impression emerges from Elmer Ruiz's comments?

4. What details of a gravedigger's job impressed you?
5. Why is this an interesting or uninteresting account?

No Madhouse

"I've been in the business quite a while now—since 1925. I was only fifteen when I started out in New Haven in an independent store. Next I moved up to an A & P chain store where I worked for three years. They didn't have meats before I got there. That was in 1928. I mean I worked in the first meat department of the chain that first sold meats. I even opened a small delicatessen out on Whalley Avenue when I quit A & P. I managed to take time off for the Olympic wrestling trials of '36, but I had to leave them early because my brother wasn't able to handle all our business alone. Well then, after the city began its redevelopment, I moved out here and rented this place from the old grocer, Frank Alba, who wanted to retire. It's my sixth year in this store."

I watched as Albert Proto flipped through order sheets and licked his thumb methodically before turning over each paper. The grocer's stubby fingers worked jerkily, but swiftly. He stopped and looked up. His features were sharp; his skin was dark; he wore glasses and had a tiny mustache. "That's my history," he continued. "Anything else?"

Wondering why he had mentioned his wrestling career, I asked him about it. "I even coached part time." He laughed slightly. "There used to be a large YMCA organization going in New Haven that sponsored meets. About seven YMCA groups from around the state competed. That's where I got my experience when I was young. The building was only a ten-minute walk from the store I was working in, and I spent many afternoons over there.

"At the delicatessen I had a fair amount of free time also. I enjoyed the bit of coaching that I did in high schools. Several volunteers and myself worked in a cycle, supervising wrestling at different high schools each year. I tried to help lay the groundwork, but after the impetus of the program dropped off, there weren't any more volunteers. But you'd be surprised how much publicity I got around the neighborhood. It helped business."

The door opened, and a bread delivery man pushed his way in, lugging a carton full of bread loaves on his shoulder. He set the box down on the closed-over ice cream freezer, located a few feet from the counter where Al was standing.

"How's it today?" the grocer greeted the man, as he walked to the freezer and then began looking through the loaves. The man nodded and asked if Al had everything he wanted. "Let's see," the short Italian murmured, "two rye, five corn and molasses, three whole wheat, and an extra club. Yeah, fine. Thanks." The delivery man nodded his head again and strode out of the market. Al swung the box onto the scarred wooden floor and piled the loaves on the shelves on the front side of the counter. Above him, there were racks on the wall, crammed with soap, brushes, towels, and detergents offering 14-carat gold-trimmed dinner plates inside the boxes. Directly behind the counter, more shelves held candy and cigarettes. A cash register sat on the counter beneath these shelves. One of the fluorescent lights in the store hung over the freezer from the low, plasterboard ceiling. Four wide stacks of sturdy metal racks filled up most of the limited space in the store, leaving room for a meat counter in the rear.

I sat upon the freezer while Al finished. "Oh, I'm sorry," he blurted out, standing up. He leaned back against the counter on his elbows. "I really forgot about you. I guess I was telling you about my wrestling times. Well, our little program fell through, and I did lose some fun of coaching. A couple of my teams had meets with Choate, Loomis, and one with Exeter. My invitation to the Olympic tryouts actually came through the head man of the YMCA in New Haven. He had some connections. The whole affair was just practice for me, but people liked to listen all about what I did and saw. The trials were, and most likely will be, the biggest venture I've ever undertaken away from the grocery business. Groceries are what I'm concerned with, but wrestling proved to be profitable as an outside activity." He smiled. "But I guess you'd be interested in what I've got here."

Happy that Al had the time to answer a few questions, I inquired about how he obtained his stock.

"It depends on the food, of course. Vegetables you have to buy every day or two, the same with milk. Meat, usually, is ordered three times a week. Generally, it's your perishable goods that you must stock up on most frequently.

"I buy food in New Haven from an association of independent merchants. It's called the 'terminal' and is located on Frontage Road, right off the Turnpike. Before I come here in the morning, I stop in there to load up.

"For the little market, the association is a great thing," Al commented. He walked over to his fruit and vegetable stand near the front window and picked over some oranges. "The association buys food wholesale for the independent grocers in the area, and sells them to us. The quantity buying, then, gives us the same lower prices as chain stores can get. If we bought individually, we could never get the discounts and never be able to sell at equally low prices as big places."

I asked if he ever got a special deal from a supermarket warehouse that could buy cheaply. "Oh, no! That would only involve another middleman and then another markup in prices, and we'd never make a profit selling at regular retail rates. Chain warehouses are supplied by large distribution centers, to our associations."

The phone in the front of the store rang. Al motioned for me to wait and rushed to answer it. "Good morning, Pine Orchard Market," he recited in a high-toned voice. "Why, yes, Mrs. Welch. Yes . . . yes. A dozen eggs, milk, and a carton of Viceroys. I'll have Ralph run them over as soon as possible. Good-bye." He hung up the phone, pulled out a pen that was hooked on his apron, and scribbled a note on a pad of paper by the cash register.

"Who's Ralph?" I asked.

"He's the fellow who cuts the meat. I guess you don't know him. But, one important fringe benefit of our association, before I forget to mention it, is the pension plan. All members are required to give money to a universal fund which later supplies money for you when you retire. All this is to help the little merchant in competing with large supermarkets."

"Do you depend much on your phone service?" I inquired.

"Yes, sir!"

"But I would think that people in the neighborhood would be inclined to buy from you simply because you are close at hand," I suggested.

"People don't come to me because I am close," Al explained. "They expect me to deliver because *I* am close to *them*." He pointed in the direction of the front window. "That lady who just called up hardly ever shows up here. She orders by phone. She would just as likely ride all the way to town to shop, where she has bigger variety to choose from, as come here."

Al walked swiftly out from behind the counter, and I followed him to the back of the store where he disappeared into a back room. "You'd better not come in here," he warned, "because it's so overflowing with stock that I can just barely keep track of it." I peered in through the doorway.

Two curtained windows filtered the bright sunlight that streamed in swirls into the opposite end of the long, narrow room. One flimsy shelf, made of now-rusted metal, ran around the room only several feet below the ceiling. A few cans of what looked like vegetable containers were set up on the shelf. The floor was cluttered with corrugated cardboard boxes, most of which had not been opened. An old TV set was conspicuous atop a table, draped with a sheet, in the center of the room. Al saw me staring at it. "When rarely there's nothing that I should be doing, I manage to take a peek at it." He yanked open a box, and pulled out some bottles of soda. He hurried back into the store and gently nudged the bottles onto a shelf between Coke bottles and a host of Campbell's soup cans.

"I don't worry about a lack of space too much," Al said. "I try, though, to keep as much stock as possible out where the customers can see it." He started back to the front of the market. "The costs of many articles will never vary, even under great quantity buying and selling. For example, you take coffee. I buy that from the association and automatically raise the price about 10 percent. All stores do the same because of the wide distribution of the product. Locally produced foods are the ones that can be found in a range of prices.

"My niece bought a boneless ham for $1.29 and ended up paying $1.49 in a supermarket in New Haven.

"I guess I am really prejudiced against chain stores, though I did get some valuable experience in one when I was young. But it's such a madhouse: millions of people milling around, yet working there is boring. I considered it impossible to get to know anybody, especially the customers, which is most of the enjoyment."

I heard the stamping of feet behind me and looked around to see a man, clad in felt hat and raincoat, close the back door of the market. He was quite a bit taller than Al, and when he hung his hat and coat on a wall hook, I saw that he was fat, bald, and had a flattened nose. I walked over to him as he reached the meat counter. He turned around.

"I guess that you're Ralph," I said amiably. "I wonder if you've worked with Al for long."

"Quite a while, I'd say," he replied, smiling mysteriously. "I'm his brother."

I felt quite embarrassed, but Ralph said, "I guess I'm just not as famous as Al." I finally asked him what he did around the store. "Little of everything—run errands, cut meat, arrange stock." He whirled around and began grinding meat.

A white grinder sat on the table against the back wall. The machine was basically cylindrical in shape, with a spout protruding from one side at the bottom. Above on a shelf, six or seven stacks of cardboard boxes, about the size of those in which French fries are often served, were piled precariously high. Ralph lifted off several boxes and laid them in a line on the table. He yanked open the heavy, iron-bound door to the freezer compartment, adjacent to the back storeroom, walked in, and reappeared a few seconds later. He was carrying a square of fresh-cut meat in each palm. He dropped them on the table, trimmed off excess fat with several swipes of a broad-bladed knife, and rammed both pieces into the top opening of the grinder.

The tottering feet of a small child caught my ear. A woman entered the store with her small son. "Hello, Mrs. Fusco," Al piped up pleasantly.

"Hello, Al. Lewis has been dying to see you," the woman replied, looking down at her boy. The youngster, giggling, tried to run away, but Al playfully swept him off his feet as he rushed by. The woman approached the meat counter. "Hello, Ralph. I'll have two pounds of your hamburg there," she said, pointing at the grinder. Ralph obliged, and he flicked the switch on the side of the grinder and pressed the meat into the machine. A dense, limp mass of red and pale pink meat poured out of the spout a few seconds later. Ralph caught the hamburg in two of the cardboard plates. He laid them down on the counter, whipped a sheet of wax paper out from under the cutting table, rolled up the boxes and slid them across to the lady. "Thanks, Ralph. Just put that on our bill." The man nodded with a smile, and the woman led her child elsewhere in the store.

On my way out, I met Al at the front counter, where he was counting the change in his cash register. "I'm glad to have been able to help you," he said, slamming the cash register shut. I thanked him for his information and started toward the front door. Al rushed in front of me and pulled the door open for me. I looked around at him, quite surprised. "Even this helps bring back business," he said.

Questions

1. How does the writer manage to convey both a sense of place and the personalities of the workers?
2. How does the writer give you the impression that the interview is happening right now?
3. How does the writer use his questions as a way of organizing the interview?
4. How is the introduction of this piece similar to the previous one? As a reader, how effective do you find these openings?
5. What overall impression of Al and his business do you receive?

The Faker: As Soft as His Ice Cream
By Marie Bradby

Sherman Beatty looks like Cookie in the Beetle Bailey cartoon strip: short, paunchy, scruffy face. A cigarette occasionally dangles from the corner of his mouth.

He also pretends he's meaner 'n heck. As he shuffles around the kitchen at Ehrmann's Bakers, where he makes ice cream, he kids his co-workers in a gruff manner. They dish it right back.

He may not be able to peel potatoes, but this guy can make ice cream. Beatty, who says he's 73 (Josef Leasure, Ehrmann's head baker, says add at least six years), has been making ice cream since he was 25. He says he started in 1927 (that adds up to 79) with F. M. Perkins and Son, a dairy store at Shelby and Main Streets.

Beatty has a habit of punching people on the leg, for emphasis, while he talks.

"I made ice cream for Harry Truman when he was inaugurated in 1948," Beatty said. (Punch.) He worked for a Cincinnati firm then. "I sent it to the White House." The flavor was Cherry White House.

"Harry didn't eat the ice cream. They sent it somewhere else. They think you're going to poison them."

Beatty talked only in between shuffling to a counter to measure out sugar and cream and then shuffling back to an old pot-bellied stove, where on Mondays he always makes six pots of caramel for his caramel ice cream. Caramel is Ehrmann's second most popular flavor. Vanilla is first.

The gooey brown mixture is boiled in an old copper bowl on top of the stove. Beatty scraped the sides of the bowl with a large wooden spatula until the confection bubbled to a dark brown. Then he dumped it out and poured in more sugar and cream for another batch.

What do you like about making ice cream?

"Well, I don't like nothing about it!" Everybody laughed. "I just started doing it. I got married when I was 17 years old. I had two kids and I had to work. It was seven days a week then."

As a young married man, Beatty first worked in a glove factory in Indiana. "That's where I got my finger cut off." He held up his left index finger, the top half of which was missing. The crew grunted. Well, Beatty admitted, he also tells people it was shot off in the war. And "I got it caught in a cash register." He grinned. (Punch.)

Beatty got tired of making gloves and took up making ice cream. He's been doing it for Ehrmann's for 12 years.

While Beatty made caramel, Leasure rolled dough for oatmeal cookies. "*That's* easy," Beatty said, pointing to Leasure. "*This* [making caramel] is hard work."

"Anybody can burn milk and sugar," Leasure scoffed. "He used to tell me you have to know how to burn it." Everybody laughed.

The caramel *is* special. It melts quickly over the tongue and tiny beads of butter stick to the roof of the mouth. There is no gradation of the word rich to describe it. Blimpo is close enough, though.

Caramel isn't the only kind of ice cream Beatty stirs up. "I make vanilla, chocolate, cherry-pecan, peach, strawberry, peppermint; and I make four kinds of sherbet: pineapple, orange, raspberry and lemon."

Each week, Tuesday through Friday, he mixes 200 gallons of ice cream, using only fresh and natural ingredients.

How do you make good ice cream?

"That's a secret," Beatty said gruffly. (Punch.)

"No, I'm not going to tell you that. I have a lot of people ask me how I make it. But I won't tell them. The only guy who knows is that guy up there [Gerald Driskell, Ehrmann's manager and a part owner] and I don't tell him too much."

"If she watches you long enough she's going to have your recipe before she leaves here today," Douglas Sexton, a baker's helper, teased Beatty.

"Oh no. I ain't telling her nothing." Beatty snapped his head and dumped in another pitcher of sugar.

Really, he's a pussy cat.

Questions

1. What did you learn about making ice cream in this essay?
2. What details do you find particularly descriptive and effective?
3. How does Sherman Beatty feel about his work? What clues tell you?
4. How does the title help or hinder the reader in understanding the point of the piece?
5. This piece originally appeared in a newspaper. What is different about its arrangement from that of the previous interview essay?

Shaping the First Draft

Your interview is done and the results are in front of you. You've seen some samples, both professional and amateur, of how similar interviews have been written into essays. The time has come to begin work on a draft. Of all your assignments, this one requires the most attention to decisions about how to present your information. The place to begin is with your notes. Study them carefully. Most writers find it useful after a visit in which notes have been taken to cluster their notes around headings of some sort. This may mean some recopying, which is not a bad idea because in recopying you may recall additional information or see where clarification is needed; as a result, you may find your notes expanding in some places, shrinking in others.

After establishing some order in your notes, you need to look for some kind of focus. What are you looking for? Ideally, you're seeking an idea that may have emerged as you conducted the interview or began to appear as you organized your notes. Maybe during the interview the particular work being done seemed boring to you, and the people involved appeared bored as well. How might you organize your material to emphasize this point and suggest what effect it may have on the work and the people? Perhaps you were surprised to discover that some ideas you had about certain types of work or people were not true; how might you explain the importance of shattering such notions or stereotypes?

At this stage you may find it useful to sit down with several of your classmates and discuss your findings. Tell them some of the things you discovered and get their reactions; ask them to indicate which observations they find most interesting. As you know, by talking through your material with someone who is engaged in the same task you are, you sometimes make new discoveries or you at least feel more comfortable with the material you have. Be sure to give as much feedback to your classmates as they give you; everyone needs help, so spread it around.

Organizing

When you sense that you have found a focus for your interview essay, the next question is how to organize the material. You have several options.

The "Stitching" Approach   If your material is almost exclusively dialogue and relies heavily on autobiographical material similar to that found in the Elmer Ruiz essay, the "stitching" approach may be useful. In this approach you take the various pieces of conversation that occurred during the interview and put them together as one continuous monologue in the words of the person interviewed. The success of this approach depends on editing out material that is uninteresting and not important to your focus while keeping a clear sense of development. You also must be careful not to distort the meaning or language of the interviewee. If you choose this approach, spend some time examining how Terkel's Elmer Ruiz piece is put together before you begin your own.

The Staccato Delivery   You frequently see this approach on television: the interviewer has some famous, or perhaps not so famous, person on camera and asks a series of questions that the person attempts to answer. The staccato approach works best when the material is relatively short and has a sharp focus. The delivery of the questions and of the answers tends to be quite rapid; an example of this approach is the interview with Studs Terkel, which appears earlier in this chapter. The approach works satisfactorily if the answers to the questions are short and other material such as description and action is not important. Again, though, the writer must have a clear point to make. Simply reproducing dialogue is not enough. There should be a sense of movement toward some important disclosure so the reader wants to continue; without this sense of movement, the reader will quickly lose interest. In this approach, questions and answers can be moved around for effect and clarity, as long as the basic meaning is not distorted. You can combine answers or questions if they deal with the same point. Repetition and imprecise wording can be edited out—something your subject will probably appreciate.

Narrative   Probably the most creative and interesting approach to this kind of writing is reflected in "Life of a Saleswoman," "No Madhouse," and "The Faker: As Soft as His Ice Cream." In these pieces, the writers chose to include observations, actions, and details along with appropriate dialogue. The result reads more like a story than a report. Careful selection of details, of speech, and of actions help place the reader with you at the time of the visit. As the teller of the story, you have a chance to offer some of your perceptions and reactions as well. In this approach, chances are good that you'll elect to use time as a basic organizing principle, particularly in the beginning; that is, you'll be inclined to start at the beginning of the visit and carry through to the end. As you have seen, the time sense can be direct, as in "Life of a Saleswoman," or more subtle, as in "No Madhouse."

These three approaches show that no one way exists for putting your interview essay together. Each interview is different and yields different results. Your main concerns are accuracy and interest.

Writing the First Draft

With your notes in some semblance of organization and a preliminary decision made about organization, get ready to plunge into a first draft. Expect this first one to be messy; don't worry if you have several false starts—that's quite natural in writing of this type. Cross-outs, notes to yourself, arrows and lines to show relationships are all part of the process. You've discovered by now that such "messing around" is quite normal and often useful in this stage of the writing. After all, you're writing to discover much of what you have to say, even though you may have a general sense of what you want to happen. But until you actually commit your thoughts and material to paper, you can't be absolutely sure of what you have.

One clue for writing this first draft is not to waste time trying to produce a perfect beginning. You've discovered by now that the introduction often comes last, after you have found the focus you want. So go ahead and write down a rough opening to get yourself started; you will have time later if repairs are needed in that area.

If you chose one of the first two approaches, your writing is going to be slower and more methodical; you will be looking for the key words and sentences to put together to create the impression you want. If that's the case, putting some of your material on cards and moving them around until you get a sequence that leads to a major point may be a useful way to proceed. If you selected the third approach, the best thing to do is to sit down and write yourself out. Using your notes and memory, re-create the visit. Leave blanks where you have temporary lapses of memory or can't find the appropriate notes. Write until you reach what seems to be a logical stopping point—maybe the point at which you concluded the interview. Then read what you have written. Make notations in places that seem weak in fact or observation or where unclear jumps in action occur. Keep asking yourself: What's the point of this, of that? Is this contributing to the main idea I started with or has a different one emerged?

If you discover that during the first draft your focus shifts and the material starts supporting a new focus, keep going with it if the direction seems promising. When you get to a stopping point, you can reread and decide if the direction is one you want to keep or if you need to return to the original focus. As you have undoubtedly discovered while writing other assignments, sometimes you make discoveries that are more valuable than the ones you thought you already had.

Re-Viewing

After reading the rough draft and determining that you have a focus (if you don't, go back and review your material, then try another draft), concern yourself with the following questions:

1. Do I maintain a clear focus throughout the piece?
   Readers are going to be looking for the "point" of your visit. Don't let them down. Does everything in the draft support that focus clearly? If something doesn't, ask why it doesn't and try to correct the problem.
2. Have I explained the information clearly?
   Depending on your approach, you may have used terms or items that some readers are not familiar with; provide some explanation, either through the words of the person being interviewed or through your own.
3. Have I used dialogue, description and action to good advantage?
   Again, depending on your approach, you should examine the use of speech: Is it clear who is speaking at all times? Of description: Have you been concrete and detailed enough? Of action: Have you shown the activity and the people to good purpose? Often more is

conveyed in how someone says something or does something than in the event itself.

4. Have I built an effective introduction and conclusion?
   Remember the importance of leading your reader into the paper; with the stitching and staccato approaches, you may have to provide a separate introduction so the reader knows what the occasion was for the interviewer's remarks. With the narrative approach, you may involve the reader right away in the action of your interview, just as you might in a story that starts off with some kind of event, remembering, of course, to orient the reader as you go.

These basic concerns should not be treated entirely separately, of course; they need to be woven together into one smooth, interesting whole. Write a second draft in which you bring all the elements together. Work on the smoothness of expression and pay particular attention to transitions within and among paragraphs. Bring to bear all that you've learned in previous writing assignments so this essay will represent the progress you have made.

Response

This second or third draft needs an audience. Find a partner or a reading group and spend some time reading and reacting to one another's papers. By now you have read enough different papers and written enough of your own to develop a good sense of what works and what doesn't, what is interesting and what's not, what is organized and what falls apart. Essays written for this assignment will offer a good test of your perception in those areas.

The following procedure can serve as the basis for your response to others' papers and their response to yours. As always, be as constructive and as specific as possible in your comments.

Read the first paragraph. *Stop.* Answer the following questions:

1. What issue or detail from this first paragraph do you expect will be developed further in the essay?
2. As a reader, how do you respond to this first paragraph as an introduction?

Finish reading the papers and then answer the following questions:

1. Review your responses to questions 1 and 2. Now that you've finished reading the essay, to what extent were your expectations fulfilled or not fulfilled?
2. What is your overall impression of the person being interviewed?

Identify specific places in the essay that contribute to this impression.

3. What do you consider three or four of the most important and/or interesting pieces of information you've gained from the essay about the person or the work?

4. Does the writer choose to emphasize the person, the work, or the environment? Which of these would you like to know more about after your reading? Which received too much emphasis?

5. How successful is the writer in creating a sense of the environment in which the interview took place? What sorts of details (facts, quotations, physical description, personal impressions) would be helpful in strengthening this aspect of the piece?

6. In light of your responses to the previous questions, what suggestions can you make to the writer about possible revisions? Does the paper need to be shortened, lengthened, reorganized? Does dialogue or description need some attention? Introduction and conclusion? Sentence structure?

The Final Draft

After carefully considering the responses you received, make the necessary adjustments to your essay, including additional revision if it seems appropriate. Then edit the essay carefully, remembering to check back to earlier essays to see what your problems were and then take the necessary steps to eliminate those problems in this essay. When you have a polished draft with which you are satisfied, submit it for evaluation.

ACKNOWLEDGMENTS

(Continued from page iv)

Joan Rivers as quoted in "The Wacky World of Joan Rivers" by Ronald L. Smith, *Writer's Digest* (September 1978). Reprinted by permission of *Writer's Digest*.

Excerpt from "Ernest Hemingway" in *Writers at Work: The Paris Review Interviews*, 2nd Series. Copyright © 1963 by The Paris Review, Inc. Reprinted by permission of Viking Penguin Inc.

James Thurber as quoted in Malcolm Cowley's Introduction to *Writers at Work: The Paris Review Interviews*. Copyright © 1957, 1958 by The Paris Review, Inc. Reprinted by permission of Viking Penguin Inc.

"Writing Habits and Influences" by Jule Cocke. Reprinted by permission of the author.

"Writing Autobiography" by Mary Yokel. Reprinted by permission of the author.

"Why I Don't Write" by Debbie Burgess. Reprinted by permission of the author.

Chapter 3

"Old Man" by Ethel Desmarais. Reprinted by permission of the author.

"Geneva" by Lisa Trovillion. Reprinted by permission of the author.

"The Way You Were" by Donna McKinney. Reprinted by permission of the author.

Excerpt from "Simple Man, Simple Dream" by John David Souther. © 1976 WB Music Corp. & Golden Spread Music. All rights reserved. Used by permission.

"Gina" by Celia Baker. Reprinted by permission of the author.

"Aunt Mamie" by Ramona Kyler. Reprinted by permission of the author.

"Snoopy" by Mary Yokel. Reprinted by permission of the author.

Excerpt from *Flowers for Algernon* by Daniel Keyes. Copyright © 1966 by Daniel Keyes. Reprinted by permission of Harcourt Brace Jovanovich, Inc.

Chapter 4

Excerpt from "The Subway" by Tom Wolfe in "The Big League Complex" in *New York, New York*. Copyright © 1964 by The New York Herald Tribune, Inc. Permission granted by The Dial Press.

Excerpt from *The Non-Runner's Book* by Vic Ziegel and Lewis Grossberger. Copyright © 1978 by Vic Ziegel and Lewis Grossberger. Reprinted by permission of Macmillan Publishing Co., Inc.

Excerpt from "How to Beat the Energy Crisis" by Paul D. Zimmerman, *Newsweek* (28 April 1980). Copyright 1980 by Newsweek Inc. All rights reserved. Reprinted by permission.

Excerpt from "How TV Violence Damages Your Children" by Victor B. Cline, © 1975 by LHJ Publishing, Inc. Reprinted with permission from *Ladies Home Journal* (February 1975).

Excerpt from "New York" by Gay Talese. Originally appeared in *Esquire* Magazine. Copyright © 1960 by Gay Talese. Reprinted by permission of the author.

Excerpt from "Reaching for Conoco's Riches" by Charles Alexander. Reprinted by permission from *Time*, The Weekly Newsmagazine. Copyright 1981 Time Inc.

Excerpt from *Death and the Magician* by Raymund FitzSimons. Copyright © 1980 by Raymund FitzSimons (New York: Atheneum, 1981). Reprinted with the permission of Atheneum Publishers.

Chapter 5

"Music" from "The Talk of the Town." Reprinted by permission. © 1980 The New Yorker Magazine, Inc.

"Recipe" by Joan Smith, *Since You Ask Me. . .* (June 1976–May 1977). Reprinted by permission.

"Scan, Scan, Bag" by Anita Strange. Reprinted by permission of the author.

"Jogging" by Linda Freeman. Reprinted by permission of the author.

"My Problems Playing Golf" by Charlotte Collins. Reprinted by permission of the author.

Chapter 6

"The Blind Men and the Elephant" by John G. Saxe. Reprinted from *Sharing Literature with Children* by Francelia

266

Butler, published by Longman Inc., New York.

Excerpt from *The Invisible Man* by Ralph Ellison. Copyright 1952 by Random House, Inc. Reprinted by permission.

"Death of a High School" by Anita Strange. Reprinted by permission of the author.

"In Florida: Jumping with the 82nd." Reprinted by permission from *Time*, The Weekly Newsmagazine; Copyright Time Inc. 1980.

From Bruce Catton, "Grant and Lee: A Study in Contrasts" from *The American Story*, ed. Earl Schenck Miers, © 1956 by Broadcast Music, Inc. Used by permission of the copyright holder.

Chapter 7

"Identity Crisis" by Carol Howard. Reprinted by permission of the author.

"An Act of Contrition" by Virgil Sublett. Reprinted by permission of the author.

"Cold Reality" by Nan Riley Flanagan. Copyright © 1967 by The Atlantic Monthly Company, Boston, Mass. Reprinted by permission of the author.

"Once Upon a Daisy" by Martha K. Lefebvre. Reprinted by permission of the author.

Chapter 8

From "Early Blooming and Late Blooming Syntactic Structures" by Kellogg W. Hunt" in Charles R. Cooper and Lee Odell, eds., *Evaluating Writing* (Urbana, IL: NCTE, 1977). Reprinted by permission.

Chapter 9

"The Fight for Integration" by Jule Cocke. Reprinted by permission of the author.

Chapter 10

Excerpt from "Teaching the Twenty-first Century in a Twentieth Century High School" by Priscilla P. Griffith in *Learning for Tomorrow: The Role of the Fu-*

ture in Education. Copyright © 1974 by Random House, Inc. Reprinted by permission.

"Surveyor in the Woods" by Kenneth Andler. Originally appeared in *Harper's* (July 1947). Copyright 1947 by Kenneth Andler. Reprinted by permission of the author.

"Surveying the Wilderness" by Donald Hall. Reprinted from *Blair and Ketchum's Country Journal* (August 1980) by permission of Country Journal Publishing Co., Inc. © 1980 by Country Journal Publishing Co., Inc.

"Shoot-out at the Red-Horse Barn" by John O'Dell. Reprinted with permission from the February 1976 *Reader's Digest*. Copyright © 1976 by The Reader's Digest Assn., Inc.

Chapter 11

"An Interview with Studs Terkel" by Gail Steinberg. Reprinted from *Writing* Magazine by permission of Curriculum Innovations, Inc. Copyright © 1981.

"Life of a Saleswoman" by Tina Poveromo. Reprinted from *The Graduate* (1981) by permission of 13–30 Corporation. © 1981 by 13–30 Corporation.

"Elmer Ruiz" by Studs Terkel from *Working: People Talk About What They Do All Day and How They Feel About What They Do*, by Studs Terkel. Copyright © 1972, 1974 by Studs Terkel. Reprinted by permission of Pantheon Books, a Division of Random House, Inc.

"No Madhouse," written by a student at Phillips Exeter Academy, from *A Student-Centered Language Arts Curriculum, Grades K–13: A Handbook for Teachers* by James Moffett, © 1968. Reprinted by permission of Houghton Mifflin Company.

"The Faker: As Soft as His Ice Cream" by Marie Bradby. Reprinted by permission of *The Courier-Journal* (Louisville, Kentucky). Copyright © 1981.

Index